HARDPRESS.NET
HOME OF HARD-TO-FIND BOOKS

The Letters of the Rev. Henry Martyn
by Henry Martyn

Address:
HardPress
8345 NW 66TH ST #2561
MIAMI FL 33166-2626
USA
Email: info@hardpress.net

THE CHRISTIAN'S FAMILY LIBRARY.

ST. JOHN'S COLLEGE, CAMBRIDGE.

3

38. I

39. WIL.

THE LETTERS OF

OCT

3..

38. P

39. WIL.

THE LETTERS OF

THE REV. HENRY MARTYN,

B. D. FELLOW OF ST. JOHN'S COLLEGE,
CAMBRIDGE; AND CHAPLAIN TO THE HON.
EAST INDIA COMPANY.

SEELEY, BURNSIDE, AND SEELEY:
FLEET STREET, LONDON
MDCCCXLIV.

Many years after the publication of Mr. Martyn's Life, a most valuable and peculiarly interesting series of letters, received from him in the course of a correspondence extending over seven years, was bequeathed to his biographer by the lady to whom the letters were addressed. These, with many others to Mr. Brown, Mr. Corrie, and other friends, were included in the publication of 'Letters and Journals,' which took place, in two volumes, octavo, in the year 1837. It has since appeared the most desirable course, to collect the whole of his Correspondence into a single volume, while his Life is at the same time enriched by fresh selections from his Diary. Thus, in two portable volumes, the public will have the whole delineation of his character, depicted by himself in the most natural and simple manner. A few sketches are also added, of the principal scenes amidst which his life was passed.

ILLUSTRATIONS.

CONTENTS.

LETTERS,

&c.

TRURO.

Page 1.

LETTERS

[illegible]

[illegible] letter [illegible] [illegible] [illegible] [illegible] [illegible] [illegible] [illegible] [illegible] [illegible] [illegible] [illegible] [illegible] visiting the sick [illegible] [illegible] [illegible] [illegible] to make your [illegible] [illegible] in Welbeck [illegible]

B

LETTERS.

I.

TO THE REV. J. SARGENT.

Swansea, August 9, 1802.

Dear Sargent,

You see by the date of my letter, that I have almost reached the end of my long pilgrimage. Our first resting-place was Wenlock in Shropshire, from whence we went on the Sunday to Madeley church. You must have heard of Mr. Fletcher, who was formerly Rector of this place. We were introduced to Mrs. F. by a young man who first introduced himself to us. We took some coffee with him afterwards, and he told us he had formerly been a cornet in the 15th Light Dragoons, but had retired from the world, and had now lived in solitude nearly three years, employed in nothing but reading the Bible and visiting the sick. He was perfectly meek and gentle in his manners, and seemed quite happy. I leave you to make your own reflections on this phenomenon. From Wenlock we became pedestrians, and went successively to Shrewsbury, the Val of Llangollen, and Chester ; from whence we sailed dow the Mersey to Liverpool. From this place I proceede to Holywell, &c. alone.

* * * * * *

Thus have I been preserved by the protecting provi dence of God, and been endued with bodily strength t accomplish my journey with ease. I have never onc wished for a companion ; even in the most gloomy mo ments I have found the Bible a never-failing source o interesting thought.

II.

TO THE SAME.

St. John's, Jan. 17, 1803.

My dear Sargent,

I find from —— that you really expect me to fulfil a promise I never made. However, as you allow me to send you even a skeleton of a letter, I sit down resolved to avail myself of the permission, if I find it necessary

* * * G—— and H—— seem to disapprove of my project much; and on this account I have been rather discouraged of late, though not in any degree convinced. It would be more satisfactory to go out with the full approbation of my friends, but it is in vain to attempt to please man. In doubtful cases, we are to use the opinions of others no further than as means of directing our own judgment. My sister has also objected to it, on the score of my deficiency in that deep and solid experience necessary in a missionary. You have taken rooms, I think, in the Temple, so that the providence of God seems to have called you irrevocably to the profession of the law. Though I cannot help regretting that one so well qualified to preach the glad tidings of salvation, should be called off to labour in the business of this world, yet we may be sure, that whatever is undertaken according to His will, will be attended with his blessing. You will, I dare say, find a double degree of watchfulness necessary to preserve a proper state of mind. In the case of those who ministe

in the sanctuary, temporal and spiritual occupations ar one; corresponding to the necessity of a superior de gree of holiness in those who are to be examples. Bu in your case, even a common degree of spiritualit; cannot be maintained without much attention. Man; have found that occasional aspirations after God hav been made the channels of the communications of hi grace in the midst of worldly business, and have lef the mind not disqualified for the employments of heaver Indeed this seems to be a good criterion of our stat‹ For surely the new-born soul never more truly acts ac cording to its heavenly nature, than when it delights t shake off the clogs of earth, and to leave the world be neath it, and to rise exultingly to God. Though it i hard to be thus minded, yet it is undoubtedly our privi lege. But nothing but almighty grace is sufficient fo these things, as the coldness we all feel manifests. I hav been reading Hopkins's sermons to-day. I would giv you my opinion of them—(I could willingly fill the sheet but the time does not allow me. Therefore, adieu.

III.

TO THE SAME.

St. John's, June 30, 1803.

DEAR SARGENT,

* * * * * *

* * * I feel ashamed that you express any satisfaction in corresponding with me. God only knows how poor and shallow I am; and if any good should ever arise to you by my means, it must be ascribed to his wisdom, who can use the meanest instruments to effect his purposes. What shall I say to him for giving me such a friend as you are likely to prove. One who fears not to give offence by speaking the truth, and who would seek to improve the spirit, rather than please the flesh. * * * * *

May you, as long as you shall give me your acquaintance, direct me to the casting down of all high imaginations. Possibly it may be a cross to you to tell me or any one of his faults. But should I be at last a castaway, or at least dishonour Christ through some sin, which for want of faithful admonition remained unmortified, how bitter would be your reflections! I conjure you, therefore, my dear friend, as you value the good of the souls to whom I am to preach, and my own eternal interests, that you tell me what you think to be, in my life, spirit, or temper, not according to the will of God my Saviour. You profess your need of humiliation. I wish my own experience could assist you in this the most important part of our sanctification. In examining myself according to your advice, on this head it seems (for the work of inquiry is so exceedingly difficult that I can hardly say with certainty what I have known, or whether I have known anything on this subject) that I seek my humility rather from views of God's greatness and the example of Christ, than of my own corruption. Now, though the former views may assist in producing the effect, yet the impressions arising from them are necessarily transient, whereas that humility which arises from just views of *ourselves* may be as abiding as our own consciousness, and be brought into exercise by everything we do, or speak, or think. It has greatly distressed me to think how slow my heart is to yield to the convictions of reason; how unable to mourn when I should be lying low in the dust. On reading the words of our Lord to the lukewarm Laodiceans, the form of the words is very striking and comforting. "Because thou knowest not that thou art wretched, &c, I counsel thee to buy of me eye-salve that thou mayest see," so that there is provision made for those whom of all others God holds most in abhorrence; the blind, (to their sins,) the hard-hearted, and the proud. Were it not so, what would become of me? Happily for us, "the covenant is ordered in all things and sure;" and it is not left to our own wisdom, but to that adorable agent, the Spirit of God, to perform that good work which he hath begun in us. May we be both conformed to the bright image of the dear Redeemer, especially in meekness and lowliness of heart. I feel for you, lest by a fatal comparison with those around you, you should be induced to lower the standard of Christian morality in your own practice. This is a temptation to which I am prone even here. But let us remember, that Go judgeth according to every man's work, and not rela tively. He marks his secret walk, and his view o him is precisely the same, whatever be the change c the opinions of the man of himself, or of others con cerning him. Let us then walk in the Spirit—

* * * * * * *

D. has heard about a religious young man of seven teen, who wants to come to College, but has only £2C a year. He is very clever, and from the perusal o some poems which he has published, I am much in terested about him. His name is H. K. White.

* * * We remembered our frien Sargent at our prayer at Mr. Simeon's room on Thurs day evening. Pray that I may have true piety an fitness for my work.

Yours ever,

HENRY MARTYN.

IV.

TO THE SAME.

St. John's, Sept. 29, 1803.

How long it seems since I heard from you, my dear Sargent; and yet I have only myself to blame, for not answering a letter you sent me in the middle of August. * * * I shall be anxious to know how you have been passing your summer: not, I hope, as I have, amidst the din of arms. I give our drilling this lofty title, because a little is sufficient to disturb me. Too many resident friends in the university have contributed not a little to the frittering away of my time. I mean, however, to leave the university corps forthwith, as the day of ordination (Oct. 23,) is drawing near. Very little indeed have I done this summer. As this is the last long vacation I shall ever pass as an 'ιδιότης, I am rather disappointed at having lost such a season of retirement. Our Lord led a very retired life; his ministers, therefore, it should seem, ought to do so too. Yet I sometimes think that it is from too much indulging solitude, that I am so easily distracted in company. But how great must be your trials from so much worldly business and worldly pleasure! How ought we, who are intrusted with the ministration of the Spirit, whose very breath ought to be prayer, to beseech God to preserve you and his other saints engaged in the business of time! May he keep you unspotted from the world, and so dwell in you by his Spirit, that while your thoughts are necessarily engaged with earthly things, your heart may b in heaven! Unhappily our treacherous hearts, if inter ested but lawfully in other things, are thereby less ap to take pleasure in religious meditation. My studie during the last three months have been Hebrew, Greel Testament, Jon. Edwards on Original Sin, and on th Affections, and Bishop Hopkins,—your favourite an mine. Never did I read such energetic language, suc powerful appeals to the conscience. Somehow or othe he is able to excite most constant interest, say what h will. I have been lately reading the first volume of th Reports of the Missionary Society, who sent out so man to Otaheite and the southern parts of Africa. You woul find the account of Dr. Vanderkemp's Mission int Caffraria infinitely entertaining. It appeared so muc so to me, that I could read nothing else while it lastec Respecting my own concerns in this way, no materi change has taken place, either externally or internally except that my sister thinks me unqualified, throug want of religious experience; and that I find greate pleasure at the prospect of it. I am conscious, howeve of viewing things too much on the bright side, and thin more readily of the happiness of seeing the desert rejoic and blossom as the rose, than of pain, and fatigue, an crosses, and disappointments. However it shall be de termined for me, it is my duty to crush the risings o self-will, so as to be cheerfully prepared to go or stay.

Your's ever,

H. MARTYN.

V.

TO THE SAME.

St. John's, Nov. 18, 1803.

I thank you, my dear Sargent, for your prayers on he day of my ordination. I rejoiced to think that many vere putting up to heaven for me ; for much indeed did : need them. Neither at that time nor since have I been luly affected with the awfulness of the charge. The ncessant employment of sermon-writing has left me ittle leisure for quiet consideration : and so my spirits iave been greatly depressed the last three weeks. The 'our sermons I have preached are on Job xiv. 14 ; John v. 10 ; Psalm ix. 17 ; Heb. vi. 11 ; two of them at Crinity Church. My Lolworth congregation is about me hundred. Now that the composition of sermons will become easier, I hope to perform all the duties of the ninistry with more attention than I have yet been able o give. Time and prayer will, I trust, through the grace of God, remove that childish thoughtlessness which ittends me still, and make me feel where I stand. * * My conversations with —— have been attended with no small advantage to me in the way of wholesome correcion. He is the only man of all my friends here that ells me the truth plainly ; and so is the only one, who, by lowering my pride, eventually promotes my sanctifiation and peace. * * * As you have read Law, ell me your opinion of him. He is rather a favourite of mine, though not without his faults. It seems by what your friends here say, that you do not engage wit sufficient earnestness in your worldly business. I hardl know what to give as my opinion on this subject. Th law is so very different from all other pursuits, in th time and labour required for it. Yet, on the other hand there is Sir Matthew Hale. * * * I never hear word about the missionary business. If you see Mr Wilberforce, and his mind is not too much occupie about the present affairs of national danger, ask him something about it.

I am, dear Sargent,

Yours ever truly,

H. Martyn.

VI.

TO THE SAME.

St. John's, January 9, 1804.

I heard of the death of your brother, my dear Sargent, some time ago: but I had neither inclination nor leisure to write to you immediately after. I hope the first impressions of grief are now somewhat worn away, but that you retain that blessed effect of sanctified sorrow, a tender spirit, which to me at this time appears so desirable, that I could be willing to suffer any thing, or do any thing, to obtain it. I should judge by your account, that he could have hardly attained the age of moral agency, and so we may hope he is among those of whom it is said, "Of such is the kingdom of heaven." I trust that the melancholy event has, in answer to your prayers, been beneficial to ——. If not in the degree you could wish, yet cease not to pray for her. But how can I encourage you to a duty, in which I am so languid myself, so seldom disposed to "stir up myself to take hold upon God?" How necessary is self-denial in this as well as every other duty, through the corruption that is in us! Sometimes I feel the most ardent and strong resolutions to fight manfully, to exert all the powers of the soul unceasingly in mortifying the flesh; but these resolves are short-lived: sometimes through forgetfulness, sometimes through weakness, I find myself giving way to ever-craving self-indulgence.

I thank you for the kind interest you take in m missionary plans. But unless providence should s fit to restore our property, I see no possibility of m going out. Most probably, after all, I shall be settl at Calcutta, in that post which Mr. Grant is so anxio to procure some one to fill: for by this the pecunia difficulties which attend my going out would be remove * * * You told me some time ago, that t multiplicity of business which would attend me as M Simeon's curate, would leave little time for reflecti on my future plans; and truly I find your predicti fulfilled: for the composition of sermons, and prepari for the societies, confines the hours of devotion into f too small a compass. Nevertheless I have found m spirit disciplined by these more active parts of t ministry, so as to perform with willingness those duti from which once I used to shrink. * *
Farewell, my dear brother,—amidst all the afflictio of the gospel, and truly they are not few, we shall al be made partakers of its consolations. The conte plation of the eternal world is of necessity my chi happiness, and your's I hope by choice: for thoug this world demands your attention more than mine, yo have learnt to give it its right value. In our Father house there are, I humbly hope, mansions prepar for us, purchased only by the blood of Jesus, wh will also keep that which we have committed to hi till that day.

H. M.

VII.

TO THE SAME.

Lamorran, August 6, 1804.

My dear Sargent,

*   *   *   *

How can I sufficiently adore the singular benefits of God to my family ; we are now brothers and sisters for eternity. How cheerfully can I now go forth to proclaim the glories of him who hath done so much for us.

*   *   *   *

Respecting your approaching union with that excellent lady, I have nothing to add at present, but that you have my prayers, both of you ; and particularly does it seem to me a necessary petition that you may not in your mutual affection forget the Saviour. May he himself show us the vanity of the enjoyments of this world ; and instead of pleasing ourselves with the prospect of a happy continuance in it, let us contemplate with greater satisfaction the moment of our departure from it.

VIII.

TO HIS YOUNGEST SISTER.

Cambridge. Sept. 18, 1804.

We should consider it as a sign for good, my deares S——, when the Lord reveals to us the almost desperat corruption of our hearts: for, if he causes us to groa under it, as an insupportable burden, he will, we ma hope, in his own time, give us deliverance. The prid which I see dwelling in my own heart, producing ther the most obstinate hardness, I can truly say my sou abhors. I see it to be unreasonable; I feel it to b tormenting. When I sometimes offer up supplica tions, with strong crying to God, to bring down m spirit unto the dust, I endeavour calmly to contemplat the infinite majesty of the most high God, and my ow meanness and wickedness. Or else I quietly tell th Lord, who knows the heart, that I would give him al the glory of everything if I could. But the most effec tual way I have ever found, is to lead away my thought from myself and my own concerns, by praying for al my friends; for the Church, the world, the nation and especially by beseeching that God would glorify his own great name, by converting all nations to th obedience of faith;—also by praying that he would pu more abundant honour on those Christians whom he seems to have honoured especially, and whom w see to be manifestly our superiors. This is at least a positive act of humility, and it is certain that not only will a good principle produce a good act, but the act will increase the principle. But even after doing all this, there will often arise a certain self-complacency which has need to be checked; and in conversation with Christian friends, we should be careful, I think, how self is introduced. Unless we think that good will be done, self should be kept in the back-ground and mortified. We are bound to be servants of all, ministering to their pleasures as far as it will be to their profit. We are to "look not at our own things, but at the things of others." Be assured, my dear S——, that night and day, making mention of you in my prayers, I desire of God to give you to see the depth of pride and iniquity in your heart, yet not to be discouraged at the sight of it; that you may perceive yourself deserving to be cast out with abhorrence from God's presence, and then may walk in continual poverty of spirit, and the simplicity of a little child. Pray, too, that I may know something of humility. Blessed grace! how it smoothes the furrows of care, and gilds the dark paths of life! It will make us kind, tender-hearted, affable, and enable us to do more for God and the gospel than the most fervent zeal without it.

I am here without a companion;—at first the change from the agreeable society in Cornwall, as also from that which I enjoyed at Plymouth, was very irksome; but it is good for me!

IX.

TO MRS. HITCHINS.

London, June 24, 1805

My dear Cousin,

The account of your ill health as described in you: former letter, affected me even to tears. I cannot in deed expect to see you any more upon earth; yet fo: my dear brother's sake, and those to whom you ar immediately useful, I wish to regard the hour of you departure as far distant—but in this and every othe particular that concerns us, God will act according t his infinite wisdom and love. As you are safe in th Lord Jesus, nothing need disquiet you, or us, on you account—whether life or death, all is yours. * * * * May God enable you, according to you desire, to continue walking as on the verge of eternity looking for and hastening to the coming of the day o God. * * * There are not many thing in the world which I would withhold from you; bu with respect to the sermons for which you ask, m mind must be changed before I send them. * * * * Sermons cannot be good memorials, be cause once read, they are done with—especially a youn man's sermons, unless they possess a peculiar sim plicity and spirituality; which I need not say are quali ties not belonging to mine. I hope, however, that I an improving; and I trust that now I am removed fron the contagion of academic air, and am in the way o acquiring a greater knowledge of men, and of my own heart, I shall exchange my jejune scholastic style for a simple spiritual exhibition of profitable truth. Mr. Cecil has been taking a great deal of pains with me; my insipid, inanimate manner in the pulpit, he says, is intolerable. 'Sir,' said he, 'it is cupola-painting, not miniature, that must be the aim of a man that harangues a multitude.' Whitsun-week was a time of the utmost distress to me; but now, through the mercy of God, I am once more at peace. What cannot his power effect? The present wish of my heart is, that I may henceforth have no one thing upon earth for which I would wish to stay another hour, except it be to serve the Lord my Saviour in the work of the ministry. Pray, my dear sister, that the Lord may keep in the imaginations of the thoughts of my heart, all that may be for the glory of his great name. The time of sailing is not yet certain. The ships are getting round to Portsmouth fast. I shall leave town this week, probably not before Thursday. As my ship is one of the latest, we shall probably not be detained long there. If we were, it would not be safe to venture to Plymouth, scarcely indeed could I wish it.

I remain, &c.

H. M.

X.

TO HIS CONGREGATION AT CAMBRIDGE.

Portsmouth, July 11, 1805.

MY DEAREST BRETHREN,

I write in great haste to thank you most affectionately for the token of your love, which our dear brother and minister has given me from you. Oh may my God richly recompense you for your great affection! May he reward your prayers for me, by pouring tenfold blessings into your own bosoms! May he bless you with all spiritual blessings in Christ Jesus! At the command of God, as I believe, I shall, in a few hours, embark for those regions where your little present may be of use to me, in guiding my way through the trackless desert. I pray that the word of God, which is your compass, may, through the Spirit, direct your path through the wilderness of this world, and bring you in safety to the 'better country' above. I beg your prayers, and assure you of mine. Remember me sometimes at your social meetings, and particularly at that which you hold on the Sabbath morning. Pray not only for my sinful soul,—that I may be kept faithful unto death;—but also especially for the souls of the poor heathen. Whether I live or die, let Christ be magnified by the ingathering of multitudes to himself. I have many trials awaiting me, and so have you; but that covenant of grace in which we are interested, provides for the weakest, and secures our everlasting welfare.—Farewell, dear brethren! May God long continue to you the invaluable labours of your beloved minister; and may you, with the blessing of his ministry, grow, day by day, in all spirituality and humility of mind; till God in his mercy, shall call you, each in his own time, to the eternal enjoyment of His glory!'

H. M.

XI.

TO HIS COUSINS.

Portsmouth, July 15, 1805.

My dear Cousins,

I went on board on Friday, expecting to sail immediately, but we have since been informed that government will not suffer us to depart till tidings shall hav been received from Lord Nelson. I make haste therefore to request you will send me another letter, directe to me on board the Union, East Indiaman. Yesterda morning I read the service and preached on deck to th ship's crew. My text was Matt. v. 2—4. Every thin was conducted with the utmost decorum. Mr. Simeo preached to them in the evening. There was the utmost attention, and one of the officers was in tears. have generally lived on board since my arrival, and fin my cabin as comfortable as my room in college, but m numerous friends here from Cambridge and London ar continually bringing me ashore. I am through merc very well, but on the road down, as I was undressing a night, I fainted, fell into convulsions and lost my senses The fit did not last long; it was brought on probabl by fatigue of mind and body. But how frail is my life I thought then that I was dying, but it pleases God t uphold me from day to day. May he also give me grac to devote myself anew to his service. God bless you, m beloved friends, remember me sometimes in your prayers

I remain now as ever, affectionately yours,

H. Martyn.

XII.

TO MRS. HITCHINS.

Falmouth, July 20, 1805.

My dear Cousin,

We sailed from St. Helen's at day-break last Wednesday morning, and to my no small surprise, I found we were bound to Falmouth. After a pleasant passage down the channel, we came to in this harbour yesterday evening, and are ordered to continue till accounts shall be received of the combined fleets. You will easily conceive my feelings at being thus brought once again to my friends; what the design of God is in this providence, I am at a loss to understand. May it be for the mutual establishment and comfort both of them and me. * * * On passing Plymouth, we were too far from the shore to distinguish the houses. I tried my spy-glass in vain, it would not bring you nearer, but my heart was with you, and I retired to my cabin to pray for you both. * * * You will have time now, I think, to send me a letter, and I need not assure you how acceptable it will be. I have sent a short letter to my cousin at Marazion. How happy should I be if she should be able to come part of the way to Falmouth to see me. But I pray that my heart may not again rove in pursuit of earthly comfort, and so subject me to new affliction.

I remain, &c.

XIII.

TO MISS LYDIA GRENFELL.

Union, Falmouth Harbour.
July 27, 1805.

* * * As I was coming on board thi morning, and reading Mr. Serle's Hymn you wrote ou for me, a sudden gust of wind blew it into the sea. made the boatmen immediately heave to, and recovere it, happily without any injury except what it had re ceived from the sea. I should have told you that th Morning Hymn, which I always kept carefully in m pocket-book, was one day stolen with it, and othe valuable letters, from my rooms in college. It woul be extremely gratifying to me to possess another cop of it, as it always reminded me most forcibly of th happy day, on which we visited the aged saint. Th fleet, it is said, will not sail for three weeks, but if yo are willing to employ any of your time in providing m with this or any other MS hymns, the sooner you writ them, the more certain I shall be of receiving them Pardon me for thus intruding on your time; you wil in no wise lose your reward. The encouragement con veyed in little compositions of this sort is more refresh ing than a cup of cold water. The Lord of the harvest who is sending forth me, who am most truly less tha the least of all saints, will reward you for being willin to help forward even the meanest of his servants. Th love which you bear to the cause of Christ, as well a

notives of private friendship, will, I trust, induce you o commend me to God, and to the word of his grace, at hose sacred moments when you approach the throne f our covenant God. To his gracious care I commend rou. May you long live happy and holy, daily growng more meet for the inheritance of the saints in light. remain with affectionate regard,

Yours most truly,

H. Martyn.

XIV.

TO MRS. HITCHINS.

* * * * *

The consequence of my Marazion journey is, that I am enveloped in gloom ; but past experience assures me it will be removed. I have taken every step that I conceive right, and now I leave the whole matter with the Lord. May he give me grace to turn cheerfully to my proper work and business, in respect of which all others sink into comparative insignificance. If she would prove a real blessing, it is not for me to complain of God, or of her, that she is withheld. * * *

* * * * * * * *

With the assurance of his love, I know that all things work together for good, and with this I may be satisfied ; yet nature mourns, restless at being contradicted. Another consequence of my journey is, that I love Lydia more than ever.

XV.

TO THE REV. ——

Falmouth, Aug. 5, 1805.

My Dear Brother,

After the many farewells you have received from me, you are surprised, though not, I am willing to hope, lispleased, at hearing once more from me. Immedi-tely after my last letter I went on board, supposing hat by this time we should be many leagues at sea; out the wind veered, and blew strong from the S. and S. W. the whole week till Saturday, when the Commo-lore, in consequence of an express he had received, ent for all the Captains in the fleet, to inform them hat government wished to muster all the effective force n the channel, to oppose the Brest fleet, which it was upposed would be soon out. The delay occasioned by his new order is unlimited, and occasions much discon-ent in the fleet; but I find continual satisfaction in ecurring to the first Great Cause of all these events—nly I sometimes doubt whether it is ever destined for ne to visit the shores of India. The belief generally revails amongst us, that the troops on board are in-ended to co-operate in taking the Cape of Good Hope; nd that we are to wait off Ireland to join another leet. These reports have set the minds of our young nen afloat; and I cannot walk the deck without inter-ering with knots of consulting politicians; my own nind is not much disturbed with speculation on human events at this time. I find the words of that hymn which I have met with in your little book far more in unison with my feelings,

> ' From earth I rise,
> And seek the joys
> At his right hand :
> I all on earth forsake :
> Its wisdom, fame and power,
> And Him my only portion make,
> My shield and tower.'

I have little expectation of finding a letter from Stoke to-night, though wishes often become expectations. I am afraid of troubling you by requesting such frequent letters from you both, but the opportunities will soon cease. I never forget to remember you twice a day in my prayers. Do you kindly continue your occasional intercessions for your unworthy brother and fellow-labourer in the gospel.

I remain with affectionate regard,
Your's in our blessed Lord,
H. Martyn.

XVI.

TO MISS GRENFELL.

Union, Falmouth, August 10, 1805.

MY DEAR MISS LYDIA,

It will perhaps be some satisfaction to yourself and our mother, to know that I was in time. Our ship was entangled in the chain, and was by that means the only one not under weigh when I arrived. It seems that most of the people on board had given me up, and did not mean to wait for me. I cannot but feel sensibly this instance of divine mercy in thus preserving me from the great trouble that would have attended the loss of my passage. Mount's Bay will soon be in sight, and recal you all once more to my affectionate remembrance. * * * * * * * *

I bid you a long farewell. God ever bless you, and help you sometimes to intercede for me.

H. MARTYN.

XVII.

TO MRS. HITCHINS.

Union, August 10, 1805

MY DEAREST COUSIN,

We are at last under sail, the pilot will carry back my last farewell to you. This morning at nine o'clock I had just finished reading 'Horne on the Psalms,' to Lydia and your mother at Gurlyn, when a messenger from St. Hilary brought an account of an express from Falmouth; how delusive are our schemes of delight. It was but yesterday that I went to St. Hilary; this morning after breakfast, Lydia and myself were to have taken a walk to view the grounds, and then to have gone to T——; and to-morrow I was to have preached at St. Hilary and Marazion, but four hours only have elapsed, and the shores of England are receding from my sight. But I bless God for having sent the fleet into Falmouth; I go with far greater contentment and peace than when I left Portsmouth; the Lord will do all things well, and with him I cheerfully leave the management of this and every other affair for time and eternity through Jesus Christ. And now, with gratitude to you for your kind counsel and sympathizing affection, I bid you once more adieu. May God bless my dear brother in his ministry, and bless you both in your family and in your own souls; this is my daily prayer, and will continue to be so. Pray that a more peculiar unction may be vouchsafed to me, now that I am actually embarked in the cause of Christ, and that I may not go forth in vain. May the Lord prosper his word in the thing whereunto he sends it. It will be a bitter disappointment if I do not receive letters from you both by the next fleet. I have not a moment more. I subscribe my name for the last time in England.

Your's with everlasting affection,

H. Martyn.

VIEW NEAR MARAZION.

Page 31.

XVIII.

TO MRS. HITCHINS.

Cork Harbour, Aug. 19, 1805.

MY DEAREST COUSIN,

I hasten to send you a few lines, in the hope of receiving one more letter from you before I leave this part of the world. No one in the fleet knew of our destination to Ireland till the Commodore opened his sealed dispatches off the Lizard, or I should have desired you to direct to me there. We continued our course the Saturday on which I wrote to you, and on the Sunday morning were becalmed in Mount's Bay. It was melancholy pleasure to have one more view of the Mount, Marazion, and St. Hilary, all of which I could see with the glass very well, though not distinctly with the naked eye. My heart was very full, as you may suppose. I would have given anything to have been ashore, preaching at Marazion or St. Hilary, where I was probably expected. I took for my text Heb. xi. 16. "But now they desire a better country, that is a heavenly, wherefore God," &c. The text was not very suitable to them but it was quite so to me. The beloved objects were still in sight, and Lydia I knew was about that time at St. Hilary, but every wave bore me farther and farther from them. I introduced what I had to say by observing that we had now bid adieu to England, and its shores were dying away from the view. The female part of my audience were much affected, but I do not know that any were induced to seek the better country. The Mount continued in sight till five o'clock, when it disappeared behind the western boundary of the bay. Amidst the extreme gloom of my mind this day I found great comfort in interceding earnestly for my beloved friends all over England. If you have heard from Marazion since Sunday I should be curious to know whether the fleet was observed passing. Whether it was or not I am very sure that more persons than one were praying for its preservation. Monday, the day after, was a day of most severe trial to me. It began to blow fresh in the morning, in consequence of which all the passengers were ill. I was thus rendered incapable of removing, by persevering prayer, the dreadful gloom that hung upon my mind; not a ray of comfort or life appeared in any quarter. We had lost sight of the land in the night, and with it I seemed to have lost all the sources of happiness. Oh this ensnaring world! What but the Almighty power of God can effectually wean us from it! I slumbered away the afternoon in darkness and stupidity, scarcely sensible of anything but the pains of memory; but reviving a little at night I was refreshed by reading some of the Psalms, and your hymns. No thoughts but those of God's covenant love and everlasting kindness would at all suit me. In such passages as these, "Why sayest thou, O Jacob," &c. I found strong consolation. I believed I should utterly have fainted, but that I was enabled to say in faith, "Rejoice not against me, O mine enemy; when I fall I shall arise; when I sit in darkness the Lord shall be a light unto me." Throughout the whole of the day, the want of Christian society, or of any friend with whom I could converse, made me scarcely doubt of the necessity of applying to Lydia immediately on my arrival in India. But I am determined by the help of God to give the matter a fair trial. I hope I shall never request her to make such a sacrifice merely for my personal relief, except so far as that may tend to promote the kingdom of God. Yesterday and to-day my sickness is removed, and my peace restored. God fulfils his promises to me in a marvellous manner. "As thy days, so shall thy strength be." He is a friend very near to me, now that all others are far from me, and refreshes my soul with long and happy seasons of prayer. He makes the great business of my ministry to be now uppermost in my mind. O let the Eastern nations at last emerge from their darkness, and let these my poor wretched countrymen who sail with me, and whom I see under the power of Satan, be turned away from their sin and enmity to God! The more I see of the world, the more deeply I am struck with the truth and excellency of the blessed Gospel. O the transcendent privilege of being enlightened by the knowledge of it. I have now free access among the soldiers and sailors, and pray that some may be awakened to a serious concern for their souls. We have a Venetian on board who speaks French; to him I have been preaching the Gospel in that language. I have given him a French Testament. Tracts and Bibles I have dispersed in numbers. Yesterday Ireland came in sight, and to-day we came to anchor in the Cove of Cork. We are in the midst of a vast number of transports filled with troops. It is now certain, from our coming here, that we are to join in some expedition, probably for the Cape of Good Hope, or the Brazils; anywhere so long as the Lord goes with me. If it should please God to send me another letter from you, which I scarcely dare hope, do not forget to tell me as much as you can about

Lydia. I cannot write to her, or I should find the greatest relief and pleasure even in transmitting upon paper the assurances of my tenderest love. And with respect to yourself, my dear cousin, I cannot but be deeply anxious, considering the very long period that must elapse before I can hear again of you. I could have wished to have left you in more established health, but I must rest contented with the happy assurance of your being under the care of a gracious God and reconciled Father in Christ, who will, in his own time, call you to your high reward. And now I reluctantly conclude, commending you both to God, and to the word of his grace. Amen.

H. MARTYN.

XIX.

TO MAJOR SANDYS.

St. Salvador, S. A. Nov. 19, 1805.

My dear Sir,

Our stay at Madeira was so short, that I was obliged to defer writing to you, till our arrival at the next port; and now we have had such sudden notice of the sailing of this packet for Lisbon, with the unfortunate Captain of the Britannia, that I shall not be able to enlarge so much as I could wish. We were present at part of the disastrous scene, the particulars of which you will have read before the receipt of this letter. The ships had gone to pieces before we arrived, but we could perceive many of the people walking about on the sands. A peculiar providence preserved us from being lost on the same rocks, for we past close to them twice in the night without perceiving them; the first time, however, we had no suspicion of being within many miles of them; and the second time, two days after, on joining the main fleet, from which we had been detached, it appeared we must have past within a mile of them, and yet could not see them, they were so low. From the time of this event we were a single ship till we reached St. Salvador. We crossed the Tropic of Cancer on the 10th of October, and the Line on the 30th. My health has continued remarkably good, occasionally indeed I suffer from relaxation and weakness; but upon the whole I bear the heat as well as any of the passengers.

I have walked here for three hours together in the noon-tide heat of a vertical sun without any sensible inconvenience. My mind through the rich mercy of God enjoys much of that peace which Christ promises to his people—"Peace I leave with you, my peace I give unto you." I seem to have lost a good deal of that saliency of spirits, which the company of my dearest friends, and the want of offensive objects around me used to inspire. Here I am, and have enough to break the heart of any one who has a concern for the honour of God. I perceive it therefore, to be my business in life, not to look for enjoyment in this world, which lieth in wickedness, but to fulfil as an hireling my day, struggling against Satan, and exposed as a sheep among wolves. God, however, has so far had compassion on his unworthy servants and the perishing souls in the ship, as to gather some of his children from amongst us. There is a small party of us, who meet every day on the orlop-deck to sing and hear an exposition of Scripture. The rest are very hardened and contemptuous; but I trust I shall have grace to instruct in meekness those who oppose themselves. In the meantime, my dear friend, you will continue to put up a prayer occasionally for me to the God of our salvation, who is the confidence of the ends of the earth, and of them who are afar off upon the sea. It is so long before we are likely to arrive in India, in consequence of the Indiamen being engaged in this expedition, that I seldom think of it. We have been already seventeen or eighteen weeks, and perhaps may be as much longer. However, my time passes very delightfully in learning the language, writing letters, and becoming more acquainted with Scripture. Major Lumsden gives me but little encouragement to hope for the conversion of the natives of India. Being strangers themselve to the power of God over their own hearts, they se only the arm of man, and therefore despair. My general reply to them is that which consoles me "With men it is impossible, but with God all thing are possible." I have not been much ashore, becaus there are no inns; but the Lord has in kindness fur nished me with a very benevolent friend in Corrè, wh has given me a general invitation to his house. I hav dined with him once, and walked round his plantation The novelty of a tropical garden afforded me no smal amusement, and much occasion of admiring the gran magnificence of the creating power of God. There i an army of 8,000 men with us, so that almost all th men I see here are military officers. This is a nev scene to me. I hear nothing but the sound of th trumpet and the alarm of war. Oh! that the day were come "when nation shall no more lift up swor against nation."

I hope, my dear Major, you maintain your groun among the enemies of the Gospel who are found i Helston. Stand fast, beloved brother, clad in th panoply of God, in truth, in righteousness, in peace, i faith, with the word of God. I delight to offer a wor of encouragement to the feeble. I know that you God in whom you trust will be your strong rock an defence. Eliza, I may venture to hope, grows in grace as she reads this, let her be assured of my affectionat remembrances. Compliments to ——. Those who ar united to me in the sacred bond of the Gospel must no be forgotten. In the utmost haste, I conclude, dear sir

H. M.

XX.

TO THE REV. J. SARGENT.

Union, in Table Bay, Cape of Good Hope
January 4, 1806, (11 *at night*.)

Dear Sargent,

* * * * * * * * * *

* * * * * * Saturday night, the instant our anchor was down, when I began this letter a signal was given for the 59th to land. I staid up till two in the morning to take my leave of them, and was grieved to find with what levity and profaneness they were arming themselves against the fears of death. Of my own men I had taken a solemn and affecting farewell, by commending them to the grace of God. They returned, however, about the middle of the next day the General not thinking it safe to land, either on account of the surf, or because he had received information of a large body of the enemy being in readiness behind an eminence to receive them. Nothing was done the remainder of that day, (yesterday) but to-day, Monday 6, three regiments have landed without opposition, as we see very plainly from our ship, and the landing of the whole army is now going on; the 59th are to leave the ship at three to-morrow morning. Poor souls! from the report we have of the force ashore, I fear many of them will never return.

* * * * * * * * *

Two days after writing the above, a battle was fought. I went ashore a few hours after it, and saw the wounded and dead lying on the field, but the particulars I have not time to relate, as I am just informed that the ship which carries the intelligence, is to sail to-morrow, and I have not written a single letter yet to my relations. I beg my kindest remembrance to Mrs. S. of whom I make mention with you without ceasing in my prayers. May you both live, my beloved friends, happy in one another, but finding your chief happiness in God. Confessing that you are strangers and pilgrims upon earth, not having here a continuing city, and seeking one to come. I beg the continuance of your prayers, especially at those seasons when you intercede for the general cause of our blessed Lord.

I remain, ever your's affectionately,

H. MARTYN.

XXI.

TO THE REV. C. SIMEON.

Union, Table Bay, Jan. 7, 1806.

* * * * * * * *

I embraced the opportunity of going to the wounded nen, soon after my landing. A party of the company's roops were ordered to repair to the field of battle, to ɔring away the wounded, under the command of Major ——, whom I knew. By his permission, I attached nyself to them, and marched six miles over a soft ›urning sand, till we reached the fatal spot. We found everal but slightly hurt: and these we left for a while, fter seeing their wounds dressed by a surgeon. A little nward were three mortally wounded. One of them n being asked 'where he was struck,' opened his shirt, nd showed a wound in his left breast. The blood which ie was spitting showed that he had been shot through he lungs. As I spread my great coat over him, by the urgeon's desire, who passed on without attempting to ave him, I spoke of the blessed gospel, and besought iim to look to Jesus Christ for salvation. He was surɔrised, but could not speak; and I was obliged to leave iim, in order to reach the troops, from whom the officers, ut of regard to my safety, would not allow me to be eparated. Among several others, some wounded, and ome dead, was Captain ——, who had been shot by a ifleman. We all stopped for a while, to gaze, in penive silence, on his pale body: and then passed on to witness more proofs of the sin and misery of fallen man Descending into the plain, where the main body of each army had met, I saw some of the 59th, one of whom, a corporal, who sometimes had sung with us, told me that none of the 59th were killed, and none of the officers wounded. Some farm-houses, who had been in the rear of the enemy's army, had been converted into an hospital for the wounded, whom they were bringing from all quarters. The surgeon told me that there were already in the houses two hundred, some of whom were Dutch. A more ghastly spectacle than that which presented itself here I could not have conceived. They were ranged without and within the house, in rows, covered with gore. Indeed it was the blood, which they had not had time to wash off, that made their appearance more dreadful than the reality : for few of their wounds were mortal. The confusion was very great ; and sentries and officers were so strict in their duty, that I had no fit opportunity of speaking to any of them, except a Dutch captain, with whom I conversed in French. After this, I walked out again with the surgeon to the field, and saw several of the enemy's wounded. A Hottentot, who had his thigh broken by a ball, was lying in extreme agony, biting the dust, and uttering horrid imprecations upon the Dutch. I told him that he ought to pray for his enemies ; and after telling the poor wretched man of the Gospel, I begged him to pray to Jesus Christ. But our conversation was soon interrupted : for, in the absence of the surgeon, who was gone back for his instruments, a Highland soldier came up, and challenged me with the words, 'Who are you?' 'An Englishman.' 'No,' said he, 'you are French,' and began to present his piece. As I saw that he was rather intoxicated, and did not know but that he might actually fire out of mere wantonness, I sprang up towards him, and told him, that if he doubted my word, he might take me as his prisoner to the English camp,—but that I certainly was an English clergyman. This pacified him, and he behaved with great respect. The surgeon, on examining the wound, said the man must die, and so left him. At length, I found an opportunity of returning, as I much wished, in order to recover from distraction of mind, and to give free scope to reflection. I lay down on the border of a clump of shrubs or bushes, with the field of battle in view; and there lifted up my soul to God. Mournful as the scene was, I yet thanked God that he had brought me to see a specimen, though a terrible one, of what men by nature are. May the remembrance of this day ever excite me to pray and labour more for the propagation of the gospel of peace. Then shall men love one another: "Nation shall not lift up sword against nation, neither shall they learn war any more." The Blue Mountains, which formed the boundary of the prospect to the eastward, were a cheering contrast to what was immediately before me; for there I conceived my beloved and honoured fellow-servants, companions in the kingdom and patience of Jesus Christ,* to be passing the days of their pilgrimage, far from the world, imparting the truths of the precious gospel to benighted souls May I receive grace to be a follower of their faith and patience; and do you pray, my brother, as I know that you do, that I may have a heart more warm, and a zeal more ardent in this glorious cause. I marched back the same evening, with the troops. The surf on

* Missionaries of the United Brethren at Grœnekloof and Gnadenthal, and those belonging to the London Missionary Society at Bethelsdorp.

the shore was very high, but through mercy, we escaped that danger. But when we came to our ship's station, we found that she was gone; having got under weigh some hours before. The sea ran high. Our men were almost spent, and I was very faint with hunger; but after a long struggle, we reached the Indiaman about midnight.'

XXII.

TO MISS L. GRENFELL.

Serampore, July 30, 1806.

My dearest Lydia,

On a subject so intimately connected with my happiness and future ministry, as that on which I am now about to address you, I wish to assure you that I am not acting with precipitancy, or without much consideration and prayer, while I at last sit down to request you to come out to me to India.

May the Lord graciously direct his blind and erring creature, and not suffer the natural bias of his mind to lead him astray. You are acquainted with much of the conflict I have undergone on your account. It has been greater than you or Emma have imagined, and yet not so painful as I deserve to have found it for having suffered my affections to fasten so inordinately on an earthly object.

Soon, however, after my final departure from Europe, God in great mercy gave me deliverance, and favoured me throughout the voyage with peace of mind, indifference about all worldly connections, and devotedness to no object upon earth but the work of Christ. I gave you up entirely—not the smallest expectation remained in my mind of ever seeing you again till we should meet in heaven: and the thought of this separation was the less painful from the consolatory persuasion that our own Father had so ordered it for our mutual good. I continued from that time to remember you in my prayers only as a Christian sister though one very dear to me. On my arrival in thi country I saw no reason at first for supposing tha marriage was advisable for a missionary—or rather th subject did not offer itself to my mind. The Baptis missionaries indeed recommended it, and Mr. Brown but not knowing any proper person in this country they were not very pressing upon the subject, and accordingly gave no attention to it. After a very shor experience and inquiry afterwards, my own opinion began to change, and when a few weeks ago we receive your welcome letter, and others from Mr. Simeon an Colonel Sandys, both of whom spoke of you in referenc to me, I considered it even as a call from God to satisf myself fully concerning his will. From the accoun which Mr. Simeon received of you from Mr. Thomason he seemed in his letter to me to regret that he had s strongly dissuaded me from thinking about you at th time of my leaving England. Colonel Sandys spoke i such terms of you, and of the advantages to result fro your presence in this country, that Mr. B. became ver earnest for me to endeavour to prevail upon you. You letter to me perfectly delighted him, and induced hi to say that you would be the greatest aid to the mission I could possibly meet with. I knew my ow heart too well not to be distrustful of it, especially a my affections were again awakened, and accordingly al my labour and prayer have been to check their influence, that I might see clearly the path of duty.

Though I dare not say that I am under no bias, yet from every view of the subject I have been able to take, after balancing the advantages and disadvantages that may ensue to the cause in which I am engaged, always in prayer for God's direction, my reason is fully con-

'inced of the expediency, I had almost said the necesity of having you with me. It is possible that my
eason may still be obscured by passion; let it suffice
ıowever to say that now with a safe conscience and
he enjoyment of the divine presence, I calmly and de-
iberately make the proposal to you—and blessed be
God if it be not his will to permit it; still this step is
ıot advancing beyond the limits of duty, because there
s a variety of ways by which God can prevent it, without suffering any dishonour to his cause. If He shall
forbid it, I think, that by his grace, I shall even then
be contented, and rejoice in the pleasure of correspond-
ng with you. Your letter dated December, 1805, was
the first I received, (your former having been taken in
the Bell Packet)—and I found it so animating that I
could not but reflect on the blessedness of having so dear
a counsellor always near me. I can truly say, and
God is my witness, that my principal desire in this
affair is, that you may promote the kingdom of God in
my own heart, and be the means of extending it to the
heathen. My own earthly comfort and happiness are
not worth a moment's notice. I would not, my dearest
Lydia, influence you by any artifices or false representations. I can only say that if you have a desire of
being instrumental in establishing the blessed Redeemer's kingdom among these poor people, and will
condescend to do it by supporting the spirits and animating the zeal of a weak messenger of the Lord who
is apt to grow very dispirited and languid, 'Come, and
the Lord be with you!' It can be nothing but a sacrifice on your part, to leave your valuable friends to
come to one who is utterly unworthy of you or any
other of God's precious gifts—but you will have your
reward, and I ask it not of you or of God for the sake

of my own happiness, but only on account of the Gospel. If it be not calculated to promote it, may God in his mercy withhold it. For the satisfaction of your friends, I should say that you will meet with no hardships. The voyage is very agreeable, and with the people and country of India, I think you will be much pleased. The climate is very fine—the so-much-dreaded heat is really nothing to those who will employ their minds in useful pursuits. Idleness will make people complain of every thing. The natives are the most harmless and timid creatures I ever met with. The whole country is the land of plenty and peace. Were I a missionary among the Esquimaux or Boschemen I should never dream of introducing a female into such a scene of danger or hardship, especially one whose happiness is dearer to me than my own,—but here there is universal tranquillity,—though the multitudes are so great, that a missionary needs not go three miles from his house without having a congregation of many thousands. You would not be left in solitude if I were to make any distant excursion, because no chaplain is stationed where there is not a large English Society. My salary is abundantly sufficient for the support of a married man, the house and number of people kept by each company's servant being such as to need no increase for a family establishment. As I must make the supposition of your coming, though it may be perhaps a premature liberty, I should give you some directions. This letter will reach you about the latter end of the year,—it would be very desirable if you could be ready for the February fleet, because the voyage will be performed in far less time than at any other season. George will find out the best ship ; one in which there is a lady of high rank in the service would be preferible. You are to be considered as coming as a visitor to Mr. Brown, who will write to you or to Colonel Sandys, who is best qualified to give you directions about the voyage. Should I be up the country on your arrival in Bengal, Mr. Brown will be at hand to receive you, and you will find yourself immediately at home. As it will highly expedite some of the plans which we have in agitation that you should know the language as soon as possible, take Gilchrist's Indian Stranger's Guide, and occasionally on the voyage learn some of the words.

If I had room I might enlarge on much that would be interesting to you. In my conversations with Marshman, the Baptist missionary, our hearts sometimes expand with delight and joy at the prospect of seeing all these nations of the East receive the doctrine of the cross. He is a happy labourer : and I only wait, I trust, to know the language to open my mouth boldly and make known the mystery of the gospel. My romantic notions are for the first time almost realized,—for in addition to the beauties of sylvan scenery may be seen the more delightful object of multitudes of simple people sitting in the shade, listening to the words of eternal life. Much as yet is not done; but I have seen many discover by their looks while Marshman was preaching, that their hearts were tenderly affected. My post is not yet determined ; we expect however it will be Patna, a civil station, where I shall not be under military command. As you are so kindly anxious about my health, I am happy to say, that through mercy my health is far better than it ever was in England.

The people of Calcutta are very desirous of keeping me at the Mission Church, and offer to any evangelical clergyman a chaplain's salary and a house besides. I am of course deaf to such a proposal; but it is strange that no one in England is *tempted* by such an inviting situation. I am actually going to mention it to cousin T. H. and Emma. Not, as you may suppose, with much hope of success; but I think that possibly the chapel at Dock may be too much for him, and he will have here a sphere of still greater importance. As this will be sent by the Overland Dispatch, there is some danger of its not reaching you;—you will therefore receive a duplicate, and perhaps a triplicate, by the ships that will arrive in England a month or two after. I cannot write now to any of my friends. I will therefore trouble you, if you have opportunity, to say that I have received no letters since I left England, except one from each of these—Cousin T. and Emma, Simeon, Sargent, Bates—of my own family I have heard nothing. Assure any of them whom you may see, of the continuance of my affectionate regard—especially dear Emma. I did not know that it was permitted me to write to you—or I fear she would not have found me so faithful a correspondent on the voyage. As I have heretofore addressed you through her, it is probable that I may be now disposed to address her through you—or what will be best of all, that we both of us address her in one letter from India. However you shall decide, my dearest Lydia, I *must* approve your determination, because with that spirit of simple-looking to the Lord, which we both endeavour to maintain, we must not doubt that you will be divinely directed. Till I receive an answer to this, my prayers, you may be assured, will be constantly put up for you, that in this affair you may be under an especial guidance, and that in all your ways God may be abundantly glorified by you through esus Christ. You say in your letter that *frequently very day* you remember my worthless name before the hrone of grace. This instance of extraordinary and ndeserved kindness draws my heart toward you with tenderness which I cannot describe. Dearest Lydia, n the sweet and fond expectation of your being given o me by God, and of the happiness which I humbly ope you yourself might enjoy here, I find a pleasure n breathing out my assurance of ardent love. I have ow long loved you most affectionately, and my attachent is more strong, more pure, more heavenly, beause I see in you the image of Jesus Christ. I unwilingly conclude, by bidding my beloved Lydia, adieu.

H. MARTYN.

XXIII.

TO THE SAME.

Serampore, Sept. 1, 1806

My dearest Lydia,

With this you will receive the duplicate of the lette I sent you a month ago, by the overland dispatch May it find you prepared to come! All the thought and views which I have had of the subject since firs addressing you, add tenfold confirmation to my firs opinion; and I trust that the blessed God will graci ously make it appear that I have been acting under ; right direction, by giving the precious gift to me an to the church in India. I sometimes regret that I ha not obtained a promise from you of following me, a the time of our last parting at Gurlyn—as I am occa sionally apt to be excessively impatient at the lon delay. Many, many months must elapse before I ca see you or even hear how you shall determine. Th instant your mind is made up, you will send a letter b the overland dispatch. George will let you know hov it is to be prepared, as the Company have given som printed directions. It is a consolation to me durin this long suspense, that had I engaged with you befor my departure I should not have had such a satisfactor conviction of it being the will of God. The commande in chief is in doubt to which of the three followin stations he shall appoint me, Benares, Patna, or Moor shedabad; it will be the last most probably; this i only two days journey from Calcutta ; I shall take my departure in about six weeks. In the hour that remains, I must endeavour to write to my dear sister Emma, and to Sally. By the fleet which will sail hence in about two months, they will receive longer letters. You will then, I hope, have left England. I am very happy here in preparing for my delightful work, but I should be happier still if I were sufficiently fluent in the language to be actually employed ; and happiest of all if my beloved Lydia were at my right hand, counselling and animating me. I am not very willing to end my letter to you ; it is difficult not to prolong the enjoyment of speaking, as it were, to one who occupies so much of my sleeping and waking hours ; but here, alas ! I am aware of danger ; and my dear Lydia will, I hope, pray that her unworthy friend may love no creature inordinately.

It will be base in me to depart in heart from a God of such love as I find him to be. Oh that I could make some returns for the riches of his love ! Swiftly fly the hours of life away, and then we shall be admitted to behold his glory. The ages of darkness are rolling fast away, and shall soon usher in the gospel period when the whole world shall be filled with his glory. Oh my beloved sister and friend, dear to me on every account, but dearest of all for having one heart and one soul with me in the cause of Jesus and the love of God, let us pray and rejoice, and rejoice and pray, that God may be glorified, and the dying Saviour see of the travail of his soul. May the God of hope fill us with all joy and peace in believing, that we may both of us abound in hope through the power of the Holy Ghost. Now, my dearest Lydia, I cannot say what I feel—I cannot pour out my soul—I could not if you were here ;

but I pray that you may love me, if it be the will of God; and I pray that God may make you more and more his child, and give me more and more love for all that is Godlike and holy.

I remain, with fervent affection,
Yours, in eternal bonds,
H. Martyn.

XXIV.

TO THE REV. J. SARGENT.

Sept. 14, 1806.

MY DEAR SARGENT,

It is now four months since I landed in this country, but I have seen little more of it than what lies between Serampore and Calcutta; and the little time that can be spent out of doors affords very small opportunities of acquiring local knowledge. My whole employment is preparing sermons and learning the language. * *

* * * * * * * *

I have grievous complaints to make, that the immense work of translating the services into the language of the East is left to Dissenters, who cannot in ten years supply the want of what we gain by a classical education. * * * Suppose D. F. &c. would devote ten or fifteen years of their lives in this country to the sole work of getting the Scriptures translated into some of the languages of the East, they might accomplish it easily, and they would very soon be able to superintend the learned natives who should be employed in the work. Were not the zeal of our forefathers almost evaporated in these times, a body of pious and learned young clergymen would come forth with joy to so glorious a work * * * * * * * * * You address me as a missionary, and as if there were hardships in my way—externally there are none, except temptations may be called so, as perhaps they ought to be. The air is so soft and serene that you might sleep at night under a tree, and maintenance so easy that a wholesome meal may be purchased for a farthing or two.

* * * * * *

I am this day appointed to Dinapore, in the neighbourhood of Patna.

With great regard, I remain, my dear brother,

Sincerely your's,

H. M.

XXV.

TO MISS L. GRENFELL.

Serampore, Sept. 1806.

How earnestly do I long for the arrival of my dearest Lydia. Though it may prove at last no more than a waking dream that I ever expected to receive you in India, the hope is too pleasing not to be cherished till I am forbidden any longer to hope. Till I am assured of the contrary, I shall find a pleasure in addressing you as my own. If you are not to be mine, you will pardon me; but my expectations are greatly encouraged by the words you used when we parted at Gurlyn, that I had better *go out* free, implying as I thought, that you would not be unwilling to follow me if I should see it to be the will of God to make the request. I was rejoiced also to see in your letter that you unite your name with mine, when you pray that God would keep us both in the path of duty—from this I infer that you are by no means *determined* to remain separate from me. You will not suppose, my dear Lydia, that I mention these little things to influence your conduct or to implicate you in an engagement.—No, I acknowledge that you are perfectly free—and I have no doubt that you will act as the love and wisdom of our God shall direct. Your heart is far less interested in this business than mine, in all probability; and this on one account I do not regret, as you will be able to see more clearly the directions of God's providence. About a fortnight ago I sent you a letter accompanying the du plicate of the one sent over-land in August. If thes shall have arrived safe, you will perhaps have lef England before this reaches it. But if not, let m entreat you to delay not a moment. Yet how wil my dear sister Emma be able to part with you an George—but above all your *mother?* I feel very muc for you and for them—but I have no doubt at all abou your health and happiness in this country.

The commander-in-chief has at last appointed me t the station of Dinapore, near Patna, and I shall ac cordingly take my departure for that place as soon a I can make the necessary preparations. It is not ex actly the situation I wished for—though in a tempora point of view it is desirable enough. The air is good the living cheap, the salary £1000. a year—and there i a large body of English troops there. But I shoul have preferred being near Benares, the heart of Hin dooism. We rejoice to hear that two other brethre are arrived at Madras on their way to Bengal, sent, trust, by the Lord, to co-operate in overturning th kingdom of Satan in these regions. They are Corri and Parsons, both Bengal chaplains. Their station will be Benares and Moorshedabad—one on one side o me, and the other on the other. There are also now ten Baptist missionaries at Serampore. Surely good i intended for this country!

Captain Wickes,—the good old Captain Wickes, wh has brought out so many missionaries to India, is now here. He reminds me of Uncle S. I have been jus interrupted by the blaze of a funeral pile, within a hundred yards of my pagoda—I ran out—but th wretched woman had consigned herself to the flame before I reached the spot—and I saw only the remain of her and her husband. O Lord, how long shall it be? Oh! I shall have no rest in my spirit till my tongue is loosed to testify against the devil, and deliver the message of God to these his unhappy bond-slaves. I stammered out something to the wicked Brahmins about the judgments of God upon them for the murder they had just committed, but they said it was an act of her own free-will. Some of the missionaries would have been there, but they are forbidden by the governor-general to preach to the natives in the British territory. Unless this prohibition is revoked by an order from home it will amount to a total suppression of the mission.

I know of nothing else that will give you a further idea of the state of things here. The two ministers continue to oppose my doctrines with unabated virulence; but they think not that they fight against God. My own heart is at present cold and slothful. Oh that my soul did burn with love and zeal! Surely, were you here I should act with more cheerfulness and activity with so bright a pattern before me. If Corrie brings me a letter from you, and the fleet is not sailed, which however is not likely, I shall write to you again. Colonel Sandys will receive a letter from me and Mr. Brown by this fleet. Continue to remember me in your prayers, as a weak brother—I shall always think of you as one to be loved and honoured.

H. MARTYN.

XXVI.

TO THE REV. D. BROWN.

Berhampore, Oct. 27, 180[illegible]

MY DEAR SIR,

I have enjoyed uninterrupted health and spiri[illegible] through divine mercy till to-day. * * Wh[illegible] did not I write from Gazipore? Why because, Sir, [illegible] could hear of no such place. I was rather anxio[illegible] about your little boat the day you left me, it blew [illegible] violently. As soon as you were out of sight, the me[illegible] laid down the rope, and would not track any more f[illegible] the day. They were about to put back into a null[illegible] but found that pre-occupied by so many boats, that w[illegible] were obliged to lie on the naked shore, exposed to th[illegible] direct stream and wind. The budgerow made a goo[illegible] deal of water by beating about on the ground, but I a[illegible] happy to say, she has not leaked since.

18. The day after, lay to in a nulla, a little abo[illegible] Troksaugur.

19. The first solitary sabbath spent among th[illegible] heathen, but my soul not forsaken of God. I thin[illegible] some of you were praying for me that day, for I e[illegible]joyed almost the same communion with you, as if yo[illegible] were present.

20. At a village which the boatmen said was Nu[illegible]dea, (which could not be if the map is right, in placin[illegible] it the other side of the river,) I had some stammerin[illegible] conversation with a Brahmin at the worship of Dhoorg[illegible]

He disputed with great heat, and his tongue ran faster than I could follow, while the people that were about us shouted applause. But I continued to ask questions without making any remarks upon the answers, and among the rest, could not help enquiring whether Marshman's stories about Khrishnoo and Bramha stealing the horse, &c. were true. He confessed the truth of them, and seemed to feel the consequences, which I forbore to press, but told him of the way of the gospel. He grew quite mild, and asked me at last with apparent seriousness, what I thought? Was idol-worship really true or false?

21. Came to at a desert place on the eastern bank.

22. In my morning walk, the musalchee brought an old fisherman to, and was about with all arrogance to make a requisition of his fish without paying for them. The old man was overjoyed at receiving money. I recollected your advice, and threatened to send them all to prison, if I found out any thing of the sort again.

Passed through a number of boats preparing to commit the effigies of Dhoorga to the water. Came to for the night near Agaradeep, where I walked. The women and children fled at the sight of me.

23. Dispatched my hirkaru to Cutwa, to announce my approach to Mr. Chamberlain, and in the evening arrived there myself. The curious appearance of the interior of his bamboo house, seemed to mark it for the residence of a recluse. In the garden behind there was a white circular building. I asked, What is that? The tomb of my first dear wife. I strenuously recommended him to demolish it.

24. Mr. Chamberlain came on with me to a village called Serampore. We passed the time in reading and mutual prayers for one another, and for you all. Thus

once more I received that refreshment of spirit whic comes from the blessing of God on Christian commu nion. Just before we parted the tow-rope broke. W were carried down with great rapidity, running foul c several boats, none of which however would lend an help. The mangee and his assistant at last jumpe overboard, and succeeded in reaching the shore wit the rope. I thought there was great danger, and there fore saw reason to bless God for the deliverance.

25. Returning to the boat rather later than usual from the evening walk, saw a wild boar galloping par allel to the river. I had not a gun with me, or I migh have killed him, as he was within reach of a fusee ball.

26. Yesterday I again enjoyed a happy sabbath Through the different hours of the day, I was wit you in spirit, and particularly remembered Mr. Jefferies All, I suppose, are still looking anxiously to him.

Tell Marshman, with my affectionate remembrances that I have seriously begun the Sanscrit Grammar, bu cannot say whereabouts I am in it, being enveloped a present in a thick cloud, occasioned by the counte operations of Goor, Ouddhi, Loop, Lop, Look, &c. wit the exceptions, limitations, anomalies, &c. If the mys teries I meet with should not clear up, I shall troubl him with a question or two respecting them.

In the tract in the Persian character, I have found th inclosed errata, which I thought it right to send to Mr Ward. With the moonshee I have began to translat the Acts, in order to give him some employment wher away from me. I wish Mr. Marshman would say whe ther this man can be of any use in going on with th Arabic Hindoo translation, and if so, whether he shal proceed with the Acts and Epistles, or take some part of the Old Testament.

The servants continue sufficiently attentive. The goat yields milk enough for breakfast, and more is procured every day from the shore. The toast and biscuits are still good. Two kids were met with at Cutwa. Besides that, my gun supplies me with snipes, minas, &c. enough to make a change with the curry.

28. Last evening after writing the above, I looked round the cantonments and walked into the hospital. While I was talking to one of the sick, a surgeon entered. Not knowing what he might think of it, I went up and made a speech. I did not know him, but I was immediately recognised by my old schoolfellow and townsman, Marshall, for whom I had brought letters. This morning I went at daylight, in hopes of getting the men together to preach to them, but after wandering through the wards of the hospital, I could not make them rise and assemble. But as Marshall says that at nine they will be together, I think it right to wait till then. In the meantime, let me chide you for letting me find no letter from you at the dawk-house.

* * * * *

Berhampore, with respect to appearance at least, is the finest thing I have seen in India. After waiting till eleven I can get no permission, and so I go on my way. Remember me most affectionately to all.

I remain, your's most truly,

H. MARTYN.

XXVII.

TO THE SAME.

Rajemahl, November 8, 1806

MY DEAR SIR,

At Jungypoor I found Mr. C——'s letter, and received another from Mr. R——, the commercial resident there, offering his assistance, and inviting me to spend the day with him. Accordingly I called upon him intending to be guided by circumstances, but found his conversation so much less cordial than his letter that I concluded his invitation must have been purely a form, and so after staying two hours to say all I could, I took my leave. On Sunday, November 2 we entered the Ganges, and arrived at Chandny on Monday. I found Messrs. Ellerton and Grant, and went up with them the next day to Gomalty, stopping by the way to look at one of their schools. The cheerful faces of the little boys sitting cross-legged on their mats round the floor, much delighted me. While they displayed their powers of reading, their fathers, mothers, &c. crowded in great numbers round the door and windows.

Thursday I baptised Mr. C——'s child, preached and administered the sacrament. Sir H. V. D. who was godfather, stayed to hear the sermon, but did not communicate. I found no opportunity of a private conversation with him, though I sought it. Friday I left Gomalty with Mr. Grant, who is now in the budgerow with me, and to-day we arrived at Rajemahl.

Your letter, together with Parsons' and Corrie's, reached me at a time when I needed spiritual refreshment, and they had the effect of reviving my heart. I hope that our God is making our faith and love to grow exceedingly. Glory be to his name, that he is with us too in India. We may surely hope that something good is near at hand for the heathen. But I am somewhat surprised at the extraordinary fear and unwillingness of the people to take the tracts. I have at this place again met with a rebuff. Only one person, a Brahmin, would take a tract, and he, I believe, chiefly from respect to Mr. Grant. The Dawk moonshee, when he found what it was about, returned the tract he had received, saying, that a person who had his legs in two different boats, went on his way uncomfortably.

I wished for more particulars about Jefferies' sermon. I wish much to see Buchanan's letter. There is a box of books in a corner of the room I inhabited at the college, for Elliott I believe; will you be so good as to forward it. We must stay no longer. With much affection for you all,

I remain, my dear Sir,

Your's in the best of bonds,

H. MARTYN.

XXVIII.

TO THE SAME.

Monghir, Nov. 17, 1806.

MY DEAR SIR,

I am now within eight days of my journey's end and, blessed be God, in perfect health and spirits. This mode of travelling is so very agreeable, that I could almost wish I had farther to go. At the different villages through which I have passed, I have never been able to leave a tract, except by forcing one or two upon a man, till Saturday, at Jangheera, when I stood in the bazaar, and gave away a good many. Last night, at another village, finding as usual that no one could read I inquired if there was no Brahmin—There was, but he was gone to another town—Then give him these when he comes back, said I, putting into his hand a few tracts. This morning we visited the hot spring in our way to this place. After examining the waters, and listening with due attention to the legendary tale, I felt a desire of leading some of these lame and impotent folk to our Bethesda, and so began to question the Surdar Brahmin; they all spoke a language different from mine. I see from this, and numberless other instances that I shall have almost a new language to learn, in order to be intelligible to the lower Hindoos. But to return; not finding utterance, I began to speak to them by means of Marshman's paper, and gave away a great number of tracts. They followed me to the budgerow and there I gave some Testaments. My fame arrived here before me, and some men had travelled on from the spring, having heard that Sahib was giving away copies of the Ramayon! I told them it was not the Ramayon, but something better, and parted with as many or more than I could spare. One poor fellow who was selling gun-rods begged and intreated me for one, after I had refused to give any more, even with tears. So, I could not hold out—when he got it, he clasped it with rapture, still thinking it to be the Ramayon. Thus, the word of God gets the honour which belongs to it, from persons who do not intend it, as our Saviour on the cross had his proper titles superscribed by a person who meant no such thing. They scorned the tracts because they were small—all wanted a bura kitab.

At Rajemahl, where I wrote my last letter to you, I met with some of the hill-people, and took down in writing a few names of things in their language—*abba* is father. The same night we met with a mangee, or chief of one of the hills—I told him that wicked men when they die go downward to the place of fire—but good men upward to God. He seemed much concerned at the former truth and remained pensive—nothing gained his attention but that, which he repeated—go to a place of fire! They sacrifice buffaloes, goats, and pigeons, and drink the blood. Perhaps this universal prevalence of sacrifices may be used at last for the universal conversion of the world. My employment at this time consists chiefly in arranging and writing on the parables;—these I hope to have ready by the time the children of the schools are able to read,—and in translating the Acts with moonshee, who takes great delight in this work. Sanscrit sleeps a little, though I am daily more convinced of the absolute necessity of it in order to know the country Hindoostanee. I wis Marshman would say whether we can be of any use i helping forward the translations by taking any par Diffusion of the Scriptures must be our great engin Happily our enemies do not equal us in generosity—n Korans or Ramayons to give away.

Let me beg you to send me all the *texts* that ar given out at the two churches. The delightful intelli gence your letter contained about the prosperity ‹ ministers and people continues to refresh my soul, an the kind remembrances of me which so many of ther make in their prayers are, I believe, drawing down th supplies of grace which I need. Dear little George an Hannah I will endeavour to remember as you desir May the Lord take them for his own.

My most affectionate love to all the church which i in your house. Greet them that love us in the faith.

I remain, my very dear sir,

Your's in everlasting bonds,

H. Martyn.

XXIX.

TO THE SAME.

Dinapore, Nov. 29, 1806.

MY DEAR SIR,

Having met with nothing worth mentioning since I last wrote to you from Monghir, I sit down to mention merely that I arrived here in safety on the 26th. I wished to be able to tell you that I was comfortably settled, and *that* has been the occasion of my delay. The bustle is now over, and I am quietly seated in my apartments at the barracks, which I have taken at 50 rupees a month; but General Clarke tells me I must not stay here, but get into others differently situated before the hot season. It is hot even now; I can scarcely bear any thing on me at night, though in the budgerow I passed many a cold night for want of clothes. General Clarke has been exceedingly civil; on account of Dr. Stacey's absence, he seems to consider himself as my only friend, and so has invited me continually to his house. On Monday I propose going to Patna to consult with Mr. Gladwin about getting a good pundit, for I find Gilchrist's Hindoostanee too fine to be understood by any but the servants of the English. A Hindoo may be probably able to teach me something of the language of the villages. Even my own Hindoostanee I speak with greater hesitation than ever, insomuch that I feel reluctant in uttering a single sentence! yet I find by the translation that I write it more correctly. The sight of the multitudes at Patna and on the banks toward this place, filled me with astonishment and dread, from which I have not yet recovered; and the crowds in the bazar here have had no tendency to diminish it. What shall be done for them all? I feel constrained to pray and to beg your prayers, for a double, yea, for a tenfold portion of the Spirit to make me equal to my work. There are four hundred European troops here, and forty-five officers. The sight of these men recalls the sorrowful remembrance of what I endured on board ship from my disdainful and abandoned countrymen among the military; they are 'impudent children and stiff-hearted,' and will receive, I fear, my ministrations, as all the others have done, with scorn. Yet we are unto God a sweet savour even in them that perish. I expected without a doubt to find a letter here from you; and perhaps some from Europe. I shall endeavour for the future to expect no letters, and then I cannot be disappointed.

Let me know when a ship is to sail for Europe, that I may get my letters ready, though I confess I am very loth to give an hour to letter-writing, when life is slipping away, and I have done nothing yet towards this immense work. About the time that Corrie and Parsons are leaving you, I shall have a great list of books and other articles ready, but I cannot recollect any now. When you are certified of my arrival here I shall hope for letters to be flowing in from all quarters. But I forget the resolution recorded at the top of the page. I remember you all affectionately, but not so much so as I ought. A brand plucked from the burning ought to love and honour the people of God more. Mrs. Brown and the children have a constant place in my prayers. My kindest love to them all.

May the Lord be with my two dear brethren under your roof, and strengthen their hearts and their hands, —so will they work wonders. Remember me very kindly to all the missionaries, and all the church at Calcutta.

I am, my dear friend and brother,

Your's most sincerely,

H. Martyn.

XXX.

TO THE SAME.

Dinapore, Dec. 3, 1806.

My dear Sir,

From a solitary walk on the banks of the river, I ha just returned to my dreary rooms, and with the reflec tion that just at this time of the day I could be thank ful for a companion, was taking up the flute to remin myself of your social meetings for worship, when you two packages of letters, which had arrived in my ab sence, were brought to me. For the contents of them all I can say is, bless the Lord, O my soul! and all tha is within me bless his holy name! The arrival o another dear brother, and the joy you so largely par take of in fellowship with God and with one another act as a cordial to my soul. They shew me what want to learn, that the Lord God Omnipotent reignet —and that they that keep the faith of Jesus are thos only whom God visits with his strong consolations. want to keep in view that our God is the God of th whole earth—and that the heathen are given to hi exalted Son,—the uttermost parts of the earth for possession.

I have now made my calls and delivered my letters and the result of my observations upon whom and wha I have seen is, that I stand alone. Not one voice i heard saying, I wish you good luck in the name of th Lord; not one kind thought towards me for the truth' sake. Sunday morning, by the general's order, the men were ordered to attend at one of the barracks, where the only article of ecclesiastical furniture was a long drum. On this I read prayers, but as there was no seat for any one, I was desired not to detain them by a sermon. Monday I went without any introduction to Mr. G. and by the influence of your name found a very kind reception; I spent the day with him very agreeably, talking about Persian, Hindoostanee, &c. but chiefly about religion. He evidently did not speak about it merely in compliment to me, for many times he chose the subject himself. He made me a present of his works, promises to get a good pundit; and what is best of all, has almost engaged to undertake a Persian translation of the New Testament. He begs to know if you have got chapter 13 of Matthew, which Mr. Chambers translated—and desires the missionaries to send him a copy of every thing they have printed. On my way back I called on the judge, and offered to come over to Bankipore to officiate to them on the Sabbath. They are going to take this into consideration.

I have found out two schools in Dinapore. The masters have waited on me with specimens of their Nagree writing—the Devu Nagree tracts they could not read at all—the common Nagree of the Testament they could make out pretty well. I shall set on foot one or two schools here without delay, and by the time the scholars are able to read we can get books ready for them.

Since I began this letter I have been chiefly thinking of Hannah. You have indeed good reason for supposing that God hath loved her. Dear child! if she should be at this time taken to his glory, I could almost envy her lot in being removed from a world of sin and sorrow so soon. Give my love to her—I hope we sha see together that great and glorious day which Jesı has made.

I hasten to write a few lines to each of my brethreı who have so kindly remembered me, and therefore conclude. You do not mention Mrs. Brown in any ‹ your letters—I do not know why; I am sure she senc her love to me.

Believe me to be, my very dear sir,

Your's most affectionately,

H. Martyn.

XXXI.

TO THE SAME.

Dinapore, Jan. 9, 1807.

MY DEAR SIR,

The melancholy intelligence you give me about —— affects me much. I feel for him all the affection of a brother, and I have been praying for him, if my prayer was not too late, that the Lord our Saviour might be with him in the awful hour. I shall much rejoice if Corrie can be fixed at Fort William. * * * * They have completed the translation of about forty parables into the Bahar, which are all I shall select; and I am just finishing the exposition of the last in my own Hindoostanee. To put this into easier language, for the accommodation of my dull pundit, and the understandings of the poor people hereabout, will be a work of time and considerable difficulty. But my moonshee is happily very intelligent, and enters into my views fully; he is about learning Hebrew. I have thought much of late of getting a short Hebrew grammar translated into Persian or Arabic, for the use of the Arabic scholars among the missionaries. Their pedantry would induce them to study it, and I need not mention the many important advantages to result from their having in their own hands the original of the Old Testament. * * *

I remain, my very dear sir,

Yours, ever affectionately,

H. MARTYN.

XXXII.

TO THE SAME.

Dinapore, January 29, 1807.

My dear Sir,

Your letter and Corrie arrived the same hour. W should have been still better pleased, had you bee present yourself, comforting and edifying us as in time past. I cannot say how much I am pleased with th plan and objects of the association, and the manner i which it has been formed and conducted. I am sure i will serve as a perpetual stimulus to us all. But I hav one fault to find. He that is at the head of it, ha placed his name, I do not know where. It looks lik the lowest place, only that the lowest place is very ofte the highest. You are saying, I know, Nolumus Epis copari ; but, my dear Sir, we must have a head, and i you will allow yourself to possess no other claim to tha place in our body, yet let at least the accidental circum stances of age and seniority fix you there. "Let al things be done in order." I dare not be sanguine abou our future proceedings, when the beginnings are thu disorderly. But enough of this. Corrie left me to-day Our communion has been refreshing, at least to me and the Lord has sanctified our meeting by his presenc and gracious influences. We parted contented an happy. The fondness of friendship gave way, as i ought, to the pleasure of seeing one another repair t his appointed place in the vineyard. He preached her on Sunday on "Not every one that saith," &c. a solemn and awakening sermon. Some seemed more than ordinarily impressed, others scoffed. The General with whom we breakfasted next morning, was fretted, I think, with this, and the former sermons he has heard. His behaviour to me was manifestly less kind and respectful. He is determined to have a recess from Divine service in the hot season, at which I say nothing, though I wish it, as it will afford me an opportunity of penetrating a little southward. We dined also at Colonel W.'s and Major Y.'s; the latter behaves to me with the kindness of a father. The former was bred a Roman Catholic, and is therefore well-disposed to favour missionary efforts. My intentions towards the heathen have become pretty generally known here; for notwithstanding my resolutions of silence on the subject, it has inadvertently slipped out, and I have argued with an intemperate heat about it, for which I shall have cause to repent many days hence. But everything at present goes on smoothly. I became the tenant of a piece of ground, without asking anybody's leave; the school is nearly built; the book for their use will soon be ready, and the people all delighted with the generosity of the Padre Sahib, and the wisdom of his shaster. The expectation from prophecy is very prevalent hereabouts, that the time is coming when all the Hindoos will embrace the religion of the English; and the pundit says, that in many places they had already begun. About Agra, and Delhi, and Narwa, in the Mahratta dominions, there are many native Christian families, as I hear from Colonel W., some officers lately in the Mahratta service, and letters I have lately received from the missionaries at Agra.

Pray always mention your family: hardly any subject interests me more. I pray for them daily, and now wishing you all spiritual blessings in Christ Jesus, and fellowship in the common salvation, I subscribe myself, my dear Sir and brother, your unworthy companion in the kingdom and patience of Jesus Christ.

H. MARTYN.

XXXIII.

TO THE SAME.

February 9, 1807.

My dear Sir,

I inclose two Europe letters, and am glad of the opportunity of asking you how you do. Really, Calcutta seems as far from me as England, and yet I suppose you cannot spare time to write to me oftener. If there were any one else in Calcutta to whom I could give commissions, I should not trouble you; but the cause of my present request is an urgent case; I tell the men to read their Bibles, and they tell me they have no Bibles to read. Be so good as to purchase for me a few, and any other religious books: for I rejoice to see that they are wanted here. The ruling powers are kindly affected towards me still, except the general, who grows daily more and more cold, chiefly, I have reason to believe, on account of what I have said about the natives. However, through grace, I am enabled to smile at contempt and opposition, and I feel determined the more I am opposed, the more vigorously to go forward. My school-room is finished, and schoolmasters applying from all quarters for the other schools I am expected to institute. If my pundit does not deceive me, which is very probable, it is the general opinion that the Gospel will soon spread over the country. Deus faxit! This opinion, whether founded, as they say, on their own prophetical books, or not, may be a great means towards its actual fulfilment.

The married families whom, in compliance with their wish, I have visited, are now inviting me round; perhaps also I shall think it expedient to pay the same compliment to the families at Bankipore, as they have expressed a wish for it. Love to you all.

Yours affectionately, ever,

H. Martyn.

XXXIV.

TO THE SAME.

February 10, 1807.

My dear Sir,

Since my last I have heard from nobody, nor has any thing occurred, but I go on with my work in high spirits. I feel, however, a want of more frequent communication with Corrie and Parsons, and especially with Calcutta. I fear we shall lose our love to one another, if such long chilling intervals occur. I do not, for my own part, mean to grow cold; and therefore I threaten you all with letters, whether you answer them or no. Next Monday I set out on a journey to Buxar, (D. V.) to marry Lieutenant ——, to Miss ——. A few days ago a Portuguese couple applied for marriage, who could not speak a word of English; I thought it certainly a very idle business to read the service in English, and so I translated the service, and married them in Hindoostanee. There seems no approach to seriousness in any here, except perhaps one soldier. They slumber away their time in idleness, and they have lately set on foot something worse, viz. theatricals. * * * * * I have to repeat my requests contained in the last letter, particularly for books. * * * * * *

Yours with true affection,

H. Martyn.

XXXV.

TO THE REV. D. CORRIE.

Dinapore, Feb. 21, 1807.

DEAR BROTHER,

The moonshee will bring this. He has been paying me a daily visit ever since I wrote to you, and was overjoyed when he found that you were expecting him. Your letter is in a mournful strain. It seems to be the way of Satan to cast us down on our first arrival. You know it was the case with me, and as you sent me a consolatory letter from Malda, so now I would repay your brotherly love by praying the Lord to strengthen your hands and your heart; so always whether we be afflicted or comforted, I hope it will be for one another's comfort and salvation. I know how to sympathize with you at——'s coldness. However, ere this I trust he has opened a little, and offered you a place in his house; if not, beware how you get into that hole of which you speak. You will be overtaken by the hot winds and suffocated. Every one speaks of the unhealthiness of Chunar. Your conversation with Mr. —— on missions was precisely such as I had with Mr. ——, a sort of candid representation of the utter impossibility of converting the natives. I trust God will soon prove all his enemies to be liars. I rejoice in your determined silence on the subject of missions. When he is actually teaching in our schools, then they will believe the thing is practicable, and not before. My Dinapore school Mr. ——

has begun, and rooms are hired at Patna and Bankipore. My pundit and moonshee went together on this business. In Patna the people gathered round them in multitudes, and expressed a wish that I would have a school for teaching the Persian character also. I took the opportunity of sending them while I was myself called away to marry a couple at Buxar. While you were writing to me I was within twenty hours of you, or less. One morning there I went to hear a Brahmin read and expound the Shasters to some of the servants of a Rajah. Having a copy of the Nagree Gospels with me then, I sent it to the Rajah, but I have not heard whether he has accepted it. My little parables go on, but the moonshee and pundit have both done making objections; and the pundit is far less pleased since I have given him the way of salvation by Christ. He now says, they will never walk according to this. I have had a letter from dear Mr. Brown, which has overwhelmed me with shame. Such profound self-abasement makes me feel my own pride and hardness of heart greater than ever.

XXXVI.

TO THE REV. D. BROWN.

Dinapore, Feb. 27, 1807.

MY DEAR SIR,

Except a Grammar in Latin, I have but one Syria book, which is the New Testament, Dr. Vanderkemp' gift to me; but I am sure he had rather it should be i the hands of those who can read it, than lie on my shel I transfer it in his name to the Syrian church.

For myself, I have, and see perpetual ground fc thankfulness, but I should go on better, were I nc crippled for want of books to give away. * *

The letters from Europe contain nothing particula There is one point on which I should sometimes writ were I sure you were the only one to see my letters. remain patient and contented—time will shew us whe the Lord intends. I pray for you and your's, my des Sir and brother, and beg the continuance of your brc therly love and intercession for me at the throne c grace.

In great haste, I subscribe myself

Your's ever affectionately,

H. MARTYN.

XXXVII.

TO THE REV. D. CORRIE.

Dinapore, March 10, 1807.

DEAR BROTHER,

My tongue is parched and my hand trembles, from the violent onsets I have had this day with moonshee and pundit, and now I hope to find some relief in communion with one, who does not deny the Lord who bought us. Ever since declaring the way by Christ, the serpent has thrown off the mask, not being able to conceal his hatred of the adorable name. Moonshee's contemptuous rejection of the truth has a tendency to dispirit me in this way. I reflect that I shall never have the power of explaining so fully and so variously divine truths to any one as I have to this man. News have also been brought to me that the school at Patna was at first filled with thirty or forty children, when the alarm spread that Sahib was going to make them all Christians, and there are now only six or seven left. The schoolmaster went round to the parents and very sensibly said to them, 'Has he made me a Christian when I am become one then do you begin to fear;' and so the master now says, (fearing, I suppose, I should give up the concern,) in a month or two after the approaching festivals of the Hindoos and Mahomedans the school will begin to fill again. The same fear kept back the children from the school at Dinapore, till the pundit assured them there was no fear, and so brought eleven or twelve more. But observe, brother, how early Satan has begun to shew his opposition. O wicked Spirit, Jesus has bruised thy head, and shall bruise thee under our feet shortly ! Oh let us triumph in the victories of our exalted Lord !

I have just received intelligence, that similar troubles have broken out in Bankipore. The Zemindar who had engaged to let me have a place for a school, has withdrawn his assent, from a fear that I am going to make them Christians. How shall I advise you to proceed, my dear brother?—the Lord direct us!

XXXVIII.

TO THE REV. D. BROWN.

Dinapore, March 23, 1807.

My dear Sir,

* * * I mentioned to you the measures I had been taking about the schools. At first my proceedings excited general admiration among the natives; but there has taken place a very sudden and lamentable change. For an alarm was spread that I meant to make the children Christians, in consequence of which several Zemindars, who at first promised to let me have houses or ground to build on, refused, and the children are not suffered by their parents to come. However, there are a few at the school here and at Patna. Your letter of the 16th is this moment arrived. * * * I feel bound to bless our God for the arrivals of Mr. and Mrs. T., ——, and ——, and Dr. Buchanan. To the latter I beg my kindest love, congratulations on his personal preservation, and thanks in the name of the whole church for those MSS. he has brought away. My expectation dwells upon the lids of those chests. Who knows how important the acquisition of them may be?

My communication with Corrie is regular, and useful to me in the highest degree. What a singular mercy to have a brother so spiritual near me, in a land where I almost expected to be alone all my days! Indeed, from the first day I came into Asia I have been crowned with loving-kindness and tender mercies.

H. Martyn.

XXXIX.

TO THE REV. D. CORRIE.

March 23, 1807.

It is with no small delight that I find the day arrived for my writing to my very dear brother. Many thanks for your two letters, and for the consolation contained in them, and many thanks to our Lord and Saviour, who has given me such a help where I once expected to struggle on alone all my days. Concerning the character in the Nagree papers you have sent me, I have to say, it is perfectly the same as the one used here, and I can read it easily; and the difference in both the dialects from the one here so trifling, that I have not the smallest doubt of the parables being understood at Benares and Bettea, (a Roman Catholic village,) and consequently through a vast tract of country. A more important inference is, that in whatever dialect of the Hindoostanee the translation of the Scripture shall be made, it will be generally understood. The little book of parables is at last finished, through the blessing of God. I cannot say I am very well pleased with it on the reperusal; but yet containing, as it does, such large portions of the word of God, I ought not to doubt of its accomplishing that which he pleaseth. The day we finished it, I asked moonshee what he thought would be the success of it; he said, with dreadful bitterness and contempt, that, after the present generation should pass away, a set of fools would perhaps be born, such as the gospel required, who would say, This is the word of God, and every word of God must contain truth, and would believe that God is man and man God. Behold how they oppose themselves and blaspheme! Nothing has exasperated him more than the declaration in 1 Cor. i. and Matt. xi. Even the dark pundit has learned to ridicule the idea of there being a Lamb in Heaven. I am sometimes astonished that they (and particularly the moonshee) speak as freely as they do; it is manifest that my countenance does not betray the feelings of my heart, for he sometimes cuts me to the very soul. I am never likely to find more severe trials of my temper hereafter than I meet with from them, and thus their conduct may be the means of fortifying my mind, and enabling me to maintain an undisturbed serenity in disputing with those that oppose themselves. A few days ago I went to Bankipore to fulfil my promise of visiting the families there; and amongst the rest called on ——, a poor creature whose black wife has made him apostatize to Mahomedanism and build a mosque. Major —— went with me, and the old man's son-in-law was there. He would not address a single word to me, nor a salutation at parting, because I found an occasion to remind him that the Son of God had suffered in the stead of sinners. The same day I went on to Patna to see how matters stood with respect to the school. Its situation is highly favourable, near an old gate now in the midst of the city, and where three ways meet; neither master nor children were there. The people immediately gathered round me in great numbers, and the crowd thickened so fast, that it was with difficulty I could regain my palankin. I told them that what they understood by making people Christians was not my intention; I wished the children to be taught to fear God and become good men, and that i after this declaration, they were still afraid, I could d no more, the fault was not mine but theirs. My school have been heard of among the English sooner than wished for or expected. The General observed to m one morning, that that school of mine made a very goo appearance from the road; 'but,' said he, 'you wil make no proselytes.' If that be all the opposition h makes I shall not much mind. The Sunday before las I gained a point, which I trust may prove highly use ful. I had translated the church service, and signifie to Colonel —— that I was ready to minister in th country language to the native women belonging to hi soldiers of the European regiment, which he approved but told me that it was my business to find them a order, and not his. So I issued my command to th serjeant-major to give public notice in the barracks tha there would be divine service in the native language o the morrow. The morrow came, but the Lord sent tw hundred women, to whom I read the whole of th morning service. Instead of the lessons I began Mat thew, and ventured to expound a little, and but a little Yesterday we had a service again, and I think ther were not more than one hundred. To these I opene my mouth rather more boldly, and though there wa the appearance of lamentable apathy in the counte nances of most of them, there were two or three wh understood and trembled at the sermon of John th Baptist. This proceeding of mine is, I believe, gene rally approved among the English, but the wome come, I fear, rather because it is the wish of their mas ters. The day after attending service, they went i flocks to the Mohurrun, and even of those who are bap tized, many, I am told, are so addicted to their ol

eathenism, that they obtain money from their hus-
ands to give to the Brahmins. Our time of divine
ervice in English is seven in the morning, and in
Iindoostanee two in the afternoon. Very few officers
ttend in the morning. Our Sunday and Wednes-
ay evening society now consists of a private, a cor-
oral, a serjeant, and one of the young merchants,
vho attends to help in singing. He acts as clerk in
he church, and yesterday gave us a psalm. Being
ne of Mr. Burney's scholars, he has a regard for
eligion. Moonshee has just read his ten command-
nents, and has, I find, altered several words, and made
he whole more fine than as I read it at the church.
Vhy did you translate from the Septuagint? It is not
n general nearly so close to the original as the English.

XL.

TO THE SAME.

* * * * * *

April 3, 1807.

If there is nothing on the rock of Chunar which occasions your frequent illness, I am sure I am not one to advise you to leave the flock. But if there is,—as I have much reason to believe,—then the mere loss of your services to the few people there, is, I think, not sufficient reason for hazarding your life, in which the interests of millions of others are immediately involved. Consider, you bring a fixed habit of body with you, and must humour it as much as possible at first. When, after the experience of a year or two, you know what you can bear, go, if you please, to the extent of your powers. It is not agreeable to the pride and self-righteous parts of our nature, to be conferring with flesh and blood: nature, under a religious form, would rather squander away life and strength, as David Brainerd did. You know that I regard him as one "the latchet of whose shoes I am not worthy to unloose:" and yet, considering the palpable impropriety of his attempting to do what he did, when he ought to have been in medical hands,—and not being able to ascribe it to folly, in such a sensible man,—I feel disposed, perhaps from motives of censoriousness, to ascribe it to the desire of gaining his own good opinion. I long to hear of a Christian school established at Benares;

it will be like the ark of God brought into the house of Dagon. But do not be in a hurry: let your character become known, and you may do anything. If nothing else comes of our schools, one thing I feel assured of,—that the children will grow up ashamed of the idolatry and other customs of their country. But surely the general conversion of the natives is not far off:—the poverty of the Brahmins makes them less anxious for the continuance of the present system, from which they gain but little. But the translation of the Scriptures is the grand point. I trust we shall have the heavenly pleasure of dispersing the Scriptures together through the interior. Oh! the happiness and honour of being the children of God, the ministers of Christ!'

XLI.

TO THE REV. D. CORRIE.

April 6, 1807.

I this day send away my report, as you do yours. How much this blessed association will tend to unite us in heart, and cause the love of every one towards each other to abound. You need not be at all troubled about books for your schools, for if the parables should not be understood, the Scriptures will. In my Dinapore school there are thirty-two. I think, brother, we ought to praise our blessed Lord for all this unmerited, unexpected success, which we have both been favoured with. If I should be called down to Calcutta this summer, I can get the Hindoostanee service transcribed for you; here there is no one that I know of able to do it. I do not read from Mirza's translation, but have written from it a copy in the Roman character, and with moonshee's help simplified the sentences and changed the words; they say still that they understand very well, and consider it as quite an honour to have service performed for them, and are at a loss to know why I should take so much trouble on their account. It is not on their account alone that I go, my hope is to see some of the heathen come to hear, but they do not as yet. I have been pleased, however, to observe the Sepoy on guard at the place listening with attention. Dr. Kerr has written to me about a Musselman converted, an expounder of Mahomedan Law, who rom persecution of the cross of Christ wishes to go to Prince of Wales' Island to make converts. I do not hink that either of us can prudently employ him yet is a preacher, for it would bar up all our doors of usefulness, and would be the ruin of all my schools; but as a moonshee he might be of use to you, for he is a great scholar. I have desired Dr. Kerr to send him to Serampore, to undergo an examination by the synod of divines here touching both his learning and religion. My own moonshee has fallen into deep disgrace. The Khansaman brought charges against him for dishonesty in his accounts with me, and by the witnesses he brought, he charges were fully established. After an absence of two days he sent a most humble letter, begging his dismissal, as he could not endure the shame of living here, or of ever showing his face to me. However, on further consideration, he has consented to stay. I fear I shall never have the heart to converse with him about Mahometanism again, lest he should think I meant to reward him. I have begged Mr. Brown to order you away from Chunar. My dear brother, for the Church's sake begone without a moment's delay! Let the consequence be what it will, go before the hot winds blow harder. Every one says that residing there will be your death. The Lord preserve you and give you every spiritual blessing.

XLII.

TO THE ASSOCIATED CLERGY, &c.

April, 1807.

I begin my first communication to my dear and honoured brethren, with thankfully accepting their proposal of becoming a member of their society, and I bless the God and Father of our Lord Jesus Christ for this new instance of his mercy to his unworthy creature. May his grace and favour be vouchsafed to us, and His Holy Spirit direct all our proceedings, and sanctify our communications to the purposes for which we are united.

On a review of the state of my mind since my arrival at Dinapore, I observe that the graces of joy and love have been at a low ebb. Faith has been chiefly called into exercise, and without a simple dependence on the divine promises I should still every day sink into fatal despondency. Self-love and unbelief have been suggesting many foolish fears respecting the difficulties of my future work among the heathen. The thought of interrupting a crowd of busy people like those at Patna, whose every day is a market-day, with a message about eternity, without command of language, sufficient to explain and defend myself, and so of becoming the scorn of the rabble without doing them good, was offensive to my pride. The manifest disaffection of the people, and the contempt with which they eyed me, confirmed my dread. Added to this the unjust proceedings of many of the principal magistrates hereabout led me to expect future commotions in the country, and that consequently poverty and murder would terminate my career. "Sufficient for the day is the evil thereof"—"as thy days are so shall thy strength be," were passages continually brought to my remembrance, and with these at last my mind grew quiet. Our countrymen, when speaking of the natives, said, as they usually do, that they cannot be converted, and if they could they would be worse than they are. Though I have observed before now, that the English are not in the way of knowing much about the natives; yet the number of difficulties they mentioned proved another source of discouragement to me. It is surprising how positively they are apt to speak on this subject, from their never acknowledging God in any thing: "Thy judgments are far above out of his sight." If we labour to the end of our days without seeing one convert, it shall not be worse for us in time, and our reward is the same in eternity. The cause in which we are engaged is the cause of mercy and truth, and therefore in spite of seeming impossibilities it must eventually prevail.

I have been also occasionally troubled with infidel thoughts, which originated perhaps from the cavillings of the Mahometans about the person of Christ; but these have been never suffered to be more than momentary. At such times the awful holiness of the word of God, and the deep seriousness pervading it, were more refreshing to my heart than the most encouraging promises in it. How despicable must the Koran appear, with its mock majesty and paltry precepts, to those who can read the word of God. It must presently sink into contempt when the Scriptures are known.

Sometimes, when those fiery darts penetrated more deeply, I found safety only in cleaving to God as a child clasps to his mother's neck. These things teach me the melancholy truth, that the grace of a covenant God can alone keep me from apostasy and ruin.

The European society here consists of the military at the cantonment and the civil servants at Bankipore. The latter neither come into church, nor have accepted the offer of my coming to officiate to them. There is, however, no contempt shown, but rather disrespect. Of the military servants very few officers attend, and of late scarcely any of the married families, but the number of privates, and the families of the merchants, always make up a respectable congregation. They have as yet heard very little of the doctrines of the Gospel. I have in general endeavoured to follow the directions contained in Mr. Milner's letter on this subject, as given in Mr. Brown's paper, No. 4.

At the hospital I have read Doddridge's Rise and Progress, and the Pilgrim's Progress. As the people objected to extempore preaching at church, I have in compliance with their desires continued to use a book. But on this subject I should be glad of some advice from my brethren.

I think it needless to communicate the plans or heads of any of my sermons, as they have been chiefly on the parables. It is of more importance to observe, that the word has not gone forth in vain, blessed be God ; as it has hitherto seemed to do in most places where I have been called to minister ; and this I feel to be an animating testimony of his presence and blessing. I think the commanding officer of the native regiment here, and his lady, are seeking their salvation in earnest ; they now refuse all invitations on the Lord's Day, and pass most of that day at least in reading the word, and at all times discover an inclination to religious conversation. Among the privates, one, I have little doubt, is truly converted to God, and is a great refreshment to me. He parted at once with his native woman, and allows her a separate maintenance. His conversion has excited much notice and conversation about religion among the rest, and three join him in coming twice a week to my quarters for exposition, singing, and prayer.

I visit the English very little, and yet have had sufficient experience of the difficulty of knowing how a minister should converse with his people. I have myself fallen into the worst extreme, and from fear of making them connect religion with gloom, have been led into such shameful levity and conformity to them, as ought to fill me with grief and deep self-abasement.

How repeatedly has guilt been brought upon my conscience in this way. Oh, how will the lost souls with whom I have trifled the hours away look at me in the day of judgment! I hope I am more and more convinced of the wickedness and folly of assuming any other character than that of a minister. I ought to consider that my proper business with the flock, over which the Holy Ghost hath made me overseer, is the business of another world; and if they will not consider it in the same light, I do not think that I am bound to visit them.

About the middle of last month, the church service being ready in Hindoostanee, I submitted to the commanding officer of the European regiment, a proposal to perform Divine service regularly for the native women of his regiment, to which he cordially assented. The whole number of women, about 200, attended with great readiness, and have continued to do so. Instead of a sermon, the psalms, and the appointed lessons, I read in two portions, the Gospel of St. Matthew regularly forward, and occasionally make some small attempts at expounding. The conversion of any of such despised people, is never likely perhaps to be of any extensive use in regard to the natives at large; but they are a people committed to me by God, and as dear to him as others; and next in order after the English, they come within the expanding circle of action.

After much trouble and delay, three schools have been established for the native children, on Mr. Creighton's plan; one at Dinapore, one at Bankipore, and one at Patna; at the last of which the Persian character is taught as well as the Nagree. The number of children already is about sixty. The other schoolmasters, not liking the introduction of these free-schools, spread the report, that my intention was to make them Christians, and send them to Europe; in consequence of which the Zemindars retracted their promises of land, and the parents refused to send their children; but my schoolmasters very sensibly went to the people, and told them, 'we are men well known among you, and when we are made Christians, then do you begin to fear.' So their apprehensions have subsided; but when the book of parables, which is just finished, is put into their hands, I expect a revival of their fears. My hope is, that I shall be able to ingratiate myself a little with the people before that time; but chiefly that a gracious God will not suffer Satan to keep his ground any longer, now that the appointed means are used to dislodge him. But, though these plans should fail, I hope to be strengthened to fight against him all my days. For, from what I feel within and see without, I know enough of him to vow, with my brethren, eternal enmity against him and his cause.

Respecting the state of the natives hereabouts: I believe that the Hindoos are lax—for the rich men being few or none, there are few Brahmins and few Tumaskus, and without these idolatry droops. The Mahometans are numerous and ignorant, but from the best of them I cannot learn that more than three arguments can be offered for their religion, which are,—the miracles wrought by Mahomet; those still wrought by his followers; and his challenge in the second chapter of the Koran, about producing a chapter like it, all of which are immediately answered.

If my brethren have any others brought forward to them, they will, I hope, mention them; and if they have observed any remark or statement apparently affect a native's mind, they will notice it.

Above all things, *seriousness* in argument with them seems most desirable, for without it they laugh away the clearest proofs. Zeal for making proselytes, they are used to, and generally attribute to a false motive; but a tender concern manifested for their souls is certainly new to them, and seemingly produces corresponding seriousness in their minds.

From an officer who had been in the Mahratta service, I learned sometime ago that there were large bodies of Christians at Narwa, in the Mahratta dominions, Sardana, Delhi, Agra, Bettea, Boglipore. To obtain more information respecting them, I sent a circular letter to the missionaries residing at the three latter places, and have received two letters in reply. The Padre at Boglipore is a young man just arrived, and his letter contains no information. From the letter of the Padre at Agra, I subjoin some extracts, premising that my questions were :—1. By whom were you sent?—2. How long has a mission been established in the place of your residence?—3. Do you itinerate, and to what distance? 4. Have you any portion of the MSS. translated, or do you distribute tracts?—5. Do you allow any remains of caste to the baptized?—6. Have you schools? are the masters heathen, or Christians?—7. Is there any native preacher or Catechist?—8. Number of converts.

In concluding my report, I take the liberty of proposing two questions, on which I should be thankful for communications in your next quarterly report.

1. On the manner in which a minister should observe the Sabbath; whether he should make it a point of duty to leave no part of his discourses to prepare on that day? Whether our particular situation in this country requiring redoubled exertion; in those of us, at least who are called to the heathen, will justify the introduction of a secular work into the Sabbath, such as translating the Scriptures, &c.?

2. In the commencement of our labours among the heathen, to which model should our preaching be conformed,—to that of John the Baptist and our Saviour or that of the Apostles? The first mode seems more natural, and if necessary for the Jews, comparatively so enlightened, how much more for the heathen, who have scarcely any notions of morality. On the other hand the preaching of the cross has in all ages won the most ignorant savages; and the Apostles preached it at once to heathens as ignorant perhaps as these.

XLIII.

TO THE REV. D. CORRIE.

Dinapore, April 17, 1807.

I have just received your letter, and being about to leave this place for Monghyr (to marry a couple) before the usual day of writing, I sit down at once to answer you. I write in such a noise and confusion from incessant interruption, that I scarcely know what I write. The children flock to the schools. There are now hardly fewer than one hundred. Even the English smile on these attempts, and begin to think for the first time, that it is *possible* to instruct the natives. They observe that if government knew of my proceedings, they would be disposed to continue me here beyond the regular time. Father Angelo has sent me another letter from Agra, in French, which gives an account of other Christians in different places, and the state in which they are, according to his views; but the Catechism which he was writing out for me was destroyed by some robbers, who broke into his house one night and robbed him of every thing he had. He complains grieviously of the same Father Gregory; who, amongst other things, gave a feast and had Mahomedan dancing-girls on Good Friday, and forbids people to eat pork, and does all he can to ingratiate himself with the Mahomedans. There is reason to suspect this man to be an emissary of France!

XLIV.

TO THE REV. D. BROWN.

Patna, April 19, 1807.

My dear Sir,

* * * * * * * * * * No words can describe my pleasure in reading Dr. B.'s correspondence. It is indeed most interesting, and I beg you to get the whole of the papers you sent us transcribed for me, and indeed all the letters from the first of May. His return by the way of Mesopotamia and Antioch was exactly the work I carved out for him in my mind, in case he should return at all. * * * * * But you must not let him go without a promise of returning, for there is a great deal of work for him here. The ten tribes can be no where but in the N. W. parts of India, Cabul, Afghanistan, &c. and who so proper to visit them as he? * *

Believe me with great regard,

Ever your's,

H. M.

XLV.

TO THE SAME.

Dinapore, April 28, 1807.

I am sorry to find that the accompanying papers ırrived the day after I left Dinapore for Monghyr ; thus you have been all this while deprived of the pleasure you have so long expected. There is in them much to refresh your spirit, as it has done mine, particularly what is said of ——. After all, any thing like a real work on the heart is more reviving than to hear of he most grand plans of spreading the gospel in the world. How much of self and carnality is there apt o be in our speculations on these subjects! Dr. Buchanan's letters describe a scene which makes one need to be reminded of the caution, *Arise! for this is not your rest*. It will read like a romance in England, and the people of God will be in an extasy. But while so many things are calling us to look abroad into the earth, may the good Spirit of God make all his people mind their own hearts as their primary concern. Seven chaplains are mentioned by Mr. Brown, O that every one of us may be a host! I pray for you all, and for myself, that we may be eminent in holiness. Might we but in some little degree receive from God the zeal, simplicity, and seriousness of the fathers in the faith, it would be a sign that the Lord would no longer delay to work a great work in this land. If I must remain but weak, yet I will bless and glorify God, if you all become eminent. I am particularly drawn forth in prayer to God for you, especially on the Sabbath morning at the appointed hour, that you may be eminently holy—that we may be saved from that levity and conformity to the world, under all which I groan. Of what importance is our walk in reference to our ministry and particularly among the natives. For myself I never enter into a dispute with them without having reason to reflect that I mar the work for which I contend, by the spirit in which I do it. During my absence at Monghyr, moonshee went to a learned native for assistance against an answer I had given him to their main argument for the Koran, and he not being able to render it, they mean to have down their leading man from Benares to convince me of the truth of their religion. I wish a spirit of inquiry may be excited, but I lay not much stress upon *clear arguments*; the work of God is seldom wrought in this way. To preach the gospel, with the Holy Ghost sent down from heaven, is a better way to win souls.

XLVI.

TO THE REV. D. CORRIE.

Dinapore, May 4, 1807.

DEAR BROTHER,

You have received, I hope, my letter, accompanying the two great parcels of Dr. B.'s correspondence. Your surmise about the apparent necessity of our continuing in this world in order to the diffusion of divine knowledge here, has sometimes been mine. It is useful to be reminded of our insignificancy. The Lord is not beholden to us for what we do, but in his good pleasure appoints us to this work, out of numberless other instruments no less worthy, and if we are cut off in the midst of our plans, his great scheme is not in the least degree disordered. I think you need not delay the institution of a school for the Persian character. Our premises will require us to limit the number of schools. I think that instead of having schools in all those places which you can see from your hill, you must look at the map. It will not be advisable to appoint any at a greater distance from Chunar than three days, that you may be able to go and return between Sabbath and Sabbath. Superintendance is absolutely necessary. I had a great deal of trouble with the Patna school-master on this account; but have now made an agreement with them all, that if they are out of their places at the appointed hours they shall lose their situations. The promise of a reward to the first boy that shall be able to read, I hope may prove an incentive to the boys and master. At Dinapore, where there are forty-five, two or three who were at school before are able to read: for them I am preparing some MS. copies of the Sermon on the Mount. The unexpected quickness of the boys (for they will all be able to read in two months, the master says) has rather put me out. I intended to keep the parables by me a little to abridge, alter, and elucidate, which are operations they need in no slight degree. I am preparing for the assault of this great Mahomedan Imaun. I have read the Koran and notes twice for this purpose, and even filled whole sheets with objections, remarks, questions, &c. but alas! what little hopes have I of doing him or any of them good in this way. Moonshee is in general mute. My native congregation grows thin. I told them yesterday that I should be glad to see a greater number. On my return from Monghyr, I found poor B., the pious young man, so cast down at the persecution of the other soldiers, who had been bringing him infidel books, and suggesting infidel thoughts, that I felt alarmed for him. But through mercy he is revived. Every blessing attend my dear brother.

H. M.

XLVII.

TO THE SAME.

May 18, 1807.

I think it will be better for us to write to one another every Monday instead of every other Monday. A fortnight's interval is really too long for me. Long before the day of receiving and writing comes, I am impatient, so it is my intention to write to you next Monday. In the ordinary course of things, you will have to wait some months at least before any of the poor men declare themselves for God. I feel anxious for your health at this time, and shall so till the rains. Through great mercy my health and strength are supported as by a daily miracle. But O the heat! By every device of darkness and tatties I cannot keep the thermometer below 92°, and at night in bed, I seem in danger of suffocation. Let me know somewhat more particularly what the heat is, and how you contrive to bear it. The worst effect I experience is the utter loss of appetite. I dread the eating time, and when I succeed in swallowing anything nourishing, I rejoice that it is over. You must feel the solitude of your situation very distressing, especially as you have been always accustomed to a domestic life. A long residence in college has rather prepared me for it; but what a privilege it is that in this dry and thirsty land, where no water is, we have a fountain of living water opened which is sealed to the world. I am however peculiarly blest here in my society. For the ——s, though they know little, are seeking to know more. They have a great wish for my company, and for conversation on religion, and read the books I give them; so that I am with them almost every day; yet they fear to break decidedly with the world. Contrary to their maxim, they went to the General's last Sunday evening, where the Major began to propose something for the better improvement of the Sabbath. It was this, I believe, which gave occasion to a general banter upon him for the change that had lately taken place in him. This annoyed him so much that he soon took his departure, but it does not appear to prove a stumbling-block to him. He says that his former conduct was different, because he never had an opportunity of hearing any thing about religion till lately. Still I have many fears for them both. That same night at the General's, our two characters and proceedings were fully discussed, to your praise and my censure. Captain ——, who met with you at Ghazipore, describes you as a cheerful, agreeable man, and yet a decorous clergyman; and he said that he would not for the world have offended you. It was observed, that it would be better if I mixed agreeably in the same way with them, though some remarked that I should only be a stern monitor. Those who knew me (among them the General) denied this with great warmth. So by way of imitating your good example, I took an early occasion of calling on multitudes of others whom I had before neglected. A Lieutenant —— has been a little excited to employ himself properly, and comes to me for mathematical instruction. He is very clever, and says that he has been of a serious turn from his infancy, but does not show any good marks of it. Yesterday was in general a happy season to me. In every ministration my heart was enlarged. The Hindoostanee congregation was considerable, but I was distressed for want of words, while trying to speak a little on "I came not to call the righteous but sinners to repentance." The unceasing repetition of the same words will I fear prove fatiguing to them. One of the women had been heard in the week before making very light of the service. She said that the Roman Padre used to cross himself and do many other fine things, but all my service was *story-telling*. This instance of contempt proved somewhat of a trial to me, as I feared they would all forsake me; their numbers and attention yesterday were an answer to my prayers. Difficulties respecting the schools have also been a trial to my spirits. As some boys were ready and no books, I got the Sermon on the Mount altered from Mirza's and written out, upon which the Dinapore schoolmaster said, that if the first book I gave them was a new strange one, the fears of the parents, already much excited, would be confirmed, and every child taken away. So with much reluctance I withdrew my book from them, and let them have their own, which is an account of Krishna's birth, or something like it, which if it do no good can do no harm, for the language of it is so old, that the children cannot understand a word of it. Some orders I had given for schools at other places I was obliged to recal, till these are pretty firmly established. The more Satan tries to baffle us, the more closely may we cleave unto the Lord for wisdom and strength. No opposition from without disconcerts me, for sooner or later the world must yield to the great Messiah. But when my expectations are strong, that even in our life-time we shall see many a Christian Church emerging from this darkness, I am damped at not finding that Holy Spirit of grace and supplication poured out on me (one of the supposed instruments) which is the general forerunner of a work of grace. However let us not despair even of *this*. If the Lord has a work to perform, all the intermediate steps are easy to him. My reading has lately been Persian, Forster's travels over-land to England, and Leland's view of Deistical writers. Writing sermons and learning Sanscrit, my proper employments, I make the heat too often an excuse for neglecting. Moonshee has been some time ill, which has delayed the translation.

XLVIII.

TO THE REV. D. BROWN.

Dinapore, May 18, 1807.

My dear Sir,

Dr. Kerr's account of Nathaniel Sabat, as well as I can remember, is this:—he is a man of good family in Arabia—was till lately employed as an expounder of Mahomadan law at Masulipatam, I believe, and according to Mr. Falconer the Persian interpreter, well acquainted with the literature of his country; I requested Dr. K. to send him to Calcutta to be examined by you, or the Synod there, and we should then be able to determine where he would be most useful. If —— is for Arabic, &c. Sabat is the man for him. At all events, if no one else would take him, I would receive him into my service with pleasure. * * * * *

The Persian translation has appeared to me of late of incalculable importance. One may safely say, it is of more consequence than any three of the Indian languages, Sanscrit excepted—spoken as it is all the way from hence to Damascus; and as the missionaries have not particularly directed their studies this way, or are likely to be able to do it with their present engagements, I look to —— for great help to the church in this department. The Missionaries will not, I think, be offended at the mention of this. As God has honoured them with the work of translating the Scriptures, I can truly answer for myself and brethren, that we are willing to be their servants in this work and not their rivals, and will do just what part of the work they will assign us.

* * * * * * * * * * * Things remain here too much in *statu quo*. Complaints are made by some that their padre does not mix enough with them,—while others think that the less of my company the better.

I meant to have filled the sheet, but the Dawk will be going. Yours ever truly,

H. Martyn.

XLIX.

TO THE REV. D. CORRIE.

May 25, 1807.

Pursuant to my promise I begin our weekly correspondence; but this last week has been so peculiarly barren of events, that I hardly know what to say. My chief employments have been as usual, Sanscrit nouns, Persian, and Hindoo translations. The Revelations are almost finished; so except ——— appoint me to some of the Epistles, I think of beginning to translate the Pentateuch. I feel the want of this for my female native congregation, and my servants, with whom it would be desirable to begin by reading Genesis; for the Gospel is so exclusively an account of the miracles of Christ, that I find them prejudiced against it. My society of Hindoostanee Beebers (women) still attend very well. I feel quite thankful to them, and the Lord who sends them. If anything is done, it will be manifestly not by the wisdom of words. In my feeble attempts I remember the words, "Who hath despised the day of small things?" A young Bengalee Sircar is to begin to-day to write out a copy of the service, and the Gospel of St. Matthew for you. They shall be upon two quartos, and room left in the latter for the other Gospels. Mrs. —— is I trust under deeper divine impressions. In her distress you will conceive she is doubly dear to me. But it is her conformity to the world that keeps her in doubt. I have been as faithful as possible, but the fear of singularity is a clogging weight to us all. Your friend Mrs. —— has been the occasion of mischief both to the bodily and spiritual health of Mrs. ——, by instituting routs. The men at the hospital, where the numbers are increasing as the heat advances, are much taken with the Pilgrim's Progress. The poor old General is become a little more serious since the late afflictions in his family, and has promised to read Law's Serious Call, which is now in the hands of his new aide-de-camp, a Roman Catholic. I spoke to —— about converting the large house in your cantonments into a church. Your letter, a part of which I quoted to him, says it might be put into a state of repair at a moderate expense. In this view of the case —— seemed to acquiesce in your proposition, and suggested your writing the public letter you proposed. Some months ago, I observed in a conversation with the Governor-General on the disgrace of there being no places of worship at the principal subordinate stations, upon which directions were given to prepare plans of building for that purpose, and estimates of expense attending them. At all events, therefore, you are likely in time to have a church. I am much gratified at hearing that your school is making a pleasing progress; from such beginnings, though to the eye of reason small, I anticipate a large increase at the latter end. The other day the question was publicly agitated, whether the convicts should work on the roads on Sabbath days. *I* thought they certainly should not, but *we* determined that they should, lest, should they be excused from labour on Sunday, the natives should suppose we meant to convert them to Christianity. What pity it is that we will not do what is right, and leave consequences to God. The prejudices and jealousies of the natives are truly astonishing, and they require to be treated with consummate wisdom. They attempted to take the city by storm, by battering the walls with ridicule, &c. and they have not found it answer. This is an additional reason for trying the opposite experiment, and seeing what caution will do. But here we must be prepared to encounter the suspicions of our religious friends, who will be continually asking, Why are you not testifying in public the Gospel of the grace of God? I trust we shall have grace to keep our eyes fixed on the fiery cloudy pillar. If you see it move when I do not, you will give me the signal, and I will strike my tent and go forward.

L.

TO THE SAME.

June 1, 1807.

'I shall send you some account shortly of a British Propaganda for uniting all the talents and industry in India,' says D. Brown in a letter I received from him since my last to you. The Hindoo translation will, I fear, be very long a source of perplexity to us. When I asked my pundit what dialect of the Hindawee would be most generally understood, he replied, That in which Toolseenas' Translation of the Ramayuna is made ; not one line of which can I understand. The dialect of Benares, in which the missionaries wish it to be done, will not, I suppose, be understood here, and one would augur that the book of the parables will not be understood there. But, however, you will be happy in having the word of God itself. Your schools flourish, I see, blessed be God ! more than mine, I think. Without any ostensible cause, the Patna school keeps very low, not above fifteen or twenty. The Dinapore one is resorted to from all quarters. Let us remember Mr. Newton's story of the gardener and the oaks. We are sowing acorns. I trust our motto shall still be, *constant, though cautious.* As we are military chaplains, I use military allusions, and say the breach will by and by be declared practicable, and then we may enter sword in hand. You do right in being on your guard against the D—— H——, though he is probably in eariest. By conversation and disputes, whether his own ieart be right or no, he may do a great deal of good. How are your communications carried on with him? You must have attained great proficiency in Hindoos-anee. His forms of prayer I should much like to see. Last Friday I sent a native Christian with money to arry him to Chunar, and a note to you to forward him he remainder of his way to Lucknow. No Hindoo would take him into his boat here, and Mr. ———, a ivil servant of Bankipore, saw him driven from the Ghaut, lest he should defile the sacred Ganges by his presence. Three or four natives came to my Hindoos-anee service, and listened some time, but on hearing he word *pyghumbur*, they walked away. It is a sin for them so much as to hear this word; and I confess, hat my disgust is little less than theirs, at a name ap-plied to a filthy debauchee by the most wicked race of mortals under heaven. I shall be careful for the future never to use it, though before this probably those three Hindoos have gone and spread an evil report of the blasphemy that is to be heard in my Church. The Lord help us all, blind and ignorant as we are! The veil hat is spread over all nations shall at last be taken away.

LI.

TO THE SAME.

June 8, 1807.

I return the inclosed with my thanks; it shows a Christian simplicity, and must have been very reviving to your spirit. How are we made to share the Apostle's feelings about the state of his people! "Now we live, if ye stand fast in the Lord." As the whole morning is almost gone in writing to Mr. Brown, I have scarcely time to send you anything, but know the translations are arrived, and the Hindoo is such as will be perfectly understood at Chunar, and in all the lands between Agra and Moorshedabad, so we need not have a particle of care left on this head, blessed be our God! My Hindoostanee congregation is small, generally about fifty. Yesterday I found more liberty of speech than hitherto with them. The young Brahmin who was engaged to write out the things for you has absconded, so the work remains untouched. Pundit having taken the Sanscrit translation, went and gathered about him eleven other Brahmins, and began to expound. A Mollah passing by, and understanding it was the Gospel, shut his ears and went away. My employment all day, Hebrew, Persian, and translations in Hindoo; and, how swift the weeks fly away! May the most spiritual parts of our ministry be equally delightful to us. God bless you, brother!

LII.

TO THE REV. D. BROWN.

Dinapore, June 8, 1807.

MY DEAR SIR,

T. writes as usual, out of breath from emotion. A conversation on justification by faith, at a large dinner-party with a lady, suggests to me the idea of zeal without knowledge, but I judge my brother uncharitably. Lord William's opinion of Mr. Martyn seems to have undergone a complete revolution. How short-lived are the smiles of the great! I sent the passage in your letter about the Persian translation to Mr. G., but have received no answer. It does not appear to me that he would be at any great loss, considering his time of life, want of Greek, and want of taste; for his translation of Sadi does, I think, betray the latter defect. Since your first letter, commanding me to change my studies, the dust has been collecting on Mr. Carey's great Grammar, and the time formerly devoted to Sanscrit is given to Persian and Hebrew. I am too shallow in both of these to touch the Arabic yet. In Hindoostanee translations, I begin to feel my ground, and can go on much faster than one moonshee can follow. I have some thoughts of engaging another. * * * *
In the meantime we are going on with the translation of Genesis. For this work I want the first volume of Poole, and the Arabic and Persian versions. * *
* * * *

You have left me still in the dark respecting the new Propaganda, but I see enough to rejoice in the zeal that animates you all; and in time I hope to catch the flame, and with you to become a living sacrifice. I should have mentioned before, that the translations have arrived from Serampore. The Hindoostanee I like very much—the Persian not so well. * * * The Sanscrit translation I consigned for a time to my pundit, who went away and collected eleven Brahmins, and began to expound. The measures you recommend for introducing proper books into the schools will not, I think, be necessary. The present delay is merely occasioned by the time necessary for making copies of the sermon on the Mount. The masters admire it much, and call it '*gyan ba bat*,' —words of wisdom.'

My cry to you still is for books. I wish to consult you and Dr. B. on some point of Hebrew philology, but I have no room here. From what version is Sabat to translate? What accounts have you of the massacre of Mangalore? The blessing of God be with you and the family.

Ever affectionately your's,

H. Martyn.

LIII.

TO THE SAME.

Dinapore, June 13, 1807.

MY DEAR SIR,

I write in reply to your letter of the 4th inst., containing a proposal for my being more directly concerned in the Hindoostanee translations. I have to say, first, that you can command me in any service which you can prove to be most favourable to the interests of Zion; and secondly, that a Hindoostanee translation of one kind is, I believe, within the reach of my powers—but there must be *two*. One which may be called Hinduwee, and depending on the Sanscrit for the supply of difficult words. The other, Hindoostanee, depending on the Persian and Arabic. For the former I am not qualified. * * * The other, Hindoostanee, though not nearly so important in my opinion as the Hinduwee, must nevertheless be executed,—and if you wish me to go on twice as fast in it, be so good as to send me a good moonshee from Calcutta, and it shall be done. Two moonshees are as much as I can employ. When Hebrew becomes a little more familiar, I may be able to keep three at work.

It is indeed, a lamentable and vexatious circumstance, as you observe, that the Hebrew and Persian attempts have so failed—and yet Mirza's Hebrew version of the Gospels, and Colebrooke's Persian, might be very speedily prepared by such a man as Sabat for the press.

What is chiefly defective in them is the arrangement of the words—the words themselves are in general well chosen—Mirza's words indeed are rather too high. If you have no better plan, I should recommend that Sabat write out Mirza's version, properly arranged in the Persian character, and send the copy to me. I should be able to reduce it to a conformity with the Greek, and also substitute simpler words by the help of my present moonshee, who being a Bengalee, is excellently qualified for that part of the work. By the time this is done I think I could get the rest of the New Testament finished, which might then be corrected by him, checked by the missionaries with their Greek Testament. About the Old Testament I can suggest nothing yet till I know more of your plans, or how Sabat is to make his translations; only it would be expedient that he should make a Persian translation of one book while I am about the Hindoostanee of another: so his performance will be a great help to me. Have you no thoughts of employing Mirza? With a person by his side to explain to him the force of the original, I think the best possible translations might be made, for his versions are very spirited, and highly idiomatical.

Before undertaking the Arabic version, you will, I suppose, first learn the state of the present version, and the opinions of the learned. Our Arabic Professor, Palmer, as I told you, was at Damascus, solely for the purpose of ascertaining how far the Arabic Scriptures are intelligible.

In my last I begged for an Arabic copy of the Pentateuch from you. Since that, Mr. G. has sent me one made by some Jews in Arabia, who, scrupulously adhering to the order of the Hebrew, have merely written the Arabic word for the Hebrew. My moonshee declares it is barbarous; however, it is of use in supplying proper words.

Marshman sent me, you know, some translations. The general style of the Hinduwee is just adapted to the most general use—it will be understood by millions; but it ought to be done with more care. Many important sentences are wholly lost, from faults in the order or other small mistakes. The errors of the press are also very considerable. Remind them, though not from me, that 'the more haste the worse speed.' Their Persian I have also read and compared with Colebrooke's. They have altered his order for the better and his words for the worse. So that upon the whole my moonshee prefers Colebrooke's. I hope they will not go on with it. What a gratification would it be to me to lean my head across your long table, to hear what you and your colleague are planning. But I hope you will send me constantly intelligence. Your wish to hear from me can never equal my desire of receiving your letters. The Lord love you and yours. How soon shall our separations be no more necessary!

Believe me, ever, most affectionately, your's,

H. M.

LIV.

TO THE REV. D. CORRIE.

June 15, 1807.

I begin my weekly labours with the very agreeabl one of a little communion with you. For whom do yo intend the history of Joseph? The circumstance of th story's being among the Mussulmans will rather be a obstacle to its admission among the Hindoos. Howeve if you can succeed in getting it read among the Hindo boys, it will be a great point gained. No part of th Scripture history is so calculated to excite an interes Respecting the execution of your translation, I have t observe that it is very plain. Mr. Brown has sent pro posals to me to go on with the Hindoostanee Scripture as a translator in their service, to which I very cond tionally assent, if they choose to consider me qualifie What their plans are I know not; only as they offe me any assistance I want, it is to be supposed there i some institution. Now, I rejoice in the zeal that an mates Mr. B. and Dr. B. O, may we all, in our respe tive places, with one heart and one mind strive togeth for the faith of the Gospel. I have been reading th missionary translations, and have been rather disa pointed in the Hindoostanee, from its being done wit carelessness. There are so many important errors bot in the language and printing, that I should think it us less to be put into the children's hands. The Persia is also bad; they have altered Colebrooke's translatio in most places for the worse. I trust they may be induced to lay this last aside, and leave it to Dr. B.

I am going on with Genesis in translation. This with my other studies makes the weeks fly like days; but I fear I make these things, which are professional for the Lord, an excuse for a carnal spirit. May I be taught to sit loose to every species of this world's work, and be glad at a moment's warning to lay it aside and pass into eternity. I have heard nothing about my schools lately.

LV.

TO THE SAME.

June 22, 1807.

The copies of the Sermon on the Mount which have been given to the schools have been received without hesitation. I hear they are reading them at the Dinapore school. The greatest difficulty will be about the printed books, because the lazy gooroos do not like the trouble of learning the Nagree; and besides the Brahmins will take care to say that it is a sin for the Sooders to read in that character. I shall be curious to hear more about that poor shopkeeper. What has Christianity got to contend with in this land! With the superstition and wickedness of some of its professors, and the folly and frenzy of others, what can make it triumph but Divine interference? My pundit has been gone some time to his native place, and so I have not had any intelligence about his Hindoo friends, who talk with him about the Gospel. A wayfaring man brought intelligence into these parts concerning the number of your schools, but observed to your discredit that you had no pundit in your service. I did my best to palliate this criminal defect, by observing that you probably thought yourself hardly ripe enough to profit by the assistance of such profound doctors. I went yesterday to the native congregation, with sorrowful conviction that I was utterly unable to say anything of use unless it would please God to put it into my mouth, and prayed for a tender concern for their souls, as more desirable than the gift of speech without it, and accordingly I was helped from above, and came away refreshed in my spirit. Six soldiers came last night. To escape as much as possible the taunts of their wicked companions, they go out of their barracks in opposite directions to come to me. To encounter such scoffs spontaneously gives one a hope of their sincerity. I go on briskly with Genesis and Romans. It is delightful to see the precious truths in the latter in their Hindoostanee dress.

LVI.

TO THE SAME.

Dinapore, June 29, 1807.

Those sequestered vallies seen from Chunar presen an inviting field for missionary labours, only that si and prejudice have found their way into every corne of the earth; still, however, as the people are probabl poor, and therefore not pestered with hungry Brahmin fewer obstacles would occur there than among other But I do not see how, with our inability to remai among them, any thing can be effectually done withou having some of the word of God among them.

B—— exerts himself indefatigably in bringing sol diers to our society. Three more have been to reques to join us. Few women came yesterday; but as the are always the same set, it is to be hoped they deriv benefit. They have observed that there was far greate difference between their (i. e. Portuguese) religion an ours than they imagined, particularly on the subject o images. A native acquainted with the Padres at Betti promises to come and make salam to-night. Pundit just returned from Davodnagur on the Soane, report that there is a great desire in the people there to hav a school, but those of Morea at the junction of th Soane and Ganges are suspicious. No particular pla is fixed between us about the translations. I have sug gested one to Mr. B., but have not heard the answe I hope and trust the work will neither be so long nor s engaging as to take me away from the desire of itinerating. Preaching the Gospel of Christ is, after all, our most honourable and delightful work ; and yet it cannot be denied, that seemingly the word of God must first be translated to produce any lasting benefit. I am arrived as far as 18th of Genesis with moonshee. The Epistle to the Romans I am doing alone first, that I may consider it at my leisure. The paucity of Hindoostanee prepositions renders a faithful translation of this book exceedingly difficult. There is not likely to be a recess from church now or in succeeding seasons, so I shall be at a loss to know how to itinerate. But the Lord will open a way in due time.

LVII.

TO THE SAME.

Dinapore, July 13, 1807.

I have received your two letters and the report, and hope to be able to dispatch it to-morrow to Berhampore. Another copy of it shall be made out for you. It was only a change of scene and air that you required, and I bless God that the change has had the desired effect. If Mirza had been at Benares, he would certainly have made himself known to the English: yet it will be worth your while to make your moonshee write to the Mufti, or Cutwal; they will say where he is to be found. In a letter from our beloved Hierarch is the following, 'Sabat is applying to Syriac, and two months will be sufficient for him to attain Hebrew. These are the originals from which he will make his translations. He will delight your heart, for he is a gentleman, a scholar, and a Christian. I have made a private communication to him of our intention of placing him in your hands, which is what he desires above all things.' In a note of Dr. B's to Mr. Brown, which he sent me, is this; 'We shall give to Martyn, Mirza and Sabat, and announce to the world three versions of the Scriptures in Arabic, Persian, and Hindoostanee, and a threefold cord is not easily broken.' This plan of placing the two with me I accord with, as it seems to be the will of God; but annunciations I ıbhor, except the annunciation of Christ to the Geniles. To announce Arabic and Persian translations to ;he world by men under my direction, who am beginıing the grammar of one, and have yet to open the ;rammar of the other language, seems to be plainly conradictory to good sense ; and what end does it answer? :t will tend to bring upon us the contempt of those, at east in India, who know the difficulty of acquiring hose languages, and can count the number of months : have been here. These are the present thoughts of ny mind, which I open to you ; perhaps farther infornation from Calcutta will sweeten some of my sour maginations. Mr. W—— has also sent me a long and earned letter. He is going to print the parables withıut delay, for me, and the modern Hindoostanee version ıf them for themselves. He says, 'The enmity of the ıatives to the Gospel is indeed very great, but on this ›oint the lower orders are angels compared with the noonshees and pundits. I believe the man you took rom Serampore has his heart as full of this poison as nost. The fear of loss of caste among the poor is a ;reater obstacle than their enmity. Our strait waistoat makes our arms ache. P. S. My best regards to Ir. Corrie when you write.' Yesterday I had nearly hundred women again, and found my mouth open nd my heart enlarged. Thus the Lord graciously nswers prayer. The good news of the Gospel seems o have no effect upon them, but the fear of God's udgment upon sin certainly has. Fear and hope take heir turn in my mind respecting the ——. The Major vas telling me yesterday, almost with tears, of the neers he met with from nearly all for his religion. I rust that something stronger than human wisdom upıolds his soul. He longs to be in England to follow religion unmolested. Mrs. —— exhibits more of Christian simplicity, meekness, and good temper every day. One would hope, from your accounts of the poor serjeant, that he has been accepted of God. Grace be with you.

LVIII.

TO THE SAME.

Dinapore, July 20, 1807.

Milner, your letter, note, and appendix have arrived safe. The latter is certainly too interesting not to be forwarded. I detain it awhile to read to the —— and B. or rather to my society. May the solemn account of this poor man's departure make us all think what manner of persons we ought to be, in all holy conversation and godliness. I groan within myself at witnessing the want of spiritual power upon the hearts even of those who do know something of the power of the world to come. Alas! I fear we are all of us, minister and people, but half awakened. The native of Bettea is likely to be useful. I would give much to hear one or two of his Lectures, that I might know how to address my Portuguese congregation. Employed as he is, you are certainly right in maintaining him, whether his heart is upright or no, provided his life is not a scandal to the Gospel. A word for church I have not yet found, as moonshee knows no word in Arabic or Persian to express it; but no doubt there is some word in one of the oriental versions, which I shall find out before anything is printed. I have written, *the company of the chosen*, which, comes most near to the εκκλησια. If the single word which may occur should not readily express this idea, I would rather use a phrase explanatory as above, than leave such a word as church is in English, to which very few affix the right idea.

LIX.

TO MRS. BROWN.

Dinapore, July 21, 1807.

MY DEAR MRS. BROWN,

That part of Mr. Brown's report which relates to yourself is so wonderful, that I cannot forbear taking notice of it by answering your kind letter immediately, instead of deferring it to another day, as I at first intended. What a scene of terror for a mother to witness! and the dear little infants too, unconscious of their danger. How was our God nigh them to cover them! I join with you in adoring his mercy, his distinguished mercy to you and your's. "Thou shalt tread upon the lion and the adder, the young lion and the dragon shalt thou trample under feet." The whole of Psalm xci. you read as if written for you. Let us indulge the hope that the Lord has interposed for the deliverance of these dear little ones, because he has set his love upon them. Perhaps gratitude on being reminded of this event in after days will be the band of love by which he will keep them for himself. So you intend the new little one for me; I accept the boon with pleasure. * * * * * * * *

It appears that the letter by the overland dispatch did not reach Lydia. Again, the Sarah Christiana packet, which carried the duplicate, ought to have arrived long before the sailing of these last ships from England, but I see no account of her. It is probable therefore that I shall have to wait a considerable time longer in uncertainty; all which is good, because so hath the Lord appointed it.

It is a delightful sign when we love our Christian friends for their Christian virtues, as I see you do Mrs. J. It shows us ripening for the society of an innumerable company of angels, and the general assembly of the first-born. There may we meet, and may your children after you, walking in your steps, follow us to glory. Tell James and Charles that I expect to find them great scholars when I next see them, and shall examine them strictly. My prayers and praises for you all continue.

Believe me to be yours affectionately,

H. Martyn.

LX.

TO THE REV. D. BROWN.

Dinapore, July 21, 1807.

MY DEAR SIR,

Yours of the 29th June and of the 11th July have come to hand. From the former I had been led to expect that the promised papers would speedily succeed it, but the second has removed my hopes to a still greater distance. Till the prospectus of the institution arrives, or some further development of your plans, I forbear saying all that is in my mind, for fear of saying what had better be left unsaid. Your declared intention of placing Sabat and Mirza with me has produced a variety of new sensations in me and my moonshee. It has made him more humble and diligent. For myself I hardly know in what light to consider it. You have carved out many years work for me, which it must be owned would be well spent if we were sure of producing some good translations. Yet mind, I never give up the idea of being an itinerant, and when I feel myself qualified and the time come, I shall neglect the translation without scruple. The hint you give in your second letter about my coming to Calcutta vexed me for three days, and as usual has made me ill. So you must be careful how you mention such disagreeable subjects any more. If ever I am fixed at Calcutta I have done with the natives; for notwithstanding previous determinations, the churches and people at Calcutta are enough to employ twenty ministers. This is one reason for my apparently unconquerable aversion to being fixed there. The happiness of being near and with you, would not be a compensation for the disappointment I should feel; and having said this, I know no stronger method of expressing my dislike to the measure. If God commands it, I trust I shall receive grace to obey, but let me beseech you all to take no steps towards it, for I shall resist as long as I can with a safe conscience. * * *

I was rather disappointed in not finding further mention of Sabat in your last. When may I expect him? Corrie has inquired in vain for Mirza at Benares; from which I conjecture that he is rioting at Lucknow, a place congenial to his propensities.

Ever affectionately yours,

H. MARTYN.

LXI.

TO THE SAME.

Dinapore, Aug. 1, 1807.

My dear Sir,

I have this day written to —— according to your d sire. But how can I offer advice to a Christian mini ter? Every one will say to me, "Physician, heal th self!" Yet I have done violence to my feelings an said something about his neglect of prayer. Dear —— he seems far from happy. * * *

It is a thought that has lately occurred to me, th if Dr. B. is disposed to add another to his acts of m nificence, he might revive Arabic and oriental literatu in Cambridge, by establishing an annual prize ther Its efficacy will not depend on the greatness of the sun so much as on the eclat attending it, and therefore ought to be a gold medal given to the inceptors in ar at the time of their taking their M. A. degree, and a companied with some recitation in Arabic on the Com mencement Tuesday. From those feelings of vanity have but lately escaped, and am therefore qualified t speak of the effect such a thing would have on th minds of the young men. I know for myself, I shoul have taken fire at the idea of appearing an Arabi scholar before the assembled university. Arabic an Persian Bibles will soon have to undergo a rapid su cession of editions in England, and it is therefore d sirable that many persons should be at hand qualifie

to superintend the printing of them. * * *
You will do me a great favour if you will get a correct Greek Testament doubly interleaved, and sent to me. A list of such books in the Mission library, as any way concern me, will also be very acceptable.

I long for Sabat, that we may begin. I have laid my plans in such a way, that if Mirza can be kept sober, the translation will go on rapidly.

Yours ever affectionately, my dear Sir,

H. Martyn.

LXII.

TO THE SAME.

Dinapore, Sept. 18, 1807.

MY DEAR SIR,

I hasten to reply to two of your letters. For the consolation contained in the first, I feel grateful to your kindness. The second, I am almost disposed to call the first angry letter I have received from you. However, I know it is only your love and zeal that make you grieve at my not standing forward to help your beloved church. You ascribe it to the agency of Satan. Let us hope, my dearest sir, that we shall live to see it fall out rather unto the furtherance of the gospel. I have now no choice left, as you tell me, and therefore it is perhaps superfluous to state again my reasons of dissent from your and Dr. B.'s opinions; yet I *must* write them down. 1st. The evangelization of India is a more important object than preaching to the European inhabitants of Calcutta. 2nd. Therefore he that is qualified for the first object in any degree by his youth and inclination for the work, should give himself to it, as he may hope that he has a divine call. But 3rd. The two objects cannot be combined in such a place as Calcutta. One consequence of my joining you would be that we should get no one from England; for they would say, Calcutta is very well supplied, Mr. Brown and Martyn are there. No, let them hear, if it must be so, that Calcutta is destitute of the gospel. Corrie and myself can always plead that we are engaged about a more important object, and then it will rest with the consciences of the ministers at home, young and old, whether they ought not to leave a small parish for the benefit of a great city. I am now supposing you actually gone; but blessed be God, we have you still, and therefore I suffer no uneasiness.

The translation in the Persico-Arab dialect and character, which Mr. Ward wanted, has been long ready. But I have been waiting to read it over with Sabat. My spirits are tolerable in general; a little depressed at this time from seeing yours so much so. My dear sir, it is our privilege to live without carefulness; especially may we be assured that the care of the churches is with Him who has the government upon his shoulder. May he graciously direct all our ways! If Dr. B. is not yet gone, assure him of my affectionate wishes for his safety and happiness.

I am, dearest sir,

Yours with unfeigned regard,

H. Martyn.

LXIII.

TO THE SAME.

Dinapore, Sept. 26, 1807.

MY DEAR SIR,

My first remark is,—another letter from Mr. Brown and again no mention of Sabat! That your silence about him is designed I cannot doubt; and I am now therefore beginning to indulge gloomy surmises: perhaps his goodness has proved like the morning cloud and early dew.

Mirza is heartily tired of sitting on the stool of blind expectation, as also am I. Instead of going to Lucknow as he threatened, he is coming here, uncalled by me, professedly on his private affairs, but probably to know what is in the wind. If he should not be engaged by the superintendant of the Christian Institution, I shall endeavour to make some terms with him myself, though his extravagance leaves me small hopes.

* * * * *

So Dr. B. is going home over land. Is he not afraid of being taken by the Turks? Yet with all the dangers of the journey, I would gladly accompany him in order to salute the churches of Asia.

I am, my dear Sir,
Most affectionately, yours,
H. MARTYN.

LXIV.

TO THE REV. D. BROWN.

Dinapore, Oct. 26, 1807.

My dear Sir,

I have received your two letters of the 14th and 17th, the last contained a letter from Lydia. It is as I feared. She refuses to come, because her mother will not give her consent. Sir, you must not wonder at my pale looks, when I receive so many hard blows on my heart. Yet a Father's love appoints the trial, and I pray that it may have its intended effect. Yet if you wish to prolong my existence in this world, make a representation to some persons at home who may influence her friends. Your word will be believed sooner than mine. The extraordinary effect of mental disorder on my bodily frame is unfortunate; trouble brings on disease and disorders the sleep. In this way I am labouring a little now, but not much; in a few days it will pass away again. He that hath delivered and doth deliver, is He in whom we trust that he will yet deliver. * * *

The queen's ware on its way to me can be sold at an outcry or sent to Corrie. I do not want queen's ware, or any thing else now. My new house and garden, without the person I expected to share it with me, excite disgust.

* * * * *

Mirza came this morning, we looked over some of

our translations together, and his remarks were so excellent that we must not let him go; and so I write again, if it be not too late, to have something done for him.

My moonshee, whose look you do not like, is clever and uniformly diligent and steady, and therefore improveable; I cannot part with him. Yet I determine to engage Mirza too and pay him, though it may reduce me to some difficulties for a few months, because I am persuaded that it is for God. Sabat must be now at hand. Some difficulties have arisen about the bungalow he was to have had, but he can be accommodated for a time under my roof. * * * *

LXV.

TO MISS L. GRENFELL.

Dinapore, Oct. 24. 1807.

MY DEAR LYDIA,

Though my heart is bursting with grief and disappointment, I write not to blame you. The rectitude of all your conduct secures you from censure. Permit me calmly to reply to your letter of March 5, which I have this day received.

You condemn yourself for having given me, though unintentionally, encouragement to believe that my attachment was returned. Perhaps you have. I have read your former letters with feelings less sanguine since the receipt of the last, and I am still not surprised at the interpretation I put upon them. But why accuse yourself for having written in this strain? It has not increased my expectations, nor consequently embittered my disappointment. When I addressed you in my first letter on the subject, I was not induced to it by any appearances of regard you had expressed, neither at any subsequent period have my hopes of your consent been founded on a belief of your attachment to me. I knew that your conduct would be regulated, not by personal feelings, but by a sense of duty. And therefore you have nothing to blame yourself for on this head.

In your last letter you do not assign, among your reasons for refusal, a want of regard to me. In that case I could not in decency give you any further trouble. On the contrary, you say that '*present* circumstances seem to you to forbid my indulging expectations.' As this leaves an opening, I presume to address you again; and till the answer arrives, must undergo another eighteen months of torturing suspense.

Alas! my rebellious heart, what a tempest agitates me! I knew not that I had made so little progress in a spirit of resignation to the divine will. I am in my chastisement like the bullock unaccustomed to the yoke, like a wild bull in a net, full of the fury of the Lord, the rebuke of my God. The death of my late most beloved sister almost broke my heart; but I hoped it had softened me and made me willing to suffer. But now my heart is as though destitute of the grace of God, full of misanthropic disgust with the world, and sometimes feeling resentment against yourself and Emma, and Mr. Simeon, and in short, all whom I love and honour most. Sometimes in pride and anger resolving to write neither to you nor to any one else again. These are the motions of sin. My love and my better reason draw me to you again. * * *

But now with respect to your mother, I confess that the chief and indeed only difficulty lies here. Considering that she is *your* mother, as I hoped she would be mine, and that her happiness so much depends on you; considering also that I am God's minister, which amidst all the tumults of my soul I dare not forget, I faulter in beginning to give advice which may prove contrary to the law of God. God forbid therefore that I should say, disobey your parents where the divine law does not command you to disobey them; neither do I positively take upon myself to say that this is a case in which the law of God requires you to act in contradiction to them. I would rather suggest to your mother some considerations which justify me in attempting to deprive her of the company of a beloved child.

26. A sabbath having intervened since the above was written, I find myself more tranquillized by the sacred exercises of the day. One passage of Scripture which you quote has been much on my mind, and I find it very appropriate and decisive,—that we are not to "make to ourselves crooked paths, which whoso walketh in shall not know peace." Let me say I must be therefore contented to wait till you feel that the way is clear. But I intended to justify myself to Mrs. Grenfell. Let her not suppose that I would make her, or any other of my fellow-creatures miserable, that I might be happy. If there were no reason for your coming here, and the contest were only between Mrs. Grenfell and me, that is between her happiness and mine, I would urge nothing further, but resign you to her. But I have considered that there are many things that might reconcile her to a separation from you (if indeed a separation is necessary, for if she would come along with you, I should rejoice the more.) First, she does not depend on you alone for the comfort of her declining years. She is surrounded by friends. She has a greater number of sons and daughters honourably established in the world, than falls to the lot of most parents—all of whom would be happy in having her amongst them. Again, if a person worthy of your hand, and settled in England, were to offer himself, Mrs. G. would not have insuperable objections, though it *did* deprive her of her daughter. Nay I sometimes think, perhaps arrogantly, that had I myself remained in England, and in possession of a competency, she

would not have withheld her consent. Why then should my banishment from my native country in the service of mankind, be a reason with any for inflicting an additional wound, far more painful than a separation from my dearest relatives?

I have no claim upon Mrs. G. in any way, but let her only conceive a son of her own in my circumstances. If she feels it a sacrifice, let her remember that it is a sacrifice made to duty; that your presence here would be of essential service to the church of God, it is superfluous to attempt to prove. If you really believe of yourself as you speak, it is because you were never out of England.

Your mother cannot be so misinformed respecting India and the voyage to it, as to be apprehensive on account of the clime or passage, in these days when multitudes of ladies every year, with constitutions as delicate as yours, go to and fro in perfect safety, and a vastly greater majority enjoy their health here than in England. With respect to my means, I need add nothing to what was said in my first letter. But alas! what is my affluence good for now? It never gave me pleasure, but when I thought you were to share it with me. Two days ago I was hastening on the alterations in my house and garden, supposing you were at hand; but now every object excites disgust. My wish upon the whole is, that if you perceive it would be your duty to come to India, were it not for your mother,—and of that you cannot doubt,—supposing I mean that your inclinations are indifferent, then you should make her acquainted with your thoughts, and let us leave it to God how he will determine her mind.

In the mean time, since I am forbidden to hope for the immediate pleasure of seeing you, my next request is for a mutual engagement. My own heart is engaged, I believe indissolubly.

My reason for making a request which you will account bold, is that there can then be no possible objection to our correspondence, especially as I promise not to persuade you to leave your mother.

In the midst of my present sorrow I am constrained to remember yours. Your compassionate heart is pained from having been the cause of suffering to me. But care not for me, dearest Lydia. Next to the bliss of having you with me, my happiness is to know that you are happy. I shall have to groan long perhaps with a heavy heart; but if I am not hindered materially by it in the work of God, it will be for the benefit of my soul. You, sister beloved in the Lord, know much of the benefit of affliction. O may I have grace to follow you, though at a humble distance, in the path of patient suffering, in which you have walked so long. Day and night I cease not to pray for you, though I fear my prayers are of little value.

But as an encouragement to you to pray, I cannot help transcribing a few words from my journal, written at the time you wrote your letter to me. (7th March.) 'As on the two last days (you wrote your letter on the 5th), felt no desire for a comfortable settlement in the world, scarcely pleasure at the thought of Lydia's coming, except so far as her being sent might be for the good of my soul, and assistance in my work.' How manifestly is there an omnipresent, all-seeing God, and how sure we may be that prayers for spiritual blessings are heard by our God and Father. O let that endearing name quell every murmur. When I am sent for to different parts of the country to officiate at marriages, I sometimes think, amidst the festivity of the company,

Why does all go so easily with them, and so hardly with me? They come together without difficulty, and I am balked and disconcerted almost every step I take, and condemned to wear away the time in uncertainty. Then I call to mind that to live without chastening, is allowed to the spurious offspring; while to suffer is the privilege of the children of God.

Dearest Lydia, must I conclude? I could prolong my communion with you through many sheets; how many things have I to say to you, which I hoped to have communicated in person. But the more I write and the more I think of you, the more my affection warms, and I should feel it difficult to keep my pen from expressions that might not be acceptable to you.

Farewell! dearest, most beloved Lydia, remember your faithful and ever affectionate,

H. Martyn.

LXVI.

TO THE REV. D. BROWN.

Dinapore, Nov. 10, 1807.

My dear Sir,

Sabat arrived last Saturday, and he now takes up so much of the time I am free from the moonshees, that I can hardly tell where to find a moment for writing a letter. But you are anxious to know what I think of him. Truly, not to esteem him a monument of grace, and to love him accordingly, is impossible: and yet with all, as you say, he is an Arab. Your descriptions of him are wonderfully exact, though I had formed no just idea of him till he came. The very first day, we began to spar. He would come into none of my plans, nor did I approve of his; but I gave way, and by yielding prevailed, for he now does every thing I tell him. He wishes to have nothing to do with my Hindoostanee works, nor do I want him, for he knows not the common Hindoostanee of the country. He says himself that he can be of no use to me, now that I have Mirza, of whose capabilities he has a high opinion. I therefore go on with Mirza and leave Sabat to his Persian. Thus time will be saved, and the two translations being done separately will correct each other. His translation is in a high and admired style. As soon as we are settled, I shall pursue the course of Hebrew, &c. which you point out.

Sabat lives and eats with me and goes to his bunga-

low at night, so that I hope he has no care on his mind
On Sunday morning he went to church with me
While I was in the vestry, a bearer took away hi
chair from him, saying it was another gentleman's. Th
Arab took fire and left the church, and when I sen
the clerk after him, he would not return. He antici
pated my expostulations after church, and began t
lament that he had *two* dispositions, one old, the othe
new. I fear the bearer must have behaved with grea
insolence to him. Last night when I found that i
would be necessary to keep bearers for him, those I ha
before hired for him refused to enter my service. To
day, however, they consent; and I have let them an
the other servants know that he that toucheth him
toucheth the apple of my eye, and that I expect pre
cisely the same respect to be paid to him as to me. *
* * And now with respect to my own mind
I am easy on every point but Sabat—he has increase
my cares,—not that I am much afraid of this dea
brother, but I feel that much of his future usefulnes
must depend upon the good he gains while with me
Oh, what manner of person ought I to be with him, i
all holy conversation and godliness. * * *

11. Since writing the above, I have received you
kind and sympathising letter, and have been mucl
comforted by it. The Lord reward you for all you
goodness to me. Sabat has so filled me with ideas o
going to preach in Arabia or Persia, that I begin t
wish Lydia may never come. But this is the though
of a day. My health is excellent, so that I have n
pretence for accepting your invitation. * *
Your words and David's are mine too—It is good fo
me to be afflicted, yet alas, I never get the good I might

H. M.

LXVII.

TO THE SAME.

Dinapore, Nov. 26, 1807.

MY DEAR SIR,

The letter from Mr. Simeon confirms the account you sent me of his being incapacitated, finally, I fear, for public preaching. His health in other respects was not affected; but weakness of lungs, in such a climate as England, how easily does it become consumption! The other letter is from Lydia, to bid me a last farewell. My heart asks in secret, 'Why have I been so crossed, from my infancy?' Yet the Lord's wisdom and love are very apparent in all his dealings with me. I think now that I ought to urge it no more, since God so evidently forbids it. Mr. Simeon went into Cornwall and had an interview with her—and from his account there appeared no great difficulty, but her own letter conveys a different impression: but enough of this.

Sabat tells me that you have a Jew of Yemen in your house. As I wish to learn Hebrew *with* points, and cannot discover the right sounds of them from books, can you help me by writing down from him the true sounds, on Gilchrist's plan or any other? Next, cannot he or some other learned Jew write a short Hebrew grammar in Persian or Arabic? Mirza promises to learn Hebrew and translate from thence into Hindostanee. Mirza and myself go on steadily; but dear

Sabat is continually called away by his wife, who claims every attention from him in her present distress. Our hearts are knit together like the hearts of Jonathan and David. He did not seem to like me at first, but now he seems greatly attached.

I have not examined the list of the books very accurately, but no doubt they are all right. Castell's Lexicon is incomplete, &c. * * * * *

H. M.

LXVIII.

TO THE SAME.

Dinapore, Dec. 4, 1807.

My dear Sir,

With a grieved spirit I write to you, perplexed but not in despair. Your letters to us came to-day. Sabat had shewn such increasing marks of attachment to me of late, that I did not hesitate to give him your letter immediately. He begged me to explain its contents, which I did, and endeavoured to shew how happy I felt that his first unfavourable opinion had changed. He could not conceal his chagrin at my knowing what he wrote to you. But your refusing to allow him house-rent made a still deeper impression on his mind. He began to speak in a way that made me tremble for his soul; complained of the injustice of sending him so long a journey, with the loss of seven or eight hundred rupees, to no purpose: of your having dealt deceitfully with him, &c. and said that he should wait till Ameena was delivered, and then give up the work. I reasoned with him temperately, though it was not without difficulty that I kept my temper. I gave him to understand that we did not consider him as a hireling, but as a brother beloved, who had the cause as much at heart as ourselves, and who would assist us in bearing our burdens. Nothing assuaged him but my promising to pay the rent, as also the expense of his journey when able. It is really surprising that with so much unfeigned piety there should be so little sense of propriety and delicacy in him ; but, as you say, he is an Arab—half-savage. The allowance he receives, is, in my opinion, very handsome. * * * * The low state of the fund, which I have now learnt for the first time, makes me greatly regret that I was so urgent for Mirza, as I fear I may have pained Dr. Buchanan's mind—I shall continue to keep him at my own expence, and my only reason for not having determined to do so at first, was the debt I incurred in buying this house. * * * * * 5th, (yesterday) the Epistles were finished in Hindoostanee. As soon as Mirza returns from Benares, whither he is gone for his wife, we shall (D. V.) begin to revise and correct the whole New Testament * * * * * 7th. dear Sabat, since the night of the 4th, seems anxious to make amends for his conduct—he is more humble and more *affectionate* than ever : *Blessed be God!* my mind is at rest again.

Dear Sir, your's most affectionately,

H. Martyn.

LXIX.

TO THE SAME.

Jan. 1808.

*   *   *   *

Sabat and I agree better in the faith of Christ than in any thing else. He exalts logic and I decry it, or rather the pedantic use he makes of it. He looks down with high contempt upon the learning and civilization of the Europeans, scarcely allowing us to know any thing but a little arithmetic. This nettles me to take up the cudgels sometimes, to teach him that we do know something. But his ignorance of the terms of science in English, and mine of Persian, is a most happy gag to our mouths, and saves us from much vain jangling. There is scarcely any thing that needs altering in his exterior but his pedantry; his passionate temper is, I think, softened considerably. His wife's *accouchement* has scarcely allowed him to get settled yet, but he translates now a chapter a day regularly.

LXX.

TO THE REV. D. CORRIE.

January 4, 1808.

DEAREST BROTHER,

I am writing a letter in a situation in which I never wrote a letter before, sitting in my palanquin in Major Y—'s camp near Patna. I am on my way to Hajipoor across the water, to marry a couple. My regard for them both (the Y—'s,) has increased very much of late, as I have seen marks of grace more evidently. It is painful to be deprived of them just at this time, yet the Lord knoweth them that are his, and will keep them through faith unto eternal salvation. To-day we ought to send our reports, but I have found it impossible to gain a moment this last week to think of what must be said.

The circumstances that discourage us at present in our ministry, are alleviated by our both meeting with them at the same time. We shall live to see better days. Among all the different people whom I have occasion to speak to, I know not which is most hardened. How shall it ever be possible to convince a Hindoo or Brahmin of any thing. These are people possessed by Satan :—like the idols they worship, without any understanding. Truly, if ever I see a Hindoo a real believer in Jesus, I shall see something more nearly approaching the resurrection of a dead body, than any thing I have yet seen. This last week a Brahmin came three or four days following, and stayed an hour or two each time. I told him all that God had done for mankind from the beginning ; the evidence of Christianity, the nature of it, the folly and wickedness of their religion, in short, every topic that could affect a human being ; at the end of all, he was exactly as at the beginning. The same serene smile, denoting the absence of all feeling. However, I well remember Mr. Ward's words, 'The common people are angels compared with the Brahmins.' Perhaps the strong man armed that keeps his goods in peace, shall be dispossessed from these, when the mighty word of God comes to be ministered by us.

Yesterday morning, on Genesis iii. 15,—there was great attention, from my obviating, perhaps, some of the infidelity our common soldiers profess. With the women I felt greatly restrained, hesitating in the most awkward manner still, between Persian and Hindoostanee. Sabat as usual, proceeding but slowly in the translation of the Scriptures.

The reports of the Bible Society are delightful, particularly those from the Roman Catholic Doctor. In what a variety of forms grace appears, and under what dirty rags may a beautiful countenance sometimes be seen.

LXXI.

TO THE ASSOCIATED CLERGY.

Dinapore, January 7, 1808.

DEAREST BRETHREN,

I come before you again with nothing to say for myself, yet happy to be with you and to be numbered amongst you, and happy to repeat my vows of fidelity to our mutual engagements. If nature were suffered to have its way, my paper would be filled with complaints. I should tell of a year passed away at this place and scarcely the least good done; of the ignorance, infidelity, and dissipation that prevail as much as ever; but, though even Sabat wept at hearing that only one of all the number he saw was converted, I must check my propensity to despond. It took much more than a year to bring out the smallest appearances of grace in myself; and perhaps the ministers of the gospel at home would have as much reason to mourn as we have, were they, like us, confined to a single society. I will therefore rather be thankful for what the Lord has done, than querulous on account of what he has not done. He has permitted me to teach and preach Jesus Christ to the same people for a whole year, and this cannot prove finally to be in vain. Some of them, the officers and ladies of the 25th are gone to Berhampore, where they will again hear the song of mercy and judgment, (blessed be God!) from the mouth of my dear brother Parsons. May many of them be ripened under his care, and be presented by him perfect in Christ Jesus. I sometimes think I could be willing to become a neglected outcast, as unfit to be useful, provided my brethren were profitable in the ministry, building up the temple of God. And I am sure that I feel indifferent who are made the instruments of saving the people that are or have been my hearers, so they are saved ; and my brethren are of the same mind. We shall all acknowledge that he that planteth and he that watereth are one, and yet neither of them is anything ; the people are God's husbandry, God's building.

The two persons frequently mentioned by me before as serious, seemed to be rather progressive than otherwise when I parted with them. And I now commend them with much affectionate desire to Parsons, that he may exhort them with full purpose of heart to cleave unto the Lord. Since the commencement of the cold season, my congregation has been large, and the attention considerable. The Hindoostanee congregation, though much fallen off since the outset, has not diminished since my last communication.

The schools are full of boys still, but not overflowing as they were. There seems not a vestige of fear left in the minds of the people respecting my purposes. By asking the boys if they understand what they read of the Sermon on the Mount, opportunities occur at every visit of explaining to the bystanders. The schoolmasters require looking after. The boys first learnt by rote ; and what they pretended to be reading, they were saying by heart. But of late I have examined them with more strictness, and rebuked the masters sharply. My hopes of the usefulness of these schools are greatly increased.

Among the most memorable events of this last quarter is the arrival of Sabat to live with me. As a Christian brother and able teacher of Persian he is a double blessing to me. He will probably prove a distinguished instrument in preparing the way of the Kings of the East. I should be desirous of sending you tidings of him from time to time, if I were sure he would never see what is written in his praise. But I am very unwilling to feed his besetting sin, which appears to be vanity.

As much of my time as was not employed for the Europeans has been devoted chiefly to translating the Epistles into Hindoostanee. This work is finished after a certain manner. But Sabat does not allow me to form a very high idea of the style in which it is executed. But if the work should fail, which however I am far from expecting, my labour will have been richly repaid by the profit and pleasure derived from considering the word of God in the original with more attention than I had ever done. Often have I been filled with admiration, after some hours' detention about one or two verses, at the beauty and wisdom of God's word and works, and often rejoiced at meeting a difficult passage, in order to have the pleasure of seeing some new truth emerge. It has been frequently a matter of delight to me that we shall never, never be separated from the contemplation of these divine oracles, or the wondrous things about which they are written. Knowledge shall vanish away, but it shall be only because the perfection of it shall come. Then shall we see as we are seen, and know as we are known. What a source of perpetual delight have we, dearest brethren in the ministry, in this precious and wonderful book of God; and what happiness is it that the study of it is made our secular business!

Time flows by me with great rapidity ; and it seems as if life would be gone before anything is done or even begun. I mean for the natives ; for with humble deference to the superior judgment and experience of our beloved president at Calcutta, I think the missionary ardour of the Hon. Company's chaplains,—that is, of one of them,—wants strengthening rather than a check. And this seems the proper place for repelling the charge publicly brought against us in the last letter from Calcutta, for refusing to come down. I do not stand up the champion of my two brethren above and below me on the banks of the Ganges. They must defend themselves as they can ; but I say boldly for myself, that I am not afraid to work amid the fires, at the Presidency or anywhere else ; but when I see a very small party of people who choose to sit still, with their faces upon the right way and a flood of light poured upon it, and not far from these, millions, equally valuable, groping for the true way in midnight darkness, I cannot help running with a lantern to the latter. At the time of Mr. Brown's late illness, (for his recovery let us bless God,) I should have rejoiced to bear any or all his burdens, and would have floated down to his aid with all joy ; but it was to be considered that by the time I had obtained permission to leave my station, and perform my journey down, he might be recovered, that my own European congregation, being superior in numbers to those at the mission church, and inconceivably more ignorant, had at least an equal claim to my labours with the people of Calcutta ; that in my absence the light is out here, no public or social means of grace left, no sabbath kept. Moreover, I sagely reflected that it is far easier not to come to a place, than after coming to get away. Thus I have exculpated myself much to my own satisfaction, and I hope t Mr. Brown's, and if he does not accept this apolog he has only to give me the threatened meeting at Bo lipore, and Corrie and Parsons shall attend as second And now since I have noticed one part of Mr. Brown communication, and got over the most unpleasant pa of it, I join with him in praise for the happy issue the late troubles of the missionaries. The cause h received in a manner legal sanction, and the missionari have learnt, what the best and wisest of men have som times occasion to learn, how to proceed in the work God according to the will of God.

The reports of the Bible Society with which M Brown has favoured us, have filled us all, no doub with wonder and delight. Their large strides towa the great object, seem to mark a power about to be, not already, gigantic; and since their weapons a necessarily by the nature of their institution not carn which cannot with certainty be said of any missiona society, they bid fair to give a more deadly blow Antichrist, than he has yet had. It is indeed his mo tal blow, I suppose, for the lease of his life seen nearly out, according to the prophecies. Amen! th kingdom come, O Lord! Thou shalt overcome hi for thou art Lord of lords, and King of kings. Ma we thy ministering servants also overcome him, throu the blood of the Lamb, and the word of their tes mony. In thy cause let us not love our lives unto t death, but be numbered at last among those who a chosen, and called, and faithful!

H. Martyn.

LXXII.

TO MRS. Y——

Dinapore, Jan. 8, 1808.

Your departure has left the Arab and me in such gloom that I cannot yet find in his society a supply for yours. I still continue, therefore, one of your camp-followers; often every day accompanying you in my thoughts as you travel along; and I now dispatch some china-paper, to overtake you, and assure you once more of my good wishes and prayers. After leaving you on Monday, I crossed the river and solemnized the nuptials of ——, without the intervention of any thing untoward. Next morning, at Patna, I walked out in hopes of having one more sight of the battalion and my friends in it. But some of the slow-moving baggage hackeries only, in the rear, shewed where you had passed. The nearness of your second day's camp was a strong temptation to add myself again to your number; and it might have been easily accomplished; but the pain of repeated farewells deterred me from going. So I set my face towards Dinapore again, and now as often as I traverse, in my evening walk, the spot where the pale grass marks your former abode; and as often as I bring out the Koran from the book-room, without taking up the Hebrew for you, I join with Sabat in regretting that 'the faithful is gone.' But only continue to deserve the name, my dear friends, and we shall sorrow the less at your departure. Cleave to Him, in duty,—in affection,—in bearing his reproach,—and we are never separated. If I am so happy as to hear good tidings of you, and that you grow in faith and love, I shall be contented. Friendship must not selfishly repine at a separation appointed by God. Yesterday a letter came from P——, who says that trials are awaiting you;—that your gay friends will oppose, &c.—but enter Berhampore armed with strong resolutions, and depending on the grace that is in Christ Jesus, and you will stand firm.

LXXIII.

TO THE REV. D. CORRIE.

January 11, 1808.

DEAR BROTHER,

Sabat sometimes awakes some of the evil parts of my nature. Finding I have no book of logic, he wishes to translate one of his compositions to instruct me in that science. He is much given to contradict, and set people right, and that he does with an air so dogmatical, that I have not seen the like of it since I left Cambridge. He looks on the missionaries at Serampore as so many degrees below him in intellect, that he says he could write so deeply on a text, that not one of them would be able to follow him. So I have challenged him in their name, and to-day he has brought me the first half of his essay or sermon on a text: with some ingenuity, it is the most idle display of school-boy pedantic logic you ever saw. I shall translate it from the Persian, in order to assist him to rectify his errors. He is certainly learned in the learning of the Arabs, and how he has acquired so much in a life so active, is strange, but I wish it could be made to sit a little easier on him. I look forward to St. Paul's Epistles, in hopes some good will come to him from them. It is a very happy circumstance, that he did not go to preach at his first conversion; he would have entangled himself in metaphysical subjects out of his depth, and probably made shipwreck of his faith. I have, I think, led him to see that it is dangerous and foolish to attempt to prove the doctrine of the Trinity by reason, as he said he was perfectly able to do.

LXXIV.

TO THE SAME.

January 18, 18(

Dear Brother,

Your conversation at the —— was curious, and doubt not, useful to them. The Lord endue his se vants with a wisdom which all their adversaries sh never be able to gainsay or resist. If I happen to go any place, there is a dead silence on such subjects ; th seem to be afraid to open their mouths before me ; pe haps it is because I go so seldom among them, th they are so shy. I now never dine out, except once three months at the General's. Their dinner hours a at night, and that is the time when Sabat reads h chapter in English, and we pray, and I read my Persi with him, all of which is so important to him and m that I feel justified in what I confess my inclinati inculcates,—seclusion. At one family where I call this week, their unkindness amounted to incivility. C coming away, my pride told me never to enter tho doors again, but charity *beareth long and is kind,* I shall go again. You do not mention whether t pious Faqueer has been baptized yet—whether Hind or Mussulman. I rejoice to bless the Lord that yo heart, brother beloved, is so much toward the heathe I am in amazement myself that —— does not stir hin self to this glorious work. When I consider how muc greater facilities he possesses than yourself, from lo habits of study, I see that the Lord has chosen you to this honourable post. Let us pray that the Holy Spirit would endue us with great powers in the acquisition of the languages; if not by supernatural gifts, yet by keeping us attentive while we read, and giving us strong and retentive memories: may he make our spirits fervent in this business. When it pleases God to open my eyes to the state of the heathen, and to the degree of good one might do, I start at my past slothfulness, and feel excited to resolve that not a moment shall be lost again. My example in this respect has a great influence on Sabat. He is not very diligent except when he sees me so, and then he vows he will not lose a minute. He is very clever, but overrates his own abilities. One day last week, the General brought Bundu Ali Khan of Lucknow, to see Sabat and me. Sabat talked a great deal with him, and warned him to seek the salvation of his soul, as life was but five days long. Bundu Ali appeared a very gentlemanly man, and I much regretted that he was going away, and would not see us again. He did not venture to dispute with Sabat on the reasons of his change. I had almost forgotten to say that the Governor General has sent an order for building a church here. You shall hear more when I hear more. I preached yesterday on the calling of Abraham, in pursuance of a plan I have designed, for noticing the chief points of the Old Testament history, for the benefit of the infidels who swarm in these parts. The Hindoostanee women are very few.

H. Martyn.

LXXV.

TO THE SAME.

January 25, 1808.

DEAR BROTHER,

One of the Hindoostanee New Testaments will soon be ready; but I want to have a press here, for the delay of having everything done at Serampore is insufferable. There are few things I regret more, than not having learnt how to print. Before travelling westward, it would be worthwhile to go to Calcutta to learn this noble art, in order to teach it wherever we go. Yesterday we had the last of our church. The General says, I must only read the prayers for the future, as the men cannot be kept in the sun for more than half an hour. I feel at a loss to know what to do; a short sermon I must give them. The sixty-seventh is expected here in ten days. I have been employed in writing Europe letters to —— and ——. To the latter, using every argument to draw him to India; advising him to keep his fellowship, for if he gets married it will be impossible to get him out of England. I have not heard from —— since I know not when, but I am greatly concerned that he does not give his mind to the languages. What an awful thought may it be to all three of us in the neighbourhood of such cities as Patna, Benares, and Moorshedabad, that thousands are perishing with a light close at hand. But while we are *seriously* preparing and conscientiously redeeming the time for that purpose, we may hope to be free fron blood-guiltiness. Last Sunday I felt greatly fatigue with speaking, and for the first time perceived symp toms of injury, by pain in the breast. Yesterday i returned just as I began the service, and I thought i impossible that I should go through all the service o the day, but the Lord helped me. Saturday evening was reading the ordination-services, and think they ar some of the most affecting things I ever read. Wha men of God were our forefathers! Oh may I lear in the same school. The Lord bless you, brother be loved, through Jesus Christ.

H. MARTYN.

LXXVI.

TO THE REV. D. BROWN.

Dinapore, Jan. 30, 1808.

MY DEAR SIR,

Sabat to-day finishes St. Matthew, and will write to you on the occasion. Your letter to him was very kind and suitable, but I think you must not mention his logic to him, except with contempt; for he takes what you say on that head, as homage due to his acquirements, and praise to him is brandy to a man in a high fever. He loves as a Christian brother; but as a logician, he holds us all in supreme contempt. He assumes all the province of reasoning as his own by right, and decides every question magisterially. He allows Europeans to know a little about arithmetic and navigation, but nothing more. Dear man! I smile to observe his pedantry. Never have I seen such an instance of dogmatical pride, since I heard Dr. Parr preach his Greek Sermon at St. Mary's, about the τὸ 'ον.

For several days past I have had my mind full of imaginations about establishing a press in my house. The reasons are many and strong which I have to offer, but as you will probably perceive them yourself, I will not adduce them till your opposition renders it necessary. But favour me with your opinion upon it as soon as you can, because we shall soon be ready for printing.

Mr. G.'s late appointment seems to have excited in

him a spirit of thankfulness to the Giver of all good gifts. * * He always mentions you with kindness, but like most other people, has a strange prejudice against Dr. Buchanan. On his removal to Bankipore, he promises to come and stay with me. His library is most choice; every article in it is interesting to me, and he lends freely. * * * * * * * *

And now I have no more questions to ask, except about your health, and that, my dear Sir, is a question which comes from my heart. Oh may your next bring me the good tidings of your restoration to health and spirits. I have often observed, that your spirits sink with your strength, but His love changeth not.

My salvation shall be for ever, and my righteousness shall not be abolished.

We wait your order to assemble anywhere to receive your pastoral visit. Were the archiepiscopal hands on you, we could not love or honour you more. Believe this to be a true word from your affectionate

H. Martyn.

LXXVII.

TO THE REV. D. CORRIE.

February 8, 1808.

DEAR BROTHER,

This week I believe I have nothing to communicate; yet, a beginning being made, something will occur. My mind is just now much occupied with some news I have heard, that the King is dead, Ireland in rebellion, England invaded, a large French force by land and sea coming to India, &c.—if any &c. can be added to this. We deserve it all for our national arrogance, and God has threatened to bring down the haughtiness of the terrible; yet I trust that the half of this is not true nor any part of it. Yet the profound secrecy observed by the governor and council since the arrival of the last overland dispatch is enough to alarm the public mind. How will our affairs be affected by it, i. e. our *preaching?* Not at all. Our Lord's kingdom is not of this world; only we shall not be dressed in so good a coat, and perhaps shall trudge about without a palanquin, neither of which we trust are serious afflictions to us. Also the Romish missionaries will lift up their head, and the Beast triumph for a season. Oh happy our lot to have a blessed heaven above for us, where no enemy temporal or spiritual shall disturb; and a Saviour here to whom we may flee and be safe from fears. "Thou art my habitation, whereunto I may continually resort." Mirza made his appearance unexpectedly last week, and began his work forthwith. To-day we reached Matt. xiv. and in a month I expect the four gospels will be ready for the press. But not a word from Calcutta to say whether I may hope to be favoured with a press here. To print, myself, is become a hobby-horse with me. * * * Sabat continues tolerable in health, though often interrupted by headaches. He wrote a second letter to the Molwee Sahebs, at Phoolwaree, convincing them from the Koran of their unreasonableness in not arguing with him; to which they replied in a Persian letter full of Galee. I advised him to let the matter rest there; but he wrote a third time, in consequence of which one of them came and sent a note from a place in Dinapore to say, that for the sake of his descent he would meet him, but not dispute except with *learned* men. He refused to meet him, and smiled at their pretending to despise his learning. Poor Sabat's mind is a little hurt, but I rejoice that his pride has received a wound. He is thereby drawn further from the world and nearer to the Lord. To-day I hear one of these haughty Mussulmen means to visit me. I shall see what arguments he can bring for the support of his filthy religion. The more Sabat and myself talk and read about the Koran, the more he is amazed that his eyes were not opened before; and I, that 1200 years out of the 1260 have left the superstition still in such strength. I had a conversation last night at my garden gate with several Brahmins, but I have forgotten my old Hindoo words, and so our discourse was reciprocally rather dark. Before I attempt speaking in the villages, I must study the Nagree parables again with some attention. And now my paper is done, but not my desire of communicating with you.

H. MARTYN.

LXXVIII.

TO THE REV. D. BROWN.

Dinapore, Feb. 12, 1808.

MY DEAR SIR,

I have no very urgent occasion to write, but next to the pleasure of hearing from you is that of writing to you. * * * My first question is about the press. May I not have one here? St. Matthew in Hindoostanee is ready; and in a month (D.V.) all the four will be so. The Acts, by Mirza, were sent by him to you, he says, and Dr. Buchanan's secretary acknowledged the receipt of it. If you can procure it from Dr Hunter, a month's labour will be saved. For Sabat Mr. G. will provide a good scribe; is it determined whether he is to be allowed one or not? He begins to be a little peevish at not hearing from you—as he suspects that silence may be the prelude to denial. Certainly our Arabian's *natural* temper is as bad as it well can be, but he fights manfully against it. If in any of our disputes I get the better of him, he is stung to the quick, and does not forget it for days. So I avoid as much as possible all questions gendering strifes. If he sees anything wrong in me, any appearance of pride or love of grandeur, he tells me of it without ceremony; and thus he is a friend indeed. He describes so well the character of a missionary, that I am ashamed of my great house, and mean to sell it the first opportunity, and take the smallest quarters I can find. Would that the day were come when I might throw off the coat and substitute the jamer ; I long for it more and more ; and am often very uneasy at being in the neighbourhood of so great a Nineveh, without being able to do anything immediately for the salvation of so many perishing souls. What do you think of my standing under a shed somewhere in Patna as the missionaries did in the Lat Bazar. Will the government interfere ?

What are your sensations on the late news ? I fear the judgments of God on our proud nation, and that as we have done nothing for the gospel in India, this vineyard will be let out to others, who shall bring the fruits of it in their season. I think the French would not treat Juggernaut with quite so much ceremony as we do. * * * * * *
The Lord graciously preserve your bodily health, and fill you with all spiritual blessings in Christ Jesus ! So prays

Your's ever affectionately,

H. Martyn.

LXXIX.

TO THE REV. D. CORRIE.

February 22, 1808.

Dear Brother,

I generally rise fresh and strong for my work every morning, but to-day, though this is my first work, I an ready to fall asleep over it. Understand that I am a perfect giant in bodily strength for reading, and Saba a mere dwarf. He gets on very slowly in his translation, and I fear it will be a long time before the Persiar New Testament will be ready. Yet we may at leas hope that the Persian and Arabic New Testament, anc the Persian and Arabic translation of the Prophets may be done before we leave India. The rest, he says, may be done in Persia. Saturday we finished St. Mark' gospel in Hindoostanee. Sabat has rather a contemptuous opinion of my translation, merely because som of the words are mean, and not the Hindoostanee whicl he speaks, which nobody but the Nabobs and Molwee would understand. The chief defect of the translatioi in my opinion will be the exuberance of Arabic words which are now so familiar to me that I do not think o rejecting them as often as I ought. But I must be careful with Mirza, for he is like a ball of wax, easy to b moulded into any shape ; and whatever he sees me earnest for he will give up ; so I alter as little of his translation as possible, lest through his absurd pliability h should give up the true idiom in my desire of having i literal. I had the pleasure of receiving a few lines from dear Mr. Brown last Saturday after a long silence, he says, 'To carry on your operations with full efficiency, you must have a press at your elbow, a distant press will only plague you. I mean to make very particular inquiries on this subject, and to let you know how it may be carried into effect. I suppose three or four thousand rupees will establish a press, and three or four hundred rupees a month will keep it a going. Now all this the Christian Institution should and must supply, the moment it has funds, and funds I think will soon be forthcoming.' This was blessed news to me, though there may be some delay before my wishes are accomplished, for without the aid of the Christian Institution I cannot do it. So —— has been at Calcutta. Mr. B. says, 'To-morrow he preaches for me a most seasonable discourse.' How are we bound to be thankful for our dear brother, we two, especially, because we both laboured for his soul. At the time of my leaving Cambridge, I had quite given him up, but behold he is become a labourer in the same distant vineyard. Only he must have his heart toward the heathen. The women still hesitate to come to my house for Divine Service. The ladies also I observe do not come, expecting I suppose that I should give them a particular invitation, which I shall not fail to do. The European regiment was again accommodated with ease under my roof. Last Monday I began to read Genesis with my servants; they attend with readiness, and listen with interest. A schoolmaster whom my schools threw out of employ, I have lately kept in the house to teach my servants to read, and it is surprising to observe how fast some of them learn.

H. MARTYN.

LXXX.

TO THE SAME.

February 29, 1808.

If writing to you were not agreeable to me, I shou not think of trying to fill a sheet at this time, for n eyes are heavy with sleep. We are all ill here ;—Mirz Sabat, &c.—and to the inequality of the temperatu we ascribe our ailings. After my preaching yesterd my lassitude was so great that I could scarcely suppo myself; at the close of the rains my sensations we the same. The General had not given orders for chur on Saturday. I sent to inquire whether there would service or no ; in consequence of this application, after order was issued, to the no small disappointme of the soldiers, who were enjoying the idea of having service. When the order came, B. says they vent their rage in dreadful curses and execrations again me, for they lay all the blame of having the worship God on me. May I be always chargeable with th crime ! But what sort of men are these committed my care? Alas! they are men, of whom it is sai that their heart is enmity against God. On the prece ing Sabbath I had given them one more warning abo their whoredom and drunkenness, and it is the tru grappling with their consciences that makes them th furious. When we do meet, it is with little comfort, you may suppose, since I know that by far the great number come by constraint. Even Sabat, who oug to be a comforter, does by his unguarded and coar remarks often dishearten me, for he says he does n like the public worship; and were it not that he afraid he should be suspected of not being a Christia he says he would not come at all. He complains th there is no love in the people, and that he is distract and not able to pray. It must be confessed, that fro the scandalous disorder in which the Company ha left the ecclesiastical part of their affairs, so that we ha no place fit, our assemblies are little like worshippi assemblies. No kneeling, because no room; no singin no responses. Yet a judicious Christian would be with all these things, and lend a hand to countera them as much as possible. But Sabat, yet young, ju thinks of pleasing himself. But through the Lord love and mercy I do not much need the help of man. feel determined to combat the enemy of souls in eve form. Yesterday was rather a happy day; text, "B hold! I stand at the door and knock." The poor me who continue to meet me so stedfastly in the evening I begin to think are really in earnest. Another can in the week, confessing his sins with tears, and desiri a hymn-book. B—— is made the butt of the wick men, who try by every species of infidel and atheistic argument within their reach to shake his faith. At t hospital, Baxter's 'Saints' Rest' seems to cut like sharp sword. The men, when I begin, look with co tempt, but presently their high looks are brought lo by Baxter's plain home arguments. A few wome came to my quarters yesterday. The explanation the Lord's prayer from Luke xi. seemed to intere them. Saturday and to-day two merchants have be calling on me; with each of them I discoursed a lo time on the affairs of another world, telling them "N

to lay up for themselves treasures on the earth:" o
of them said these were 'words of wisdom, and
would hear me further on this matter.' Thus we go c
through evil report and good report. I have been rea
ing Sir John Chardin's Travels into Persia, and a h
tory of the Turks. I read everything I can pick
about the Mahomedans. The Lord soon destroy th
detestable dominion! But we shall soon be out of t
reach of all evil, where the wicked cease from troublir
Let us continue to pray for one another, brother l
loved, that we may be faithful unto death.

LXXXI.

TO THE SAME.

March 7, 1808.

I think you have been getting on very well to be a the 7th chapter of the Gulistan, and shall expect a let ter from you in Persian soon. Mirza recommended th plan of your and P——'s translating different parts (the Bible and sending it to him to correct :—take thi into consideration, but you ought to translate from th original. We are arrived as far as the end of Luke but Sabat carps at several things still. As I think tha no man on earth will be able to find a fault after such severe critic has let it go, I mean to make Mirza rea the whole again before him, and then we shall ampl discuss every phrase in the Epistles ; far less correctio will be necessary, as their translation is very literal, an the arrangement of the words Hindoostanee. Mirza i gone to the Mohurrun to-day ; he discovers no signs (approach to the truth. Sabat creates himself enemies i every quarter, by his jealous and passionate spirit, par ticularly among the servants. At his request I hav sent away my tailor and bearers, and he is endeavour ing to get my other servants turned away ; becaus without any proof he suspects them of having persuade the bearers not to come into his service. He can nov get no bearers nor tailor to serve him. One day thi week he came to me, and said, that he meant to writ to Mr. Brown to remove him from this place, for ever thing went wrong—the people were all wicked, &c. The immediate cause of this vexation was, that some boxes which he had been making, at the expense of 150 rupees, all cracked at the coming on of the hot weather. I concealed my displeasure at his childish fickleness of temper, and discovered no anxiety to retain him, but quietly told him of some of the consequences of removing, so it is gone out of his mind. But Mirza happened to hear all Sabat's querulous harangue, and in order to vex and disgust him effectually, rode almost into his house, and came in with his shoes. This irritated the Arab ; but Mirza's purpose was not answered. Mirza began next day to tell a parcel of lies about Sabat, and to bring proofs of his own learning. The manifest tendency of all this was to make a division between Sabat and me, and to obtain his *salary* and work for himself. Oh, the hypocrisy and wickedness of an Indian ! I never saw a more remarkable contrast in two men than in Mirza and Sabat. One is all exterior—the other has no outside at all. One a most consummate man of the world—the other an artless child of the desert.

LXXXII.

TO THE REV. D. BROWN.

Dinapore, March 13, 1808

DEAREST SIR,

It is now the evening of the Lord's day, and thou I am much tired with its duties, I seize the first r ment of leisure to answer your letter of the 5th, wh arrived to-day. The subject of it is constantly in : mind, as you may suppose; my secret reflection Lord, how long shall the ungodly triumph? and i consolation, Psalm xxxvii. —— is spreading hims like a green bay-tree; the succeeding verse I forbear mention. * * * Sir, I grieve little you; nothing can happen to your injury. "He sh bring forth thy righteousness as the light, and t judgment as the noon-day;" but I mourn for Ind Happy will it be for them if God do not in anger ta you away from them, that they may know the value what they have lost when it is too late. * But is not the Scripture fulfilled, that thus it must for an appointed time? Do we right to expect m favour from men than the Lord Jesus found? * * Sir, I am saying all this to myself. have nothing for you but the prayers which you desi I have already been interceding for the church of Ind the preservation or at least the prosperity of wh seems so intimately connected with your residence he that I should be utterly cast down if you were to ,

Dear Sabat, when I explained the matter to him, promised with tears in his eyes to add his prayers to ours. And I trust that we shall both separately and together pour forth our hearts in your behalf; or rather, as I said before, in our own behalf.

With respect to your former letter, about the press, I wrote to Mr. G. and this is his reply :—' It is absolutely impossible to make types at Patna, and I know from dear-bought experience that it cannot be done at Calcutta, without a very heavy expense, great trouble, and considerable delay, so that I am persuaded you might procure better types from England for half the sum and much less time.' * * *
To wait for types from England is a trial of patience indeed. I hope Mr. Ward has something to say in reply to Mr. G.'s statement. We are ready for printing; —the four Hindoostanee gospels will be finished this week. We must then stop till I can hear from you whether there is any hope of recovering Mirza's translation of the Acts. * * * *
May the Lord continue to keep you in peace—so prays your affectionate,

H. Martyn.

LXXXIII.

TO THE REV. D. CORRIE.

March 14, 1808.

The 67th are now all here. The number of thei sick makes the hospital congregation very considerable so that if I had no natives, translations, &c. to think o: there is call enough for my labours and prayers amon all these Europeans. The General at my request ha determined to make the whole body of troops attend i three divisions ; and yesterday morning the company' European, and two companies of the king's, came t church in great pomp, with a fine band of music play ing. The king's officers, according to their custon have declared their intention not to call upon the com pany's, therefore I mean to call upon them. I believ I told you that 900 of the 67th are Roman Catholic: It seemed an uncommonly splendid Mohurrun her also. Mr. H——, an assistant judge lately appointe to Patna, joined the procession in a Hindoostanee dres and went about beating his breast, &c. This is a plac remarkable for such folly. The old judge you know has built a mosque here, and the other judge issued a order that no marriage nor any feasting should be hel during the season of Mahomedan grief. A remarkabl sensible young man called on me yesterday wit Colonel —— ; they both seem well disposed to religion I receive many gratifying testimonies to the chang apparently taking place among the English in religiou matters in India ; testimonies, I mean, from the mouth of the people, for I confess I do not observe much myself

LXXXIV.

TO THE SAME.

March 28, 1808.

My exertions yesterday leave me to-day without strength or spirits for any thing. I had better, I believe, take warning in time, before I am put upon the shelf. My congregation last night was increased to fifty, and I expounded and preached, and sung, and prayed with them, with an exertion, the evil effects of which I did not feel then, but I do now. This week I have been about the Epistles; the corrections Mirza makes are so many, that I almost begin to despair of ever perfectly acquiring the Hindoostanee. The idioms are so numerous, perverting the most innocent phrases into obscurities, and giving another meaning to the simplest expressions, that nothing but very long acquaintance with the natives can give you any power in it. What surprises me too is that so few verbs are used in the passive voice. We began with the 2nd Epistle to the Corinthians, and have finished eleven chapters. I am now in no hurry to print, but rather to read it again and again. Mirza went to Patna because I am obliged to give so much more honour to the jealous Arab than to him; he talks of leaving me at the end of the year; if it please God to spare us to finish the New Testament, I shall be happy. The Old Testament will not require half the pains. Sabat has been tolerably quiet this week; but think of the keeper of a lunatic, and you see me. A war of words brol out the beginning of last week, but it ended in ε honourable peace. After he got home at night he se: a letter, complaining of a high crime and misdemeanoı in some servant ; I sent him a soothing letter and tl wild beast fell asleep. In all these altercations we ta! occasion to consider the extent of Christian forbearan‹ as necessary to be exercised in all the smaller occasio of life, as well as when persecution comes for religio This he has not been hitherto aware of. One night prayer I forgot to mention Mr. Brown ; so after I h done, he continued on his knees and went on and pray in Persian for him. I was much pleased at this. O of his servants, whom he has taught to read the Kor without understanding it, has taken a prodigious liki to my book of parables, and engaged a scribe to tak‹ copy for him for two and a half rupees. One day goi along the bazaar reading it, he exclaimed involuntari ‘uck, ha uck, ha,’ (very good.) Some people w‹ surprised at finding the cause of his pleasure, not t Gulistan or Bostan, but a book written by a Ferin; Padre, (Christian parson.) He said those books w‹ written in Persian, which he did not understa whereas this was his mother's tongue ; (he is a Mal medan boy of Madras ;) and ‘besides,’ said he, ‘wl is here against God and his prophets ?’ This little cident makes my sorrowful face to smile with hope, if the parables are so understood, I am sure that translation of the word of God will be understood and wide. Did you read Lord M.'s speech, and commendation of those *learned and pious men,* the n sionaries ? I have looked upon him ever since a nursing-father to the church. One letter from Euro and but one, has reached me. But I have done w

Europe, and I hope with the world, as far as affectio for it is concerned. But, oh, that I had more strengtl of body and ardour of soul to do something for th kingdom of Christ in this world of sin and woe !

LXXXV.

TO THE REV. D. BROWN.

Dinapore, March 31, 1808.

DEAREST SIR,

Your letters and the reports arrived safely * * * Now touching the various topics you have handled, first, praise to Him, the God of love, the answerer of prayer, who holds the stars in his right hand, and has granted us the continuance of the light of the brightest of them. I am become a little oriental, you will say. Sabat has made me so, yet you will not accuse him of making me insincere. Truly we ought all to bless God, and we do, that at this moment, when your presence is more necessary than ever, you are granted to our prayers.

Sabat's letter I had seen before he sent it you. I told him that I thought it so harmless, and so unlikely to effect what he was then anxious about, that I consented to his sending it you without fear.

He complains first of the bungalow. * * It is surrounded with a fine garden, in an airy situation, and far removed from noise. It is about as far from my house, as your pagoda is from your house, so that I was quite pleased at getting it. * * There is so much room, that he offered to accommodate one of the scribes there under the same roof, and it is in other respects so commodious, that, not able to live in mine on account of the dust, he has chosen to pass the day in his own in preference. But how shall I g through the number of his childish freaks ? *

The scribes—we have tried several, but all are unf for Sabat's work. His words are so high, and h writing so bad, that the poor Hindoos are as much i the dark, as if they were writing Greek. * This has tried Sabat's temper. * * * Bu what has irritated him more than all, is Mirza, thoug I cannot safely say that Mirza is perfectly innocent In some of Sabat's Arabic, Mirza accidentally remarked that another conjugation of the same verb, and havin the same meaning, was generally used, and this I a accidentally mentioned to Sabat. His heart immedi ately filled with wrath, and now he never speaks o hears of Mirza without contempt and bitterness. Bu from that time nothing would satisfy him but going t Calcutta ; the people about me were all so wicked, ther was no living with them. You may imagine some o the distress I have been in from all his madness an folly. The hours and hours I have spent in convincin him of the inconsistency of his conduct ; the disgrac he would bring upon himself and the cause, by hi fickleness ; the interruption to the work that would b occasioned by his leaving me ; the displeasure of Go if he went away, merely to please himself, without an intimation of the divine will ! This matter rested a little, then Mirza began to complain that the house I had given him to live in on my premises, was almost uninhabitable on account of the dust,—that his things were stolen, &c. I humbly represented to Sabat, that I had a small unoccupied room on the side opposite to his rooms, where I would put Mirza. He apparently consented, but instantly ordered all his things away to his own house, and declared he would never live under

e same roof with Mirza. And why? Because he
new the servants would at last say, 'This belongs to
e Hindoostanee moonshee, and this to the Arabian
oonshee,' thus equalizing him with an Indian, and
priving him of his Arabian honour. * *
order to have the Hindoostanee more correct, it was
tended that Sabat should hear it, but I tremble to
gin, lest the Arab's ungovernable temper should stop
e work at the very outset. * * *
e scarcely ever speaks a Hindoostanee sentence
ammatically right, yet withal, sometimes says that
is probably a better Hindoostanee scholar than
irza. So boundless is his vanity. He will, however,
of great use in detecting the improper use of the
rabic and Persian words. In this work of translation,
irza is invaluable, on account of his knowledge of
nglish, which surprises me. May the Lord long pre-
rve his life: but I observe with concern in him, the
arks of declining years.

I am at present employed in the toilsome work of
ing through the Syriac gospels, and writing out the
mes, in order to ascertain their orthography, if pos-
ble; and correcting with Mirza the Epistles. This last
ork is incredibly difficult in Hindoostanee, and will
nearly as much so in Persian, but very easy and
gant in Arabic. But Sabat need not talk of leaving
, for it will require the union of all the talent we pos-
s, and more too, I fear, to produce a good translation
the Epistles.

April 1. Last night and this morning we have had
great deal of conversation on the subject of your
ters. He is unhappy on account of something or
her he has read in them. * * * But
e main cause of his unhappiness is the prevalence of

the dark passions, pride, and envy, and revenge, leavin little room for the comforting influence of the Spir of God.

He has been again maintaining, seriously and stoutl his superiority to Mirza in the Hindoostanee, thoug the very mention of it is absolutely ridiculous.

* * *

I perceive no distinct ground of complaint at presen but the house. Two others were found for him som time ago, but one, he said, had been built from the tim of Noah's flood, and the other was surrounded by mea Mahometans, which would be a dishonour for an Aral Thus is this poor man made miserable by his extrava gant pride. I am still looking out for a house, to re move, if possible, all sources of disquiet.

I find some relief in venting my thoughts respectin him. Before him I endeavour to possess my soul i patience. When you write to him, I think it may b useful to touch him on the subject of his pride. An you need not fear to give him some severe admonitions tell him that to be an Arabian, or to have all the learn ing in the world, is of no account at all before God that to desire human praise, or to be uneasy at the los of it, is entirely inconsistent with the humility and hea venly-mindedness of a Christian.

With respect to his leaving me, speak of it witl decided disapprobation. He hankers after Serampore * * * I fear he has been too mucl flattered there, and his pride sighs for a repetition o this homage. * * *

But I have been writing gloomily about Sabat. D not think I love him less. He does not want integrit of heart, but to have his mind more enlightened re specting the extent of Christian obedience. One nigh

I had omitted in prayer to mention any of my brethren in India; at the close, he continued the prayer in Persian, and mentioned you by name, and your affair then pending. I was much pleased at this mark of his regard. * * *

Your kind anxiety about my health affects me much. My cares and employments are the things which seem to threaten me with most serious injury, by depriving me of sleep; but I daily experience the privilege of prayer, and the truth of the promise:—"Thou wilt keep him in perfect peace, whose mind is stayed on thee."

I could willingly prolong my letter, but other employments must be attended to.

Adieu, dearest Sir, the Lord help us to be faithful unto death.

H. Martyn.

LXXXVI.

TO THE REV. D. CORRIE.

April 11, 1808.

I am surprised that my letter of this day fortnigh has not reached you, but I have not yet found leisur to inquire at the Dawk. Your report arrived safely and is transmitted to P. I shall be curious to hea more about the Brahmin you baptised. The tiding from Bettea are also interesting. Do you know an thing more of this Padre lately from Europe, that ha his eyes opened and preaches Jesus Christ? I purpos a descent upon those Christians of Bettea the first op portunity; how many days' journey may they be fron you? All this week, night and day, I have been em ployed in getting ready for press, so that I have nothin to write about. We wait for nothing but Sabat to exa mine it; but that alas! is the greatest plague to come How shall we ever get through it? I do not expect indeed, that we shall get further than a few chapters for if every thing is not altered according to his *ips dixit*, he is angry; and this I certainly cannot do. H says, that if I print it now I shall be ashamed; yet intend to run the hazard. It is surprising, that a ma can be so blinded by vanity as to suppose, as he does that he is superior to Mirza in Hindoostanee; yet thi he does, and maintains it stoutly. I am tired of com bating this opinion; as nothing comes of our argument but strifes. Another of his odd opinions is, that he i so under the immediate influence and direction of the Spirit, that there will not be one single error in his whole Persian translation. You perceive a little enthusiasm in the character of our brother. As often as he finds himself in any difficulty, he expects a dream to set him right. One of our disputes was, whether the order of the verses should in any case be altered, on account of the Hindoostanee order. I had no doubt, but on the contrary affirmed it to be absolutely necessary; he was now determined to seek instruction from heaven; so the next morning he said he had seen a dream, and an old man said something to him in Arabic, from which he rather inferred that I was right. In Mr. Brown's late affair he took to dreaming again, and prophesied truly enough that Mr. B. would stay. My men continue steadily to come every night. Yesterday we had the band again to play two hymns, and they sung. At the hospital and with the Hindoostanee congregation, I had great numbers. One very respectable Portuguese old woman, whom I have often observed very attentive and devout with the external fooleries of the Roman Catholics, I asked, whether she understood me; she said, 'Every word, and I wished the Portuguese Padrees would expound in the same way in Hindoostanee.' I have received great encouragement from this. Thus the Lord helps us on. I am grieved to hear of the attack you have had. The same cause it is, I suppose, which has affected me. Lassitude, sickness, and head-ache, have been hanging about me all the week. We shall live as long as the Lord has work for us to do.

H. MARTYN.

LXXXVII.

TO THE REV. D. BROWN.

Dinapore, April 13, 1808.

My dear Sir,

This day Sabat dispatches his translations, and w proceed immediately to prepare for the press. We wai for nothing but his reading over the Hindoostanee of St Matthew, and it shall be sent to you. After that, th same gospel in Persian. Last night Sabat began to sa that he had been for some time past uneasy at som things in his own family, and had been venting his dis pleasure upon me. I was glad to find him disposed t unbosom himself. * * * * In the present sor state of his mind, reproof would be unsuitable ; therefor defer the admonitions I requested you to send, to future day. * * * * *
* * * * *

We are all agitated with the idea of a French arm being on its march to India. As you are nearer th centre of information, perhaps you may know the truth "The Lord reigneth, therefore will I not fear," &c.

I am yours ever, dearest Sir,

H. Martyn.

LXXXVIII.

TO THE REV. D. CORRIE.

April 18.

I began with Sabat the correction of the Hindoostanee gospels, and we are determined not to move from one another day or night till we finish it. I have begged, however, for a few moments after dinner to write to my brother at Chunar. The Brahmin ought certainly to lay aside his string, because the distinction is founded upon imposition and lies. I should also discourage his appealing to their testimony to Jesus Christ,—it is an evidence in their favour. I have written to Mr. Brown to beg he will order you to desist from so much exertion; he has written me a great deal this week. You, Parsons, Jeffries, and myself, are members of the Corresponding Oriental Committee. Padre Arratoon, an Armenian monk of Jerusalem, called on us to-day begging. His ignorance was incredibly great. This week I had news from Patna that I had become a Mussulman; when I do turn I will let you know. One day this week Major —— fell in with my men coming to me, and ordered them all back, saying he would send for a guard and fetch them away from my house if they went there. I was very indignant at first, but waited till next day and went to Colonel —— and complained. He said he would speak to Major ——, and was as polite and kind as he could be. He came the next day to me and sat a long time, looked over some of my books, and took away Wells's Geography of the Bible. The men came as usual, and Colonel —— approves of it. Thus the Lord continues his favour. Praise to his name.

H. MARTYN.

LXXXIX.

TO THE REV. D. BROWN.

Dinapore, April 26, 1808.

DEAREST SIR,

This day I sent off a chapter of Hindoostanee, of St. Matthew. The name I design for my work is—Benoni, the son of my affliction: for through great tribulation will it come out. Sabat has kept me much upon the fret this week: when he had reached the ninth chapter, the idea seized him, that Mirza might receive some honour from his inspecting the work. He stopped immediately; and, say what I will, he determines not to give me the smallest help in correcting the Hindoostanee. I argued with him, chiefly on the ground of Christian duty; but I grieve to say that he is deaf to all that I urge respecting the necessity of loving our enemies. His love to Christ, he says, will ensure him salvation, though he does disobey that one command. Hence he continues to hate Mirza with a perfect hatred, inveighing against him with dreadful bitterness, and declaring that if he were not a Christian he would destroy him instantly. * * What to do with him I am at a loss to know. I pity him, and pray for him and with him; but his poor soul is still the sport of bad passions. He is angry with me for not hating Mirza too, according to the Arabian proverb,—that a friend is an enemy to his friend's enemy. Last night he spoke to me in a more provoking way than ever. The occasion was this: In consequence c his refusing to help me in the Hindoostanee, my scribe were left without work. At last I resolved to send on away with the intention of calling him again, whe work should be ready for him, and the one I fixed or is an old deaf man who cannot hear what Mirza dic tates, while the other can. But this old man is one fo whom Ameenah made intercession some time ago, whe he was about to be sent away. When Sabat found wha I was going to do, he said that I meant to insul Ameenah; that I would not have done such things t a European woman; and that such proceedings mus produce a speedy separation between us.

I now keep the scribes to please him, though the stand all the day idle, merely through his perverseness Since the unexpected stop in the Hindoostanee, I hav been giving most of the time to his Persian—unwill ingly he thinks—but I tell him that the souls of th Persians are as dear to me as those of the Indians. H would have sent you about six chapters to-day, but h wished to take a copy of it in its corrected state. Mr G——'s scribe having proved a bad one, he has sen him away, and lays all the blame of delay at my door where I am very willing it should lie. I give way t him in every thing—too much, I fear, but I am afrai to make any experiments of a rough nature, when th success of our public plans so much depends on ou remaining together. He himself begins to acknowledg the advantage of having access to the Greek, for hi translation has in many cases already been made mor concise and elegant. But I have my doubts about it purity, at least I never saw Persian in my life s crammed with high Arabic words. If you could get a native Persian or two to give his opinion of the firs heet, it would be a satisfaction to me ; at least I should ntreat him, if necessary, to use a few more intelligible vords. Mirza laughs at what he has seen of it, but I eckon his opinion as nothing.

Well, sir, you must write to the Arabian if you lease ; but now not gently—confirm by your word vhat I have said about the danger of his soul, if he ontinues thus to hate. Next Tuesday I hope we shall e able to send you a large portion of the Persian, but he Hindoostanee, when, and as I can. * *

P— writes that Dr. Ward is coming to Calcutta. s there any truth in the report ? I do not care who oes there, provided *you* remain there, and *I* stay away rom it. Interpret this ambiguous sentence rightly.

Yours ever affectionately,

H. Martyn.

XC.

TO A FRIEND AT CAMBRIDGE.

Dinapore, Bahar, April 26, 1808.

Dear E——,

What is become of you I cannot tell, and lest you also should forget your old friend, I begin with specifying accurately the spot of the terraqueous globe where I am to be found.

The last letter I have received from you is dated about two years ago, in answer to the one I sent you from South America. I have written you one or two since that, but as you have not answered them I conclude that they have not arrived. I hope, however, that those I chiefly value continue to remember me in their prayers, as I do them without ceasing. Without this method of binding our hearts together, we should soon be as those who had never met. I freely acknowledge my own weakness. The new scenes I have witnessed these last three years have made so strong an impression as almost to efface the remembrance of England. Even so late a period of my short life as the years spent at Cambridge, seemed to have passed in a prior state of existence; and when I think of our fellows of St. John's, they flit before my fancy like the varied personages of the camera obscura. Yet there is nothing that would gratify me more than to hear of them. I have no correspondent at Cambridge but Mr. Simeon, who you know has not much to do at St. John's.

I have just been reading over all the letters I ever received from you, and cannot help expressing how forcibly I am now struck with the sense of my own conceit and ignorance in times past, and of your unequalled charity and forbearance. Oh, my dear friend, if instead of blaming your faith, I had been trying to follow your practice, how much better would it have been for me. Continue your friendship to me, a right to which I have so often forfeited, and accept one more assurance of my unalterable attachment. I fear I shall never again see your face in the flesh; every day's experience convinces me that with the power I shall soon possess of making known the gospel in two such large countries as India and Persia, I should never be able to live with a quiet conscience in England. Dr. Buchanan, whom you will have seen before this reaches you, will give you such an account of the plans we are pursuing, of which he is himself the designer, that it is superfluous for me to write about them. All I have to say is, that I am endeavouring to perform the part he has assigned to me. With my Arabian brother and Mirza Fitrut I am labouring most of the day in the Hindoostanee and Persian gospels. The translation of the rest of the Sacred Scriptures in these languages is employment enough for some years to come. At intervals I read the Persian poetry with Mirza, and the Koran with Sabat. Thus you have an account of my private studies. My European flock at this place is about 1700, consisting of two European regiments and their followers.

You will perceive that I am obliged to fag as hard as ever we did for our degrees at Cambridge. But it pleases God graciously to proportion my bodily strength to my day; and the hot winds preserve me from the intrusion of idle people, for every one is obliged to keep quietly at home. None of the officers (about eighty in number) are decidedly religious; one or two I have prevailed upon to begin Euclid and Algebra with me. In the way of preaching to the natives I have done little yet. In the morning I read Genesis to my servants, about eighteen; and on Sunday the gospels to a congregation of Hindoostanee women, but I have never yet had courage to pray extempore in Hindoostanee. In the common things of life I find infinitely more difficulty to express myself than about religion. Numberless instances occur in my translation-work in which I regret the want of learned books and learned friends. I must some day send home a list of passages to you for your consideration. I have to propose a new translation of several passages both Hebrew and Greek. But how astonishing is the accuracy of the English translation! A subject that engaged my thoughts some time ago very much was the force of some Greek particles. I wish I had more time to read the profane Greek for this curious subject. I want it to understand St. Paul's epistles.

These orientals with whom I translate require me to point out the connection between every two sentences; which is often more than I can do. It is curious how accurately they observe all the rules of writing, and yet generally write badly. I can only account for it by supposing that they have been writing too long. From time immemorial they have been authors, without progressive knowledge; and so to produce variety they supply their lack of knowledge by overstraining their imagination; hence their extravagant metaphors and affected way of expressing the commonest things. Sabat, though a real Christian, has not lost a jot of his Arabian pride. He looks upon the Europeans as mushrooms, and seems to regard my pretensions to any learning as we do those of a savage or an ape. I must make haste and conclude. Believe me to be, dear E——,

Your affectionate,

H. MARTYN.

XCI.

TO THE REV. D. CORRIE.

May 2, 1808.

You have your trials and I have mine ; and trials are necessary for us both ; the fall of one among few is very cutting. But you will soon have more to supply his place, if he is not himself restored. My greatest trial is Sabat, he spreads desolation here. Mirza is driven to Patna, declaring he will not live here to be insulted by Sabat. My Hindoostanee work is, as I told you, all stopped. My scribes, whom Sabat will not allow me to turn away, pass all their days without any thing to do. All my employment now is to compare Persian with Greek, and this, if it please God, shall be done before we part ; he talks every day of going, saying he cannot live here for these wicked people. Alas, he little thinks that his wicked heart is the cause of all his trouble. He still holds fast the diabolical doctrine, that love of our enemies is not necessary. Last night I preached to the men on humility, and angered him much. I intended it for him, he said, but that if he knew more English he could preach infinitely better. Friday morning one of our lieutenants, breakfasting out, went on the top of the house in the middle of the day without a hat, and while he was looking about, a stroke of the sun laid him dead in an instant. That night I buried him, and yesterday preached his funeral sermon. The heat here is terrible, often at 98°, and the nights almost insupportable. My employment every day is very great now. Sick and dying people are to be visited at the barrack and hopital. Sabat always calling me to the Persian, &c. But the Lord helps me through. I hope you have received the parables. Epistle ii. of Corinthians is also written out for you, but I must read it over before I send it.

H. Martyn.

XCII.

TO THE SAME.

May 9, 1808.

Sabat having one of his head-aches, leaves me at liberty to take a complete sheet. This week has passed, as usual, in comparing the Persian and Greek ; yet we are advanced no further than the end of the fifteenth of Matthew. Notwithstanding the vexation and disappointment Sabat has occasioned me, I have enjoyed a more peaceable week than ever since his arrival. I do not know how you find the heat, but here it is dreadful ; in one person's quarters yesterday it was at 102° ; perhaps it was on that account that scarcely any women came. Another reason I assign is, that I rebuked one of them last Sunday, yet very gently, for talking and laughing in the church before I came ; so yesterday they showed their displeasure by not coming at all. I spoke to them on the Parable of the Great Supper : the old woman, who is always so exemplary in her attention, shed many tears ; I have sometimes endeavoured to speak to her, but she declines conversation. I feel interested about her, there is so much sorrow and meekness depicted in her countenance ; but she always crosses herself after the service is over. Yesterday, for the first time, I baptized a child in Hindoostanee. My Europeans, this week, have not attended very well: —fifteen only, instead of twenty-five ; some of them, indeed, are in the hospital ; and the hospital is a town of itself ;—how shall I ever be faithful to them all !

XCIII.

TO THE SAME.

May 23, 1808.

The Christian boy is arrived, and I have appointed him to fill the same office which he held with Padre Marco. He seemed very indifferent about staying at all with me, but he appears pleased now, and is very active, but not sufficiently respectful ; perhaps from your having condescended more to him than I do, or from his being of Sahib's caste. He had not arrived many hours before he opened to me spontaneously his stores of knowledge, and drew forth a distinct history of Joseph, Cain and Abel, and related the parable of the Sower with its explanation. Whether anything more remains will appear in the sequel. I like the sight of the boy, because he has been with you, and I amuse myself at dinner in asking him questions about all that you do and say. We had but ten women at the service yesterday ; this is the second Sunday on which they have stayed away. So my gentle reproof to one about laughing in the house has given, I fear, lasting offence. It is lamentable that the circumstances of our situation should prevent our preaching the precious word all over the country ; we should not have nine or ten, but nine or ten thousand hearers. I preached to them on the parable of the Lost Sheep ; it excited no attention, but the poor boy gave a good account of what he had heard. Many have gone from here, appointed to Sepoy battalions. Indeed the Company's European is extin guishing very fast: a year or two more will leave no thing but corporals and serjeants. A more wicked se of men were, I suppose, never seen. The General, th Colonel of the 67th, and their own Colonel, all acknow ledge it. At the hospital, when I visit their part, som go to a corner, and invoke blasphemies upon me, be cause, as they now believe, the man I speak to, dies t a certainty—so that I am shunned as the harbinger o death. There is a half-caste of them that attends ever day; but I can never believe a half-caste's sincerity til I see him in heaven. Since I began writing, a youn lieutenant of the Company's European came to speal with me. He is a man of fine abilities and a good scho lar; and as he wishes to go into the ministry, I recom mend it strenuously, and I heartily wish —— and —— would do the same. Dear young men, I feel for then both. Send them my good wishes and prayers, tha they may with full purpose of heart cleave unto th Lord. Yesterday morning, I made an attack on th Roman Catholic principles of my congregation. Th Irishmen were not well pleased. One wished that th roof of my house would fall; another that Fathe Murphy had been there, &c. But my evening congre gation is more than a reward for all.

H. MARTYN.

XCIV.

TO THE SAME.

May 30, 1808.

Yesterday morning scarcely any but the soldiers and their adjutant were present, the heat and closeness of the air were so insupportable. Several days in the week my men were forty in number, (and promising too) so that they are a great comfort to me. Yet there are dissensions every now and then among them. I long to have the pleasure of hearing you preach to them. My purpose of emigrating to the west is not altered. Whether Sabat live or not, I shall go and plant myself among the Popish missionaries of Ispahan. Sabat's quietness is more than temporary, I think. We are a long time about our work, though we are at it all day ; but he is subject to head-aches, which deprive us of many days. Mirza sent me yesterday from Patna fifteen chapters of Exodus. Your intention of studying medicine I highly approve, and much regret that I did not follow S——'s advice to learn surgery. The Lord be with you.

H. Martyn.

XCV.

TO THE REV. D. BROWN.

Dinapore, May 31, 1808.

My Dear Sir,

Yours of the 24th arrived to-day, and reliev me from much anxiety respecting your own healt Still you do not say whether the Hindoostanee shee have arrived. I do not wonder at your enquirir about the Persian. To-day we finish comparing S Matthew with the Greek, if it may be called a con parison; for, partly owing to the errors of the scrib rendering whole verses unintelligible,—and partly account of Sabat's anxiety to preserve the rhythr which often requires the change of a whole senten for a single word,—it is a new translation. We ha laboured hard at it to-day; from six in the mornir till four in the afternoon. * * * Some days Sabat overworked himself and was laid u He does his utmost. He is increasingly dear to me, I see more of the meekness and gentleness of Christ him. Our conflicts I hope are over, and we shall dra very quietly together side by side. * *

* * * * *

The cloud hanging over —— seems to become mo thick and black. I never thought it would come this. With all their faults and prejudices I pity a love that unhappy house. O may it please God to brir them soon to a right spirit.

Yours ever,

H. Martyn.

XCVI.

TO THE REV. D. CORRIE.

June 6, 1808.

To-day we have completed the Persian of St. Matthew, and to-morrow it is to be sent off to be printed. Sabat desired me to kneel down to bless God for the happy event, and we joined in the praise of "the Father of Lights." It is a superb performance in every respect. Sabat is prodigiously proud of it: I wish some mistakes may not be found in it, to put him to shame. Among the events of the last week is the earthquake; we were just reading the passage of the 24th of Matthew, on "earthquakes in divers places," when I felt my chair shake under me; then some pieces of the plaister fell; on which I sprang up and ran out:—the doors had still a tremulous motion. This edition of the Gospel must be announced as 'printed at the expence of the British and Foreign Bible Society.'

XCVII.

TO THE REV. D. BROWN.

Dinapore, June 21, 180(

DEAREST SIR,

At length the Lord has blessed you with another son Your prayer for him I echo. May he be a missionary May he be an instrument in dispersing the thick darkness that covers the earth! Help me to understan what is the duty of a sponsor. I have never yet stoo as godfather, but I have a notion that you rather desir it, and Corrie must be the other.

The translations have met with another interruption Mirza has deserted me, and I know not how to suppl his place. Last week was spent in seeking him out i Patna, to endeavour to accommodate matters, at leas till the four gospels should be finished, but all in vain.

* * * * * * *

During my stay at Patna, I had two conference with the Nabob Bahir Ali at his house, on Mahomme tanism and Christianity. There is no appearance tha he is seeking the truth. I formed an acquaintanc also with a young Italian Padre, and tried to convinc him of his errors. Meantime the translations were a a stand, but we now go on again.

Yours ever,

H. MARTYN.

XCVIII.

TO THE REV. D. CORRIE.

Bankipore, June 23, 1808.

I groan at the wickedness and infidelity of men, and seem to stretch my neck every way to espy a righteous man. All at Dinapore treat the Gospel with contempt; here there is nothing but infidelity. I am but just arrived, and am grieved to find in my old friend —— less proofs of real acquaintance with the Gospel than I used to hope. On my way here I called on Col. ——, and advised him to marry or separate;—the alternative I am ever insisting on. As soon as I arrived, Mr. —— informed me that the reason why no one came to hear me was, 'that I preached faith without works, and that little sins are as bad as great ones,' and that thus I tempted them to become great sinners. A young civilian, who some ago came to me desiring satisfaction on the evidences of Christianity, and to whom I spoke very freely, and with some regard, as I could not doubt his sincerity, now holds me up to ridicule. Thus, through evil report, we go on. Oh! my brother! how happy I feel, that all have not forsaken Christ; that I am not left alone even in India. "Cast thy burden on the Lord, and he shall sustain thee," is the text I carry about with me, and I can recommend it to anybody as an infallible preservative from the fever of anxiety.

XCIX.

TO THE SAME.

June 26, 1808

The day after I wrote to you from Bankipore, called on the Nawaub, Babir Ali Khan, celebrated fo his sense and liberality. I staid two hours with him conversing in Persian, but badly. He began the theological discussion by requesting me to explain necessity and free-will; I instantly pleaded ignorance. H gave me his own opinion; on which I asked him fo his proofs of the religion of Mahomet. His first argument was the eloquence of the Koran, but he a last acknowledged that this was insufficient. I the brought forward a passage or two in the Koran, containing sentiments manifestly false and foolish: h flourished a good deal, but concluded by saying, tha I must wait till I could speak Persian better, and ha read their logic. His whole manner, look, authority and copiousness, reminded me constantly of Dr. —— This was the first visit, and I returned highly delighte with his sense, candour, and politeness. Two day after I went to breakfast with him, and conversed wit him in Hindoostanee. He inquired what were th principles of the Christian Religion; I began with th Atonement, the divinity of Christ, the corruption o human nature, the necessity of regeneration, and holy life. He seems to wish to acquire information but discovers no spiritual desire after the truth. S much for this mussulman lord: now for Antichrist in another shape,—the Popish padre, Julius Cæsar. I asked him whether the doctrine I had heard from the Franciscan brethren in America was his;—*Extra Ecclesiam Romanam salus non esse potest?* He said that it was a question on which disputations were constantly held at Rome. By some means we got upon the additions made to the Commandments by the Church of Rome; he said that Christianity without Councils was a city without walls; and that Luther, Calvin, &c. had made additions: all which I denied, and showed him the last verses in the Revelation. Upon the whole, our conversation seemed without benefit.

C.

TO THE SAME.

June 27, 180

Sabat is certainly wonderfully improved. He ha long since resolved never to strike a servant ; but a fe days since he gave an unfortunate blow to a person his conscience smote him immediately, and he fell upo him, kissed his hands and asked pardon, and gave hi money. An angry word never passes between us nov though our disputes during the correction of the Persia are obstinate. How much do I owe to a gracious Gc for staying his rough wind in the day of the east winc not suffering them both to blow together. Last Monda the Padre came and dined with me ; he had been se for to baptize a child of some of the 67th. At tl same time arrived a pompous Brahmin from Benare Not knowing how to dispose of them both, I consign the Hindoo to Sabat, and took the Padre myself. I d not, however, press him hard, especially as he pr mised to visit me often. He is very agreeable. The is to be a synod of divines held at Patna, to consid about the ejection of Padre Angelo from the prefectur When Joseph first saw the Padre he took off his tu ban, fell on his knees and put the Padre's hand on h head. I was sorry to see this, and took occasion question him about it ; all he had to say was, 'custon In a letter from Mr. Brown, he says, 'I hope, my de sir, you will continue to be a black chaplain, as —

calls you and Corrie, and that you will never giv up the thought, which God put into your heart, o giving light to the gentiles.' This is the first tim we have received encouragement from our dear Patriarch to continue black chaplains. I married recentl a young couple in Hindoostanee. The Lord direct al your ways.

H. Martyn.

CI.

TO THE REV. D. BROWN.

Dinapore, July 2, 1808.

Dearest Sir,

My work is very delightful in itself, but it is doubly so by securing me so much of your correspondence. My eyes seized your beloved handwriting with more eagerness than even if the letter had been from Europe. I rejoice with you, and praise God for one Gospel in Persian. With elegance enough to attract the careless and please the fastidious,—it contains enough of Eternal Life to save the reader's soul; therefore, if we do no more, we are happy that something is done. We are safe with the Hindoostanee; it wants but little correction, and in case of my death, could be easily prepared by any one. I am anxious to hear of the new plans you are about to propose to me: let them not be in the way of *recreation*: my only exertion, and that, through indolence, is small, is to keep my heart rightly disposed to minister to my congregation at night. I shrink from the idea of Sanscrit: the two or three months I spent in striving to penetrate its unwieldy grammar, were more painful to me, than any since the sorrowful days when I first began to learn Greek. * * *

* * * Sabat has no inclination to leave me whatever he may sometimes say, especially since we have begun our united work. He loves to plague me now and then, and to call forth some testimonies of my

regard, by speaking of Serampore; but if he ever goes it will only be to change the scene a little. To-day while he was dissuading me from marriage, I said, by way of trying him, 'What if I should be married; why could not our work go on as well?' 'Sir,' said he, 'it would all stop—no Hindoostanee, no Persian—I know the missionaries cannot help me, and I can do nothing by myself.' * * He is very dear to me. When I think of the circumstances of his life, and look upon him, I cannot help considering it as one of the most singular and interesting events of my life that I was brought acquainted with him. Indeed everything in the east has been interesting to me. * * Is there an edition of Aristotle's works to be had in Calcutta, or any part of them in Greek? * * At your leisure procure me an Italian dictionary.

Your's affectionately,

H. Martyn.

CII.

TO THE REV. D. CORRIE.

July 4, 1808.

I have received no letter from you this week. When Sunday came and no letter arrived from you, I began to entertain the romantic notion, that perhaps my brother himself would come, and preach for me at night. I am now on my way to Patna by water. The Italian Padre came to Dinapore again on Saturday, but did not call upon me; the men sent him a letter, to which he replied in French;—that he lamented he could not speak their language, but should remember them in his prayers, and spoke of them as brethren in Christ. When he came into the barracks, the Catholics crowded round him by hundreds, and in tone of triumph pointed out his dress,—that of a Franciscan friar,—to the Protestants; contrasting it with that of a clergyman of the Church of England, booted and spurred, and ready for a hunt. The Catholics in this regiment amount to a full thousand,—the Protestants are scarcely discernible. Who would think that we should have to combat Antichrist again at this day? I feel my spirit roused to preach against popery with all the zeal of Luther. How small and unimportant are the hair-splitting disputes of the blessed people at home, compared with the formidable agents of the devil with whom we have to combat here! There are four castes of people in India: the first, heathen; the second, Mahometans; the third,

Papists : the fourth, infidels. Now I trust that you an I are sent to fight this four-faced devil, and by the hel of the Lord Jesus, whom we serve, we will. I was rath apprehensive yesterday that my female hearers woul have forsaken me ; but they came as usual, and th words, " Search the Scriptures," occurring in the cha ter of the day, I took occasion to point out to them th wickedness of the church of Rome, in forbidding th use of the Scriptures.

CIII.

TO THE SAME.

July 11, 1808.

A loquacious Brahmin having interrupted us in our work, I leave him to Sabat, and turn my thoughts with more pleasure Chunar-ward. My last letter left me at Patna. The Catholic Padre, Julius Cæsar, had gone to Dinapore that very day, to say mass: but at Baber Ali's I met with a very agreeable Armenian Padre, named Martin, who kept my tongue employed nearly the whole of the day. I tried him once or twice in spiritual things, but on these he had nothing to say. His dress was a little black cassock, exactly such as we wear, or ought to wear: the top of his head was shaved like the Franciscans. I am almost ashamed of my secular appearance before these very venerable and appropriate figures. The Catholics in the regiment are a thousand strong; and are disposed to be malicious: they respect me, however, and cannot help thinking that I have been taught by Roman Catholics, or have been in some way connected with them at the hospital:—the greater number keep themselves aloof. My society, this week, has occasioned me great trouble; one man was the occasion of it: still his professions, and earnestness not to be excluded, make it difficult to know how to deal with him. Certainly there is infinitely better discipline in the Romish church than in ours, and if ever I were to be the pastor of native Christians, I hould endeavour to govern with equal strictness. My emale hearers do not give me half such encouragement .s yours ;- probably because I do not take such pains vith them ; yet there is no trouble I would spare, if I :new how to reach their minds. There were only foureen yesterday. I spoke to them on the text, "Lord, o whom shall we go ? thou hast the words of eternal ife." To whom shall we go ?—To the Padre,—to the Virgin Mary,—to the Saints,—to the world,—to works, —to repentance ? No ! to Christ."

CIV.

TO THE SAME.

July 18, 1808.

I mentioned to you that I had spoken very plainly t the women last Sunday, on the delusions of the Papists yesterday only seven came. I ascribed it to what I ha said; but to-day Sabat tells me that they pour contemp upon it all. Sabat, instead of comforting and encourag ing me in my disappointments and trials, aggravate my pain by contemptuous expressions of the perfect in utility of continuing to teach them. He may spare hi sarcastic remarks, as I suppose that after another Sun day none at all will come. I find no relief but i prayer: to God I can tell all my griefs, and find com fort. Last Tuesday the Padre, Julius Cæsar, came an stayed with me four hours. We argued with great ve hemence: when I found that he had nothing to say i defence of the adoration of the Virgin Mary and th saints, I solemnly charged him and his church with th sin of idolatry:—he started, and said, that if I had ut tered such a sentiment in Italy, I should have bee burned. He certainly seems sincere; and at one tim he lifted up his eyes and prayed, that I might not con vert him, and that God would never suffer the Protes tant religion to enter Italy. His main argument agains me was, the disorder and impiety prevalent among th Protestants, whom he had had an opportunity of ob serving in Geneva and Leghorn. This disputation ha brought us to be quite familiar in our acquaintance ; he looked over all my books, and found a French one, called 'the Crimes of the Popes ;' which he desired to have ; but recollected afterwards, that his coadjutor might see it. I feel a regard for him : he is a serious and unassuming young man.'

CV.

TO THE SAME.

August 1, 1808.

One day this week, on getting up in the morning, I was attacked with a very serious illness. I thought I was leaving this world of sorrow ; and, praised be the God of grace, I felt no fear. The rest of the day I was filled with sweet peace of mind, and had near access to God in prayer. What a debt of love and praise do we owe ! Yesterday I attempted to examine the women who attended (in number about thirty) in Christian knowledge : they were very shy, and said that they could say no prayers but in Portuguese. It appears that they were highly incensed, and went away, saying to Joseph, 'We know a great deal more than your Padre himself.' The Lord graciously endue me with wisdom and love to deal aright with these poor souls ! At night I preached to the men on "So run that ye may obtain." My poor weak body has been reminding me of its decay to-day. The services much fatigued me.

CVI.

TO THE SAME.

August 8, 1808.

I called on the Commander-in-chief here on Saturday morning, and was received very graciously. I told him that it was a duty we owed to God, as a nation, to erect churches: and asked whether Lord Minto was disposed to go on with it: to which he replied in the affirmative. I enlarged on the shame I felt in my disputes with the Popish Padres, as often as they threw out reflections on the utter disregard of the Protestants to religion. Julius, the Padre, has been here twice this week, but stayed only a very short time. He began to assert, with very great vehemence, the necessity of an infallible judge, in order to settle all disputes on religion; and mentioned how much he had been agitated by his last dispute with me: he could do nothing but walk about that night;—yet looked up to God and became tranquil. The men are fast dying in the hospital, yet they would rather be sent to Patna for some holy oil, than hear the word of eternal life. Two or three of my evening hearers are in the hospital; one is prepared to die: blessed sight! The Persian of St. Mark is to be sent to-morrow, and five chapters of St. Luke corrected. There is no news from down the stream; but always glad tidings for us from the world above.

CVII.

TO THE REV. D. BROWN.

Dinapore, August 9, 1808.

My dear Sir,

* * * * * * *

The farther we go in our work, the more Sabat is attached to me. By this day's post we have sent you the Persian of St. Mark. For the Hindoostanee I must look to you for help ; all the moonshees that have applied to me are fit for nothing, and now, indeed, they are afraid to come and undergo an examination. What an acquisition would Akber be ! * * * By the first opportunity, please to send back the first part of the Hindoostanee St. Matthew ; also the parables in the Persian character. * * * Remember also my request for Aristotle, particularly his ethics.

Now, dearest sir, let me beseech you to let me hear from you as soon as possible. * * * My own health is good again, but the rains try my constitution. I am apt to be troubled with shortness of breath, as at the time I left you. Another rainy season I must climb some hill and live there ; but the Lord is our rock. While there is work which *we* must do, we shall live.

Yours affectionately,

H. Martyn.

CVIII.

TO THE REV. D. CORRIE.

August 15, 1808.

Glad am I that we are likely to meet so soon; may it be "in the fulness of the blessing of the gospel of peace." Last week, Mahomed Babir, the Mahomedan lord, and Padre Martino, spent three days here. Little, I am sorry to say, has been done. Sabat did not appear to advantage; instead of speaking about the gospel to Babir, he was reciting poetry, particularly his own; and seemed more anxious to gain admirers than converts. We did, however, at last converse about religion; but Mahomed confessed himself an infidel, and required proof of the truth of any religion. Sabat was not prepared for this, so I attempted to speak to Babir upon the nature of probable evidence, but he did not understand me: so this came to nothing. One day we sat down to dinner before Sabat came; and, to our great astonishment, he rebuked us with much wrath and pride. With all Babir's gentleness, he rebuked him in his turn, and told him that the Persians and English knew how to behave, but the Arabs did not. Babir was so lavish in his compliments to us all, that it was difficult to get at his real sentiments; but he praised Sabat's Persian translation to the stars; which I was glad to hear. As for the poor Padre, with an exterior so imposing that you would think St. Peter himself was present, he knows nothing at all. I tried him on spiritual things again and again; but he could say nothing. Alas! how fallen from what their fathers were! When shall the churches of Asia recover their ancient glory? You will see both the Nabob and the Padre soon, I hope. Last Tuesday we sent off the Persian of St. Mark.

CIX.

TO THE SAME.

August 22, 1808.

Your next letter will, I hope, mention the day of your leaving Chunar. I have been looking at the list of the passengers per Preston, with almost as much anxiety as yourself. The arrival of your sister will deprive me of much of the time you would otherwise spend with me, but I ought to rejoice in all that would add to your comfort. This week the first proof-sheets of the Persian and Hindoostanee gospel arrived. Mr. Brown says, 'Through the tender mercies of the Lord we are preserved; and though the wrath of man was high, both at Calcutta and at Serampore, I am left in peace. I thank you for your advice concerning ——. I was about to give them a triumph by letting them tread me in the mire, and so I would do still if it would do them any good. But every friendly overture on my part has been fuel to their pride, and has brought upon me more bitterness and insult. This is a grievous affair, brother; let it issue as it will, it makes against the great cause, at least for a time, for finally it must prevail.' This week the Ganges inundated us; all communication between my quarters and the barracks was cut off, so that the men could not come. When the water began to subside, the smell was so intolerable, that I was obliged to make a precipitate retreat to Major Stewart's. During my absence, a child was to be buried. 'Well,' said the Papists, 'where is Mr. Martyn?' 'If I wer the god-father of that child,' said one, 'I would hav sent him to the right-about.' Thus, something or othe is constantly happening to try one's spirit. "I the multitude of my thoughts within me, thy comfort delight my soul."

H. Martyn.

CX.

TO THE REV. D. BROWN.

Dinapore, August 23, 1808.

DEAREST SIR,

I hope that by the help of our new friend the Nawuab Mahommed Bahir, we shall have a consesus of nabobs, rajahs and other Hindoostanees, to hear the Hindoo gospels, and offer their remarks. After that, no moonshee can open his mouth against them without proclaiming himself an ignoramus. * * * The few Turkish words that are used may be explained in a preface, where their use will be justified. It is curious, that in the same manner, and for the same reason that the Roman military terms found their way, or rather forced it, into Greek, and have been used in the New Testament, and the English ones into Hindoostanee; so the Turkish terms of war are used in Persian. * * * It delights me, dearest sir, that amidst all your troubles you are kept in peace. We all owe thanks for this mercy. * * *

Your's, ever affectionately,

H. MARTYN.

CXI.

TO HIS SISTER.

October, 1808.

I deserve your reproof for not having written to yo oftener: and I am pained at the anxiety I have thought lessly occasioned you. I console myself, however, b reflecting that a letter must have reached you a fe weeks after you sent your last. I am sorry that I hav not good accounts to give of my health; yet no dange is to be apprehended. My services on the Lord's da always leave me a pain in the chest, and such a grea degree of general relaxation, that I seldom recover i till Tuesday. A few days ago, I was attacked with fever, which by the mercy of God lasted but two day I am now well, but must be more careful for the futur In this debilitating climate the mortal tabernacle is frai indeed: my mind seems as vigorous as ever, but m delicate frame soon calls for relaxation; and I mus give it, though unwillingly; for such glorious fields fo exertion open all around, that I could with pleasure b employed from morning till night. It seems a provi dential circumstance, that the work at present assigne me is that of translation; for had I gone through th villages, preaching, as my intention led me to do, I fea that by this time I should have been in a deep declin In my last, I gave you a general idea of my employ ments. The society still meet every night at my qua ters, and though we have lost many by death, othe ıre raised up in their room; one officer, a lieutenant, is ılso given to me; and he is not only a brother beloved ›ut a constant companion and nurse; so you need feel ıo apprehension that I should be left alone in sickness; ıeither on any other account should you be uneasy. You know that we must meet no more in this life: herefore since we are, as I trust, both children of God ›y faith in Jesus Christ, it becomes a matter of less onsequence when we leave this earth. Of the spread f the gospel in India I can say little, because I hear ıothing. Adieu, my dearest sister: let us live in contant prayer for ourselves, and for the church.

CXII.

TO THE REV. D. CORRIE.

October 24, 1808.

You mention a letter enclosed, but none came. The intelligence, however, intended to be conveyed by it met my delighted eyes. Thomason is coming! This is good. Praise be to the Lord of the harvest, for sending out more labourers! Behold how the prayers of the society at Calcutta have been heard. I hope they will continue their supplication: for we want more yet, and it may please God yet further to bless us. You cannot leave Calcutta by the middle of November, and must therefore apply for one month's extension of leave. But you are unwilling to leave your flock; and I do not wonder, as I have seen my sheep grievously dispersed during my absence. Uncertain when I may come amongst them, they seldom come at all, except the ten or twelve who meet one another. My morning congregation increases as the cold weather advances, and yesterday there seemed to be a considerable impression. I spoke in a low tone of voice, and therefore did not feel much fatigue;—after the Hindoostanee service, I was very weak; but at night tolerably strong again. On the whole, my expectations of life return. May the days thus prolonged be entirely his who continues them! and may my work not only move on delightfully, but with a more devout and serious spirit! You are too many for me to mention each; suffice it to say, that my heart is with you, and daily prays for blessings upon you all.

CXIII.

TO THE REV. D. BROWN.

Dinapore, October 31, 1808.

DEAREST SIR,

* * * * * *

Dr. John's letter is delightful—Des Granges' hopeful, Mr. Grant's wise, ——'s empty.

The Vizagapatam missionaries set out well because, cautiously and modestly. Happy will it be for them if future success and praise should not spoil them.

Dr. John's account of the Brahmin seems to have done Sabat good. For some days before, he had been saying that he meant, after the four gospels were completed, to go to Constantinople, there recite his poetry to the Sooltan, and receive as a present at least two lacs. * * * I told him that the Turk's head would be off before he got there. * * * After the Brahmin's letter, he began to relate against himself very appropriately the fable of the ass and the camel: An ass and a camel who had been left behind by a caravan, remained in the wilderness in good pasture and grew fat. One day the ass being merrier than usual, told his comrade he would entertain him with a song; the camel intreated that he would not, as it would lead to a discovery, and then he the camel would be killed, and the meat laid upon the other's back. But the ass was obstinate and would not be persuaded, and accordingly began his note. A caravan passing by heard the braying, and caught them both, when it happened as the camel had foretold.

Sabat says that no one Hindoostanee moonshee will be of any use. The translation must be read before a company of well-educated people. Mohammed Bahir is unfortunately for us just at this moment going to Calcutta; and as for the civil servants, they might, if they pleased, assemble all Patna, but they would not touch the work with the tip of their finger. They look on me as a pest with respect to the natives, and publicly assert that I wish to *coerce* them into Christianity.

* * *

Affectionately your's,

H. MARTYN.

CXIV.

TO THE REV. D. BROWN.

Dinapore, Nov. 14, 1808.

Dear Brother,

* * * * * * *

* * At present my mind is full of disorder from Sabat's evil temper. He is now in great pride and wrath, perhaps marching to Patna. Since you went away he has changed his bearers again and again; at last he said he would have nothing to do with them—I might keep them myself; I accordingly sent for some—all refused to come except I gave my word that they should not be in Sabat's service. This I did. To-day he wanted them to go to Patna and stay with him there a fortnight. I thought that if I ordered them to do this it would be breaking my word, and therefore I gently told him what engagement I had made with them. He flew into a most violent rage, and said he would have no more to do with a man who would keep such servants, and would walk away at once to Patna. I in vain attempted to pacify him. * * * Alas! it was a poor finale to the Gospel of Luke, the revisal of which we had that moment finished. For some days past he had been particularly unpleasant. * * * * I would sooner give a thousand rupees than ask a favour for him from any European, he is so universally detested among all persons, native or English. Lately taking offence at some-

thing his landlord did, he and Ameenah employe themselves in tearing up every shrub, plant and flowe in the garden. He could not perceive that it was wrong 'Should I be at twenty-five rupees expence,' he said 'for him ?' All these evils spring from nothing bu horrible unmortified pride ; and it is this that makes m fear for his soul. How such a temper can be consisten with a state of grace I am at a loss to conceive. Yet I will continue to hope, and have been praying for him * * * * Last night I had th pain of hearing of some misconduct in D—— my ver best man. What offences daily come ! but it is all fo the trial of our faith. "In your patience possess ye you souls." * *

Your brother affectionately in the Lord,

H. Martyn.

CXV.

TO THE REV. D. CORRIE.

December 31, 1808.

On the review of the last year, I give praise to God, who hath graciously preserved my life, notwithstanding the attacks which threatened its destruction, and hath prolonged it to another year. Every day he gives me, I account gain, as it enables me to advance a little way farther in the work which I have so much at heart. O if it be his will that I should live to finish it, how happy should I be. But he knows best. To him I leave all; present mercies demand my praise; my mercies multiply as my moments; O that my praises could as constantly ascend. My progress in divine things has not been sensible, but I am more than ever convinced of the happiness of wisdom's ways.

Jan. 1—21, 1809.—Was seldom alone. On 1st, (Sunday,) preached from 1 Cor. vii. "This I say, brethren, the time is short." On 7th, Mr. J. arrived with his family, and preached on Sunday the 8th, from Galatians. "If righteousness come by the law, then Christ is dead in vain." The following week I spent with Sabat at Patna, in the Persian of St. John, and in translating some things from the Arabic.

CXVI.

TO THE SAME.

January 10, 1809.

Your letter from Buxar found me in much the sam spiritual state as you describe yourself to be in : thoug your description, no doubt, belongs more properly to me I no longer hesitate to ascribe my stupor and formalit to its right cause,—unwatchfulness in worldly com pany. I thought that any temptation arising from th society of the people of the world, at least of such as w have had, was not worthy of notice : but I find mysel mistaken. The frequent occasions of being among ther of late, have proved a snare to my corrupt heart. Instea of returning with a more elastic spring to severer dutie as I expected, my heart wants more idleness, more dis sipation. David Brainerd in the wilderness,—what contrast to Henry Martyn ! But God be thanked tha a start now and then interrupts the slumber. I hop to be up and about my Master's business ; to cast o the works of darkness, and to be spiritually-minde which alone is life and peace. But what a dangerou country it is that we are in ; hot weather or cold, all i softness and luxury ; all a conspiracy to lull us to slee in the lap of pleasure. While we pass over this en chanted ground, call, brother, ever and anon, and ask 'Is all well ?' We are as shepherds keeping watch ove our flocks by night : if *we* fall asleep, what is to be come of them !

CXVII.

TO THE SAME.

January 18, 1809.

To resume our usual correspondence, I take up my pen, but seem not to have much to say. Wars and rumours of wars reach my ears, and call me to look abroad into the earth. How interesting are the politics of the present day. Every event is like turning over a new leaf in a book of mysteries. I have sometimes some gloomy thoughts on this account, but "Cast thy burden on the Lord, and he shall sustain thee," is a sufficient support against evils present or suspected. Much of this last week I have been at Patna, with Sabat: amongst some orientals whom I met there, was a young man of Aleppo, a Christian. I talked to him in Arabic. The conversation was not very brisk, as you may easily imagine, but it gave me hope that I should one day be able to preach the Gospel all the way from Calcutta, round about unto Damascus. Oh, when will the day come, that like the great apostle I shall be no more a talker, but a doer. Your idea of going to the poor Malabar Syrians is romantic, but I am afraid we shall not get Khanu (food) there; however, learn Syriac as fast as you can. In those sweet sequestered spots, *tu lentus in umbra,* you may teach the woods to re-echo the beloved name.

CXVIII.

TO THE SAME.

January 30, 1809.

I have been seized with a sudden desire for reading Hebrew, chiefly from a wish to see language in its simplest and purest state. It is my belief that language is from God ; and that therefore, as in his other works, so in this, the principles must be extremely simple. My present labour is to find a reason for there being but two tenses in Hebrew. I have read, or rather devoured, the first four chapters in the Hebrew Bible, in order to account for the apparently strange use of these two tenses, and am making hypotheses every moment ; when I walk, and when I awake in the night. One thing I have found, which is, that there are but two tenses in English and in Persian. *I will go* :—in that sentence the principal verb is, *I will*, which is the present tense. *I would have gone* :—the principal verb is, *I would* or *I willed*. *Should*, also, is a preterite, namely, *shalled*, from *to shall*. Another thing I observe is, that both in Persian and in English the preterite is formed in the same way, viz. by the addition of *ed ; porsum, porsedum*,—*ask, asked*. I should not wonder if, in the Saxon, or some other ancient northern language, from which the English comes, it is *askedum*. Thus you have a letter of philology. If I make any other *great* discoveries, and have nothing better to write about, I shall take the liberty of communicating them. *Scire tuum nihil est, nisi te scire hoc sciat alter* ;—but this, I trust, is not my maxim. "*Whatsoever ye do, do all to the glory of God*," is much better.

CXIX.

TO THE REV. D. BROWN.

Dinapore, February 4, 1809.

DEAREST SIR,

* * * * * *

Since the attack I had in the rains, I have set ıy house in order. Every thing that you recommend ɔr the Hindoostanee has been done. The whole New 'estament is written out large and fair. Besides that, have given many directions to Sabat, who is perfectly cquainted with all the papers I have. Do not suppose, earest Sir, that I am so short-sighted as to destroy my ife by English preaching, or any other preaching. St. 'aul did much good by his preaching, but how much ıore by his writings. I have now reduced my Sun- ay's services to less than one half; the Hindoostanee rayers, &c. are discontinued. * * *
My health is as good as ever; no appearance of a con- umption yet, though I look thin. The rains would e the best time to leave Dinapore and my work, but hen that season is worse in Bengal than here: besides, am in constant expectation of hearing of a removal o the outer provinces. Meer Sheer Ullee's Hindoostanee s to my eye hideous, and so it is to Sabat's. A trans- ation in his style would be the most useless thing maginable, for his Hindoostanee is only Persian spoilt, nd every one who is scholar enough to understand it, vill certainly prefer to read the Persian gospels. *

* * I spent most of my time with Sabat at Patna, and lament to see how little of his time is given to his work. Though I am there merely to examine with him, he will not stir beyond one chapter however short, though it is done in an hour or two And there am I left fretting, that without one single cause but his idleness, the precious work is left undone It is this that makes me more bilious than any of his bad tempers. We have still five chapters to do in St John, which, however, I trust will be done next week He lives almost without prayer, and this is sufficient to account for all evils that appear in saint or sinner With all this, there are many good symptoms in him You tell me to pray; I have every encouragement to prayer, but little perseverance in it; yet it is the only way of comfort in this vale of tears.

Affectionately your's,

H. Martyn.

CXX.

TO THE REV. D. CORRIE.

February 13, 1809.

Last Friday we had the happiness and honour of finishing the four Gospels in Persian. The same evening I made some discovery respecting the Hebrew verb; but was unfortunately so much delighted, that I could not sleep; in consequence of which I have had a headache ever since. Thus even intellectual joys are followed by sorrow; not so spiritual ones. I pray continually that *order* may be preserved in my heart; that I may esteem and delight most in that work, which is really most estimable and delightful,—the work of Christ and his apostles. When this is in any measure the case, it is surprising how clear and orderly the thoughts are on other subjects. I am still a good deal in the dark respecting the objects of my pursuit; but have so far an insight, that I read both Hebrew and Arabic with increasing pleasure and satisfaction.

CXXI.

TO THE SAME.

February 29, 1809.

Your attack proves the necessity of diminishing your Sabbath services. I scarcely know how this week has passed, nor can I call to mind the circumstances of one single day ;—so absorbed have I been in my new pursuit. I remember, however, that during one night I did not sleep a wink. Knowing what would be the consequence the next day, I struggled hard, and turned every way, that my mind might be diverted from what was before it ;—but all in vain. One discovery succeeded another, in Hebrew, Arabic, and Greek, so rapidly, that I was sometimes almost in ectasy ;—but after all, I have moved but a step : you may scold me if you please,—but I am helpless. I do not turn to this study of myself, but it turns to me, and draws me away almost irresistibly. Still I perceive it to be a mark of a fallen nature to be so carried away by a pleasure merely intellectual ; and, therefore, while I pray for the gifts of His Spirit, I feel the necessity of being still more earnest for His grace. "Whether there be tongues they shall cease : whether there be knowledge, it shall vanish away ;" but "Charity never faileth." Yesterday my mind was mercifully kept free the whole day ; and I ministered without distraction, and moreover without fatigue. I do not know when I have found myself so strong. The state of the air affects me more than any thing else.—On Saturday I completed my twenty-eighth year. Shall I live to see another birthday?—it will be better to suppose not. I have not read Faber yet; but it seems evident to me that the eleventh of Daniel, almost the whole of it, refers to future times. But as the time of accomplishing the Scriptures draws on, knowledge shall increase. In solemn expectation we must wait, to see how our God will come. How interesting are his doings! We feel already some of that rapture wherewith they sing above, "Great and wonderful are thy works, Lord God Almighty; just and true are thy ways, thou king of saints!"

CXXII.

TO THE REV. D. BROWN.

Patna, March 1, 1809.

DEAREST SIR,

The gospel of St. John has been finished some time, but we have not yet been able to revise the copy for the press.

Sabat is in great distress, lest the missionaries should be guilty of plagiarism with his work, and says that if he finds his fears realised, he will write a book on purpose to put them to shame. Poor man, I have been reasoning with him in vain on the emptiness of human praise. * * *

He requires me to add, that unless his request is complied with, he will not send anything more to the press.

I am very anxious to get the first volume of Walton's Polyglott, for the sake of the Prolegomena, also Hyde, &c. Relig. veter. Pers. Any of Schulten's productions. A list of the books in the Calcutta College and Missionary Libraries is a desideratum.

Sabat sends salam ; if you will not answer his letters, he will come down to speak mouth to mouth. With John he will say something about an Arabian gospel.

Excuse my bad writing. I am sitting on the ground in the corner of a native house, with nothing but a Gulum to help myself with.

Affectionately your's,

H. MARTYN.

CXXIII.

TO THE REV. D. CORRIE.

March 3, 1809.

I did not write to you last week, because I was em-
loyed night and day on Monday and Tuesday with
abat, in correcting some sheets for the press. I begin
ıy letter, now, immediately on receiving yours of last
reek. The account of your complaint, as you may sup-
ose, grieves me exceedingly ; not because I think that
shall outlive you, but because your useful labours
ıust be reduced to one quarter of their present amount ;
nd that you may perhaps be obliged to take a voyage
ɔ Europe, which involves loss of time and money. But,
) brother beloved, what is life or death ? Nothing, to
he believer in Jesus. "He that believeth, though he
rere dead, yet shall he live : and he that liveth, and
elieveth in me, shall never die." The first and most
atural effect of sickness, as I have often found, is to
loud and terrify the mind. The attention of the soul
ı arrested by the idea of soon appearing in a new world ;
nd a sense of guilt is felt, before faith is exercised in a
ledeemer : and for a time this will predominate ; for
he same faith that would overcome fear in health, must
e considerably strengthened to have the same ascen-
ancy in sickness. I trust you will long live to do the
rork of your Lord. My discoveries are all at an end ;
am just where I was ;—in perfect darkness, and tired
f the pursuit. It is, however, likely that I shall be

constantly speculating on the subject. My thirst after knowledge is very strong; but I pray continually that the Spirit of God may hold the reins; that I may mind the work of God above all things; and consider all things else as merely occasional.

CXXIV.

TO THE SAME.

Patna, March 20.

I should sometimes with pleasure resign the translaons to others, that I might be more in the actual xercise of the ministry. But it seems the path marked ıt for me—a path, however, in which I feel that I ust be much on my guard. The ——s have been so ıtirely engaged in preparing the word of the Lord for hers, that they seem almost to have lost the Spirit of ıe Lord themselves. "My soul cleaveth to the dust, uicken thou me according to thy word." Last Tuesıy we began the Hindoostanee, and to my surprise and ortification it was found necessary almost to new odel it. Sentence after sentence was not understood ll the Persian was read. It was a satisfaction to see ›w plain the Persian was to them, so that this Persian ill probably appear to be the first useful translation in odern times. Twenty hours we were employed, and ›t no farther than the end of the second chapter. ow extraordinary is all this when you consider the ıins that have been bestowed upon the Hindoostanee.

H. MARTYN.

CXXV.

TO THE REV. D. BROWN.

Patna, March 28, 1809

DEAREST SIR,

Your letter is just come. The Europe letter is from Lydia. I trembled at the hand-writing, * * * * * It was only more last words sent by the advice of Colonel S——, lest the non-arrival of the former might keep me in suspense. * * I trust that I have done with the entanglements of this world; seldom a day passes but I thank God for the freedom from earthly care which I enjoy. I long to see Buchanan's letter.

You chide me for not trusting my Hindoostanee to the press. I congratulate myself. Last week we began the correction of it: present—a Seid of Delhi, a Poet of Lucknow, three or four literati of Patna, and Babir Ali in the chair. Sabat and myself assessors. Almost every sentence was altered. I was amazed and mortified at observing that reference was had to the Persian for every verse, in order to understand the Hindoostanee It was however a consolation to find, that from the Persian they caught the meaning of it instantly, always expressing their admiration of the plainness of that translation. After four days' hard labour, five hours each day, we reached to the end of the second chapter; so when you will have a gospel I do not know. It is to be hoped that they will get on a little faster when they are more used to the work of translation. Babir Ali, who is ambitious of the name of a learned man, thinks his own reputation involved in this work. He often tells his coadjutors to be careful, for if any error should escape, it will be said that they do not know their own language. I find that I have very little to do towards helping them out. The Persian is another Greek, so literal. This makes me more anxious about the remainder of the Persian, and less about the Hindoostanee. It is a delightful consideration, to have set these Indians at work without hire at the word of God, for their own eternal salvation. Already kings are becoming nursing-fathers to the Church. Babir Ali and his nephew are of the Soofi dynasty of the kings of Persia, and Sabat, you know, counts kings in his pedigree. I was about to say that the Euphrates was flowing towards you, but the unexpected departure of the bungy has proved a dam to it. So we must wait till next Wednesday.

Sabat is not likely to come down, except I am ordered away from this place.

Your's ever affectionately,

H. Martyn.

P. S.—I am ordered to Cawnpore, as you will know. I mean to apply for permission to stay till the rains.

CXXVI.

TO THE REV. D. CORRIE.

April 11, 1809.

I went yesterday to Bankipore, to take my leave of Babir Ali, and the civil servants, and had no time to write you. I still continue in the determination to go next Tuesday. I have applied for bearers from Aorah, Bunar, and Ghazipore. If it were cold weather I should beg you to meet me on the Friday, but now I charge you not to attempt it. I shall leave Ghazipore very early on Friday morning, and be with you about the middle of the day, please God. Preparation for departure does not disturb and disorder me as it used to do. The little things of this world come more as matters of course. Still I find it necessary to repeat often in the day, "Thou wilt keep him in perfect peace whose mind is stayed on thee." My men seem to be in a more flourishing state than they have yet been. About thirty attend every night. I had a delightful party this week, of six young men, who will I hope prove to be true soldiers of Christ. Seldom, even at Cambridge, have I been so much pleased.

H. MARTYN.

CXXVII.

TO THE SAME.

Cawnpore, May 1, 1809.

The entrance to this place is through plains of immeasurable extent, covered with burning sand. The place itself I have not yet been able to see, nor shall, I suppose, till the rains: at present it is involved in a thick cloud of dust. So much for exordium. Let me take up my narrative from Mirzupore, from whence I wrote you a note. I reached Tarra about noon. Next day, at noon, reached Allahabad, and was hospitably received by Mr. G—— : at night dined with him at the Judge's, and met twenty-six people. From Allahabad to Cawnpore, how I shall describe what I suffered! Two days and two nights was I travelling without intermission. Expecting to arrive early on Saturday morning, I took no provision for that day. Thus I lay in my palanquin, faint, with a head-ache, neither awake nor asleep, between dead and alive,—the wind blowing flames. The bearers were so unable to bear up, that we were six hours coming the last six *kos* (twelve miles). However, with all these frightful circumstances, I was brought, in mercy, through. It was too late on Saturday to think of giving notice of my arrival, that we might have service; indeed, I was myself too weak. Even now the motion of the palanquin is not out of my brain, nor the heat out of my blood.

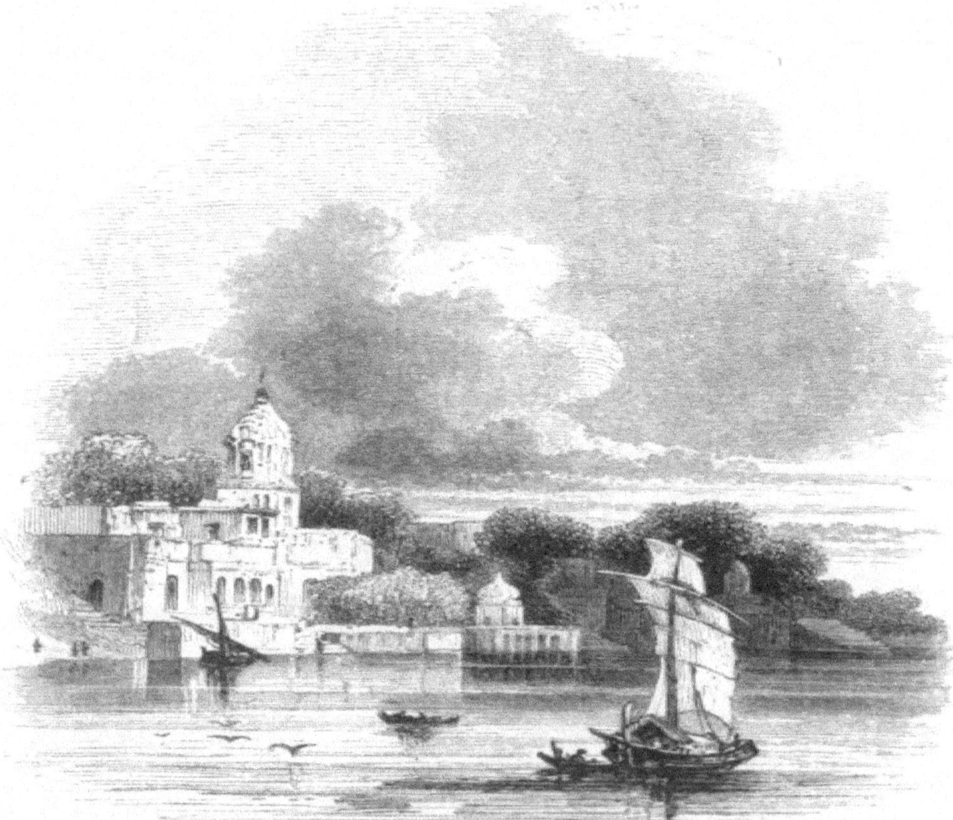

CAWNPORE.

Page 263.

[illegible]

CXXVIII.

TO THE REV. D. BROWN.

Cawnpore, May 3, 1809.

DEAREST SIR,

I transported myself with such rapidity to this place, that I had nearly transported myself out of the world.

From Dinapore to Chunar all was well, but from Allahabad to this place, I was obliged to travel two days and nights without intermission. The hot winds blowing like fire from a furnace. Two days after my arrival, the fever which had been kindling in my blood broke out, and last night I fainted repeatedly. But a gracious God has again interposed to save my life ; and to-day I feel well again. Where Sabat is, I do not know. I have heard nothing of him since leaving Dinapore. Corrie is well, but it is grievous to see him chained to a rock with a few half-dead invalids, when so many stations,—amongst others, the one I have left,—are destitute. * * *

I do not like this place at all. There is no church, not so much as the fly of a tent ; what to do I know not, except to address Lord Minto in a private letter. Mr. Grant, who is anxious that we should labour principally for the present among the Europeans, ought I think, to help us with a house. I mean to write to Mr. Simeon about this.

I feel a little uncomfortable at being so much farther removed from Calcutta. At Dinapore I had friends on both sides of me, and correspondence with you was quick : here I seem cut off from the world. Alas ! how dependent is my heart upon the creature still.

I am ordered to seal up.

Your's affectionately ever,

H. MARTYN.

CXXIX.

TO THE REV. D. CORRIE.

Cawnpore, May 15, 1809.

By all that I hear, Meerut will be a station so large as to require a chaplain, and you or J—— will be the man. For myself, I feel fixed at the last place where I shall ever live in India, and sometimes look with interest at the road that leads to Cabul and Candahar. There is a man at Lucknow, I hear, who once set up a press there, but was forbidden by the Nawaub. I shall of course find him out. I hear of a Mrs. A— as one who is religious, and is even suspected of singing psalms on a Sunday. Such flagrant violations of established rules seem to mark her for one of our fraternity. Yesterday service was performed on the parade, to the 53rd. Two officers dropped down, and some of the men. They wondered how I could go through the fatigue. When I looked at the other end of the square which they had formed, I gave up all hope of making myself heard, but it seems they did hear. There are above a hundred men in the hospital. What time shall I find for doing half what ought to be done. Major O. H—— is as kind as possible, and well disposed to religion. About a dozen of the 53rd come to me every night. I am just going to sit down to Psalm xviii. with Bishop Horsley's translation. His interpretation does not carry conviction to my mind.

H. Martyn.

CXXX.

TO THE SAME.

Cawnpore, May 22, 1809.

For the last three or four days I have been very unwell, a fever still hangs on me I believe. Yesterday I ould scarcely hold up my head, from head-ache and xcessive debility, and this morning on getting up it vas with the utmost difficulty I could keep from fainting. My situation is rather uncomfortable, in a bungalow at a distance from Captain S——'s, with none ut a few cold-hearted bearers whom no intreaties can revail upon to quicken their motions. I proposed to ne gentleman to apply to government for the billiard-oom for a church, which is better than the ball-room, ut he did not enter into the idea. Yesterday I went o the Light Dragoons. They are the finest regiment ever saw. We met in the riding-school. The effluvia vas such as would please only the knights of the turf. What must the Mahomedans think of us! Well may hey call us dogs, when even in divine worship we hoose to kennel ourselves in such places. However, ating the carpet of the room, every thing else was ecent enough; and from being within walls, I was ieard better by these five hundred than by the three undred artillery.

H. Martyn.

CXXXI.

TO THE SAME.

Cawnpore, May 29, 1809.

DEAREST BROTHER,

I raise myself from my bed to taste one of my chief pleasures, and for which I thank the Father of mercies and God of all comfort. None but those in our situation know the privilege of having a free communication. I do not think that the deadness of your poor congregation is very discouraging, for who could expect any thing better? My chief regret is that you are not sent elsewhere. What an arrant knave that Julio must be. His conscience must be convinced by the old man's questions, and yet he goes on, "having a conscience seared as with a hot iron." Observe how these priests contrive to pay the expenses of their journey. Dibdin, when making his tour of England, sung his way from town to town; so these mountebanks turn their masses to good account. But the wickedness and folly of the people! The longer I live, the more weary I become of human nature. Men love darkness, and do the deeds of it. Except a few precious saints who are redeemed from among men, I would rather pass my time with children, if I had my choice. I shall deal with Sabat no more with any delicacy, for I perceive he does not understand it. He looks upon you and Mr. Brown as two fools, because you are the two that behave best to him. We must not quite abandon our hopes of him, ill it is impossible to retain any. But he ought to be iharply rebuked on all sides. What would appear to is indelicate, and stab us to the heart, does not touch ın oriental at all. Oh! what has the gospel done for he world! We see it is the only thing that has made efinement of sentiment and conduct spread through all lasses, even of those who do not know whence they iave obtained it. Do you think that in all Christenlom any man would be found so brutish as to act as Sabat did about the goat? Now, if you had said, when ie asked for a goat, 'No, Sabat, you are rich enough o buy one for yourself;'—instead of being hurt, he vould have had a much higher opinion of you, as a man hat looked to your own interest, and knew the world. The east has been long forsaken of God, and depravity n consequence more thoroughly wrought into them. I have been very ill all this week, the disorder appearng in the form of an intermittent. In the night, cold sweats, and for about five hours in the day, head-ache ınd vertigo. Last night I took some medicine, and I hink that I am better, though the time when the fever ias generally come on, is not yet arrived. But I hardly know how to be thankful enough for this interval of ease. What millions of mercies come to us unnoticed. The General gave orders for service at his house yesterlay, after morning service, to the artillery, but there vere only nine present. We first assembled in the lrawing-room, where they began to converse as if just ıbout to enter a ball-room. I could not conceal my ndignation: but it did not last long. I read the service, ınd preached on "Except a man be born again," &c.

H. MARTYN.

CXXXII.

TO THE SAME.

Cawnpore, June 5, 1809.

Yesterday as all the regiments were out firing for th King's birth-day in the morning, there was no servic except at the General's. Rather more were preser than before. I preached on the gospel for the day, th rich man and Lazarus. A sermon on such a subjec in such a congregation, could not fail to be alarmin and they sufficiently shewed the effect in their count nances. Oh that their terror may lead to true repen ance! Sabat's behaviour since his arrival has bee unexceptionable. He is gentle, and almost as diliger as I could wish. Every thing seems to please hin His bungalow joins mine, and is very neat; so fro morning to night we work together, and the work go forward. The first two or three days he translated int Arabic, and I was his scribe; but this being to fatiguing to me, we have been since that at the Persia Sabat talks of a journey to Cashmere, in which we ma see on a small scale what we may want, when we com to travel further. When the Persian translation i finished I shall have no objection. As for the othe journey, I have no great idea that I shall ever live t accomplish it; for when my translation-work is don I shall be of little further use on the face of the eartl except indeed a more active life out of doors shoul restore strength to my feeble frame.

Yours ever,

H. Martyn.

CXXXIII.

TO THE SAME.

Cawnpore, July 3, 1809.

The surgeon of the Native Battalion is just dead; quite unexpectedly to himself, I fear, as well as others. How many will this month number with the dead! myself perhaps among the rest. On Sunday morning, while ministering to the artillery, I nearly fainted; some water and a chair enabled me to get through, by the blessing of God. Divine service yesterday was at head-quarters, where I preached to a very few on "Whosoever is ashamed of me and my words," &c. Last Saturday a philological mania again seized me; after lying an hour or two without any sleep, from some other cause, I began to think of the power of each of the Hebrew letters, and was so transported with what I thought discoveries, that I slept not a wink till daylight.

Your ever affectionate,

H. Martyn.

CXXXIV.

TO THE SAME.

Cawnpore, July 10, 1809.

DEAREST BROTHER,

Yesterday, when I should have begun to write t you, I fell asleep, and slept till the messenger was gon on his way. This omission admits of a remedy; not s the neglect of the day of grace, or the mis-spending of single day by the children of grace. I am glad yo take a liking to Hebrew. It transports me at presen My speculations occupy me night and day. They ma be said to be always in my mind. Even in my prayer I have constant occasion to seek for help against inor dinate attention to one object, to the neglect of othe things more important. Yesterday I preached to th 53rd, and felt very strong. Some of the men confesse that their hearts trembled within them. I built a schoo near the Sepoy Lines; the barrack-master sent to know who did it, but when he found that it was I, and fo what purpose, he wrote me very kindly, and said, should have a better place, even some empty Bunga lows. I spoke to the General to-day about it, and h is all cordiality. Sabat is laid up to-day. We are i Romans iv. My evening audience increases, praise be the Lord for all his mercies,—they multiply as m moments!

H. MARTYN.

CXXXV.

TO THE SAME.

July 17, 1809.

Golius' Arabic Lexicon was said by Sir W. Jones, to be not only the best *Arabic* dictionary, but the best *dictionary* in the world. Where did you get the treasure? Were you not going to learn Arabic, I should procure an order from the government (the ecclesiastical one I mean) for you to give it up. I do not know what can be done for your moonshee, but should he go, Sabat and myself have agreed on the proper person to be your Arabic teacher; a physician of Patna. My Hebrew speculations stick to me still, but instead of advancing in my pursuit, I am entangled in a jungle, without being able to see my path exactly. I think that when the construction of Hebrew is fully understood, all the scholars in the world will turn to it with avidity, in order to understand other languages, and thus the word of God will be studied universally, and from the least even to the greatest they shall all know him, and all be able to speak in other tongues the wonderful works of God. I have just returned from the General's, where I heard disastrous news from Europe. Perhaps England must fall; that is, her earthly glory. Proud and idle Englishmen, if taught a few wholesome lessons in the school of adversity, might perhaps be of infinitely greater service when dispersed through the world, than in the nest where they lie wrapped in ease and security. What horror for the high lords and ladies of England to have a French army quartered upon them. Why has England been so long spared, when the unhappy nations of Europe have been made to drink so deep of the cup of affliction! We must expect something soon. One would think, that the extreme uncertainty of all earthly possessions at the present moment, must make even the most giddy look with some desire at the portion of the godly. I have heard nothing of the Christians of Patna, except from his highness the resident, who was pleased to honour them with every expression of contempt and displeasure; adding that they made Christianity appear despicable in the eyes of the Mahomedans. To which I replied, that for the latter evil I had one remedy to propose, which was, that the English gentlemen should undertake to show the natives what true Christianity was, by observing the Lord's-day, and meeting for divine service, and observing all in short which Christ had commanded. Afterwards when we were alone, Mr. B. said, that his week-days were so much occupied by public business, that he required the Sunday for himself. He said this so humbly, and with such an appearance of regret, that it seemed as if he meant to add, "The Lord forgive thy servant in this thing;" expecting, I suppose, the prophet would say, "Go in peace." But he said no such thing, only this, "Six days shalt thou labour, and do all thy work." Yesterday I preached to the regiment of horse. The evening lecture continues to increase; the merchants in particular attend it well on Sundays. Solomon's words are true, that learning much is a weariness to the flesh. My days are almost turned into nights. I stay awake all night, and slumber all day. This deranges my nervous system, but I trust for the future to have every thought brought into subjection to the Gospel of Christ. H. M.

CXXXVI.

TO THE SAME.

July 25, 1809.

You must not be angry with me for taking a burden ›ff my back and putting it on your shoulders. In a few lays you will receive a letter from Lieut. Barber, of Preabjush in my diocese, for you to marry him. After a ;ood deal of correspondence between him, his agent, and nyself, I yesterday very unwillingly conveyed myself nto a Budgerow, and said, 'khol-do,' (loose the boat,) vhen a letter came to stop me for a time. On this I vrote to beg him to apply to you, for you were much ıearer. So this is what I have done. The travelling is ıs unpleasant to you as to me, yet think that for every lay you travel in my place one more Arabic chapter is ;ained. We are about the tenth of Romans. Sabat is ıighly pleased with his work, and wishes to stop the oublication of the Persian Gospels, till the Acts, but specially Romans, can be added. I think we had better ıtay till the whole New Testament is finished in Perian. Sabat has heard that the king of Yemen ordered he Jews there about ten years ago to make a translaion into Arabic of the whole Hebrew Bible. It would ›e worth while to make a voyage to Yemen to ascertain his ; so when my remaining four years apprenticeship ıre finished, suppose we go together. The New Testanent we have, edited by Erpenius, is indescribably bad ; t is not a translation but a paraphrase, and that always wrong. Till you are able to read Arabic you had better let us have the one I gave you, and you shall have it the moment you can use it. Last Lord's day, service was ordered for the artillery, but the rain prevented. Thus the impious neglect of Government to build a house for God, deprives us of the ordinances, and desecrates the holy day. The General has not yet forwarded to Government the proposal for a church. Mrs. —— seems equally giddy, and does not at all relish my company, if I may judge from her manner. To her daughter, Mrs. F——, I have sent White's Poems and Law's Serious Call. As she is very humble and teachable, I hope some good may be done. In Hebrew I have made few discoveries this week. The difficulties remain unsolved, and so strong is my desire of getting to the bottom of them, that I find my ignorance quite a cross. I think I have found out the meaning of every letter except the last.

H. MARTYN.

CXXXVII.

TO THE SAME.

July 31, 1809.

I fear I have done wrong in desiring you to repair to Pretabjush. If you are not recovered from the effects of your last journey, it will be madness to set out upon another. You have only to let me know on receipt of this, and I will get myself ready. Were the Hindoo woman you mention a true convert, she would be a rich reward indeed for a life's labour; but alas! I doubt of every Hindoostanee Christian in Hindoostan, the Carnatic not being excluded. I think you are quite right in not having anything to do with an Arabic moonshee now, if ever. You would learn more Arabic from a grammar in one year, than from an Eastern blockhead in ten. Whether it is a dull Rabbi, a formal Arabian, or a feeble Indian, he is a drawler in science; and those who follow them are like unto them,—e. g. what Erpenius has comprehended in a couple of pages, Mr. B. has wire-drawn through a folio. Yesterday we had service at head quarters. I have repeatedly begged the General to have two services, but he says I had better rest quiet till the cold weather. Whether it is really from a wish to spare me I do not know. I believe I shall soon clear the drawing-room. Yesterday when I came, there were the old people and one son and daughter. Three people came afterwards, and that was all. Perhaps I had better have begun more gently. Who is sufficient for these things?

May he who carries the lambs in his bosom and gentl leads those that are with young, give me wisdom an tenderness! It is extraordinary how much I am lef to myself here. In the midst of multitudes I am solitary. I have abundant leisure for my Hebrew spe culations, but the evil is, that I have too much of them For want of agreeable society to dissipate them, I carr these thoughts to bed with me, and there am I all nigh long in my dreams tracing etymologies, and measurin the power of some Hebrew letter. Yesterday I ha some very uneasy thoughts; Satan was at work in m heart; and oh, how did I envy my men at night, wh were safe from the snares of increasing knowledge. I prayer with them I could not help dwelling upon this and found relief. Truly love is better than knowledge Much as I long to know what I seek after, I would ra ther have the smallest portion of humility and love than the knowledge of an archangel.

H. MARTYN.

CXXXVIII.

TO THE REV. C. SIMEON.

Cawnpore, August, 1809.

* * * * *

Just after the last ship from Europe arrived, and I ˈas hourly expecting my letters, I was summoned to distant station to marry a couple, and did not return ill three weeks after. It was a great disappointment ɔ be thus suddenly sent to roam amongst jungles and ackalls, when I was feasting my fancy with delightful etters from my friends at home;—though Europe is o longer my home. However, my mind was soon econciled to it, and I was often able to recite, with ome sense of their sweetness, Mr. Newton's beautiful ines:

> 'In desert tracts, with thee, my God,
> How happy could I be.'

The place to which I was called is Pretabjush, in he territory of Oude, which is still under the go-ernment of the Nabob. Oppression and insecurity of roperty seemed to have stripped the country of its nhabitants. From Manicpore, where I left the river, o Pretabjush, a distance of fifty miles, I saw but two r three miserable villages, and no agriculture. The oad was nothing more than a winding footpath, hrough a continued wood, and that, in consequence of the rains, was often lost. Indeed, all the lowlands were under water, which, added to the circumstance of travelling by night, made the journey by no means a pleasant one. Being detained one Lord's day at the place, I assembled all the officers and company at the commanding officer's bungalow, and preached the gospel to them. There were five and thirty officers, besides ladies, and other Europeans. You will have an idea of the Nabob's country, when you are informed, that last September, a young officer, going from his station to Lucknow, was stopped by robbers, and literally cut to pieces in his palanquin. Since that time, the Nabob has requested that every English gentleman wishing to visit his capital, may give notice of his intention to the Resident, in order that a guard may be sent. Accordingly, a few months ago, when I had occasion to go to Lucknow, I had a guard of four troopers, armed with matchlocks and spears. I thought of Nehemiah, but was far too inferior to him in courage and faith, not to contemplate the fierce countenances of my satellites with great satisfaction.

CXXXIX.

TO THE REV. D. BROWN.

Cawnpore, August 26, 1809.

DEAREST SIR,

Three weeks ago I was sent for to marry a couple. I struggled hard to get off, as it was just at the moment when I expected a flood of letters; but I was forced, and am only this hour returned. Thirteen letters which I found on my table have almost bewildered me, but your's I answer immediately.

1. You require a table of errata. I will do my best, but it is a work of time, and to-morrow is Sunday.

2. Sabat shall pen the title-page in Persian, and I will translate it, and both may be printed on the same page, if approved.

3. The —— astonish me. Let them, with all the host of college moonshees, produce one chapter like Sabat's, and then proceed with Persian translation. If they wish to have it supposed that Sabat's work is superintended by *them*, why let them, Sir; as for my crown, the fading earthly laurel I mean, let them pluck it from my brows if they find it there, and trample it under foot, so they deprive me not of the crown of life. Most cordially do I wish to remain in the back-ground to the end of life. * * I long to see Buchanan's letters. * * What is doing at Berhampore? It is the only cloud that darkens the horizon.

Pray for us, beloved Sir, as we do for you.

Affectionately your's ever,

H. MARTYN.

CXL.

TO A FRIEND IN ENGLAND.

Cawnpore, August 30, 1809.

Dearest Friend,

I perceive from your last letter, (dated Jan. 9, 1809,) and from what I hear of you, that we approach nearer to one another in sentiment and affection. Like the sun rising to its meridian, you grow more and more warm and zealous, and my fiery zeal, if it ever deserved the name of zeal, is becoming more cool and rational. God grant that my rationality may not prove to be lukewarmness.

How do you go on in Hebrew? Though my duty calls me to other languages, I am perpetually speculating on that, and the nature of language in general; and while I remain in my present state of profound ignorance upon the latter subject, I fear I shall never be able to take up the study of any other language again without disgust. It goes against the grain with me now to read a little Arabic or Greek, as much as it once did to cram a proposition I did not understand. How or by what magic is it, that we convey our thoughts to one another with such ease and accuracy? The region I am now in invites to contemplation. The soft warm air allows of no obstructed perspiration: and lately I have been in a situation still more favourable to thought, by being called on duty to a distant station, the way to which was chiefly on the river. There, far removed rom noise, and every thing European, I glided along, peculating with as much subtlety as the visionary γυμνοσοφοι, who pursue their reveries on the banks. These hermits literally forsake the world; they build a ittle hut close to the margin of the river, and there sit nd muse. One evening, after the boat had come to for he night, I rambled along the bank into a clump of rees where one of them had fixed his residence. We oon began to converse upon religion. He defended himself with great dexterity from the charge of polyheism, and excused the worship of images in the same nanner as the Roman Catholics do. In my turn I gave him an account of God's dealings with men till the oming of Christ, and then spoke to him of the gospel. But he seemed to feel no interest in what he heard. And thus it has always been when I have conversed with them. They hear with polite attention, but start no objections, and ask no questions. I begin to doubt whether they understand my speech. But to return to he Hebrew: how happens it that the Hebrew, with its legant dialects, such as the Arabic, can do very well with two tenses, and the Greek verb should have eight or nine? Do not you think it probable that the Greek verb has really but two? As we live in days when prophecy is fulfilling, I wish you would read Genesis x. and tell me where we are to find the nations sprung from the great progenitor brothers. Am I right when I read Meshech—Muscovy, (see Ezek. xxxviii.) Ashkenaz—Scandinavia, Riphath—Riphæi, (montes,) Togarmah—Germani, Elisha— ελλας, Tarshish—Etrusci, Kittim—Catti. But above all, tell me where in Scripture I may find India. Is there any reason for thinking the Britons to be a branch of the Catti? It is probable that for some time to come, as long as I am engaged in translation, my letters as well as my thoughts wil be rather tinged with philology. The former will, I know, be not less acceptable to you on that account but on my own mind I perceive that I must keep a tight rein. How soon critical pursuits, even when the object is the elucidation of the word of God, lead away the heart from him! I pray continually for divine aid in my studies; also that I may desire knowledge, only to be qualified for translating and preaching the word of God: but the language of the heart is often at variance with the words of the prayer. I beg your prayers that after having began in the Spirit, I may not leave off in the flesh. Kindest love to Mrs. ——.

Yours ever affectionately,

H. Martyn.

CXLI.

TO THE REV. D. CORRIE.

Cawnpore, September 4, 1809.

Go on with the church, and, perhaps by the time it is built some brother from Cambridge will join us. I am rather surprised, that now the ice is broken, others are not already come. Captain R. has sent me several letters from Calcutta, all very pleasing as far as a judgment can be formed by man; there is no reason to doubt of him. The conviction of my own ignorance on all points is gaining upon me so fast, that I am become a sceptic on all subjects except the word of God. One good effect I trust may be produced,—that of my being kept from rash censures. The three weeks I was on the water, and this last week, I have been speculating incessantly without gaining one particle of knowledge. I cannot find out by what magic language conveys ideas, and while I remain in this radical ignorance, I feel that I shall never be able to relish any human compositions. The same cause does not operate to make me disrelish the word of God, because what I have learnt from that is satisfying, which nothing else in the whole world is; and also because I perceive superlative wisdom in the little I have yet been able to understand of the language of the Old Testament. Capt. and Mrs. H—— arrived on Saturday, and dined with me on that day and yesterday. In a note he sent after he went away he says, 'I have left you with warmer sentiments of religion, and with more confirmed resolutions for the future practice of it.' H. MARTYN.

CXLII.

TO THE SAME.

September 11, 1809.

The state of things in India begins to assume somewhat of an alarming aspect. Englishmen taking u[p] arms against Englishmen ! Regiments are called fro[m] Bengal, Bombay, and the Cape, to reduce the rebe[l] army. Whereunto will this grow ? The Company'[s] reign must come to an end, I suppose, or they will soo[n] have no country to reign over. It is possible that al[l] these things may be overruled for the promotion of th[e] great purpose to which all things converge ; but seeing as we do, only what is contiguous to us, we must regar[d] this rebellion as something to be lamented. "Whenc[e] come wars and fightings," &c. I hardly know what [I] have been about this week ; we go on in the Arabic o[f] 1 Corinthians. My silence about Sabat amounts to a favourable testimony for him, for when he goes wrong [I] am sure to complain to you. He much improves in hi[s] prayers. I hope he begins to see that like the rest h[e] knows little or nothing ; like the rest, I mean of men, for it is surprising how little any body knows. I suppos[e] that of all the things in the world language is that whic[h] submits itself most obsequiously to our examination, and may therefore be understood better than anything else. For we can summon it before us without any trouble, and make it assume any form we please, and turn it upside down and inside out, and yet I mus[t] confess the more I look at it the more I am puzzled. I seem to be gazing with stupid wonder at the legerdemain of a conjuror. By the bye, Sabat would have it that the Hindoostanee magicians, by some magic, could make a mango blossom and bear fruit in an hour, for he saw the thing done in his own house. I consented to be present when the same people came again. Sabat was about to be deceived again by suffering his attention to be diverted by the eggs, birds, &c. and the gibberish of the man ; but when I begged him to look at what the third accomplice was doing with the mango, he rose in great wrath (probably at having been their dupe before,) and was about to demolish them and their nobaut (goods) ; however, when he was appeased he said he should now be no more a believer in spells or charms. Thus his mind is gradually enlightening by intercourse with Europeans. The Epistle to the Romans has been wonderfully blest to him. I trust by the time we have finished the New Testament he will go forth well qualified to preach the truth, and rejoice as a strong man to run his race. Yesterday we ought to have had service at the head-quarters, but for what reason I know not, the 53rd were on orders. I was quite spent before the services of the day were over, through the abundance of extra duty. At night I had a large congregation, and there was much solemn attention ; at least my own mind was in a state in which I wish it always was.

H. Martyn.

CXLIII.

TO THE SAME.

September 18, 1809.

I have received no letter from you this week, an shall probably on that account keep this till to-morrow especially as tomorrow the Commander-in-Chief is t be here, and I must let you know whether I can ge the promise of a church from him. His family are al at General S—'s, where I breakfasted with them thi morning, and baptized a child of Mrs. C, his daughte Mrs. H. and her three daughters joined with exemplar piety in the baptismal and churching services ; an they read the responses aloud, and knelt as if the were accustomed to kneel in secret, from the manne in which they bow their knees in public prayer. Th Miss ——s are remarkably modest and correct ; a grea deal of pains seems to have been taken with them b their mother. General —— has never been very co dial, and now he is likely to be less so ; for while w were walking up and down together, I reproved hi for swearing ; though it was done in the gentlest way he did not seem to like it. It was the first time he ha been called to order for some years I suppose. 'So yo are giving me a private lecture !' said he. He the went on in a very angry and confused manner defend ing the practice of swearing. 'God judges of th heart, and sees there is no bad intention,' &c. Agains all this I urged Scripture. The pride of my heart ha discovered itself very strongly since I have entered this new circle. They sometimes take no more notice of me than a dog, at other times vouchsafe a dignified condescension ; so that were it not to become all things to all men in order to save some, I should never trouble them with my company. But how then should I be like Christ? I have been almost the whole morning engaged in a good-humoured dispute with Mrs. P——, who in an instant after my introduction to her, opened all her guns of wit and eloquence against me for attempting to convert the Brahmins.

CXLIV.

TO THE REV. D. BROWN.

Cawnpore, Sept. 29, 1809.

Dearest Sir,

I was out on another marriage expedition when you letter arrived. Thus, my time is taken up, and my strength exhausted, by travelling day and night, to immense distances. * * * Unless you can authorise me to desist from this itinerant life, I fea I shall not be very punctual in my remittances of translation. But now to your long and most acceptabl epistle; how shall I thank you for it? It has made me breathe the air of Aldeen; yet I am half afraid o its length. Such a copious shower portends perhaps a long drought to succeed it. * * *

As to the Persian and Arabic, your word is law with us. I am very curious to know the result of the criticisms to which the work is subjected. I was likeminded with the moonshee at first; as I wrote to you but now I can never look into a book of respectability without perceiving as much or more Arabic than in Sabat's. Even the Gulistan of Sadi, written six hundred years ago, has nearly as much, and since that time Arabic has been continually flowing into Persian. To an Arabic version, however, by Sabat, no objection can be made, and this I suppose is the great reason why you wish to publish that first. Well, we will do nothing else but prepare it; but I do not much like sending it by morsels, for often in one part we learn the way of rendering better what was badly done in another. Sabat will make out the list of books you wish. But now this thorn in my side—this Hindoostanee. What shall I do? I must even send down a gospel since you require it; and yet though the learned at Calcutta should approve of it, it will answer no purpose, because I could not let it go without revising it with a learned Indian; which is what I am not likely to get, and if I could I do not know where the time is to come from. I spoke to the resident at Lucknow about a moonshee, but such a one as I want, he says, would not come without a large salary. I never cease to regret the loss of Fitrut; his latter translations of the Old Testament are excellent.

Now let me congratulate you on Mr. B.; my attention was always arrested by his Christian name. Surely thought I, the friends at least of this young man must be admirers of the illustrious Wilberforce. There is another writer at the college, Henry Sargent, about whom I am much interested, because he is the brother of one of the dearest friends I have in England, if not the dearest. * * * *

I am much delighted with the picture you have drawn of the little olive-branches round about your table. I long to see them. When I have finished my first seven years in India, I am thinking of taking my furlough and floating to Aldeen. But in the meantime we shall expect that you make your purposed visitation of all the dioceses and provinces in your patriarchate * *

T. wishes * * * so do I too, and so does every body else, but the *quomodo*. The time does not seem come when Churchmen and dissenters shall feed together. Till the arrival of the wished-for period, the farther asunder, the more peac

* * * * *

You have a hard battle to fight. You may now se the immense advantage resulting from your presenc Without you * * * would have ha their own way. Sacks of rupees would be expended o translations, which would be waste paper almost as soo as published: * * in short, nothin would have been done. Twenty years patient waitin Sir, are not too many when you consider what you seniority and experience enable you now to do. Saba is now for the first time in his life happy, and I mus confess does a great deal to make me happy. If wrat rises, he goes and prays, and soon returns with a smilin countenance and quiet heart. We are left entirely t ourselves. In this crowded station we are in perfe solitude.

I forgot to write about books. We have three Arabi versions—one printed at Rome with Vulg.—one edite by Erpenius, and the one printed in England. Wa ton's Polyglott you will buy of course.

I remain, dear Sir,

Your's ever affectionately

H. Martyn.

CXLV.

TO THE REV. D. CORRIE.

Cawnpore, October 9, 1809.

Sabat is gone to Lucknow, and to-day a letter arrived from him. Julio shewed him great attention; so did the Mahomedans he visited. I had a letter a day or two ago from Mirza Fitrut at Lucknow, offering to become my moonshee provided Sabat was not with me. My heart is full of delight at the thought of having a Hindoostanee Testament ready soon. I trust that it will now be accomplished, because if Mirza does not come here, I can go for a month now and then to Lucknow. What will friends at home think of Martyn and Corrie. They went out full of zeal, but behold! what are they doing? Where are their converts? They talked of the banyan-tree before they went out, but now they seem to prefer a snug bungalow to field-preaching. I fear I should look a little silly if I were to go home just at this time; but more because I should not be able to make them understand the state of things, than because my conscience condemns me. Brother, what can you do? If you itinerate like a European, you will only frighten the people; if as a native, you will be dead in one year. Yet the latter mode pleases me, and nothing would give me greater pleasure than so to live, with the prospect of being able to hold out a few years.

H. MARTYN.

CXLVI.

TO THE SAME.

October 16, 1809.

One day this week dining at —— I had a stiff dispute with ——, an elderly man. It began by my rebuking him for swearing. Instead of taking it as they usually do, he kindled, and used some harsh language and harsher looks. But I was not in the smallest degree disconcerted, but persisted that I had done my duty. He then went on to ridicule the Scriptures, declaring his contempt for Christianity, *i. e.* the story and theory of the business, as he expressed it. We were happily at opposite corners of the table, so that the discussion, which lasted a long while, was a sermon to all present: though he never allowed me to finish a sentence fairly, I got out enough to make me pleased that the thing had taken place. He was continually withdrawing, concealing his wish for time under the mask of respect for my profession; but I would not allow him. 'No,' I said, 'I provoke discussion. Many here, perhaps, are as infidel as yourself. Let us hear what can be said against the prophet Jonah and the whale.' The conception of our Lord, and the Song of Solomon, were the chief objects of his attack. I could not get to say one twentieth part of what I wished, but still it was better than nothing. The ice being broken I went on to tell the company present how shameful it was to defile their mouths with the allusions which I had heard but would not notice before. Sabat has sent me two more letters, the first runs thus :—'My brother, object of my eyes, and beloved of my heart ; God give thee peace and long life, and feed me near thee, and associate me and thee ! Amen. I had an interview yesterday with the great Ameer nobleman, and found him better than I thought. He kept me near him, and gave me a room, omitted no mark of respect, and seemed wanting in nothing becoming a true Christian, and a believer in the Lord, except that he kept me from coming to thee, and confined me from proceeding to thee. By Christian love ? No ! but by chains and fetters. When I come I will tell thee all his goodness. I have found Mirza Fitrut again, and mean to bring him to thee. The peace of God and the Saviour be with thee. The Mussulman physicians are not inclined to cure me. Besides, the Ameer—God prolong his life—does not consent that I should return to them.' So I understand it. The second letter !—'Peace on the peculiar one of his elect ! in the name of his gracious Son. I have received your letter in answer to my first. With respect to Mirza Fitrut, I told you in my last of my desire to bring him with me. I visited him with the utmost humility, and though he should reject me with ignorance and pride, I shall overcome him with gentleness, if it please God, and bring him with me. Peace on thee, and the mercy of Christ.'

CXLVII.

TO THE REV. D. BROWN.

Cawnpore, October 17, 1809.

Beloved Sir,

There is a book printed at the Hirkara Press, calle Celtic derivatives—this I want ; also grammars an dictionaries of all the languages of the earth. I hav one or both in Latin, Greek, French, Italian, Portu guese, Dutch, Hebrew, Rabb. Hebrew, Chaldee, Syria Ethiopic, Samaritan, Arabic, Persian, Sanscrit, Ben galee, Hindoostanee.

I want them in the languages of *Northern* Europ such as German, Danish, Icelandic, &c.—languages c Ireland and Scotland, Hungarian, Turkish, moder Greek, Armenian. But do not stare, Sir, I have no am bition of becoming a linguist, but they will help me i some enquiries I am making, closely connected wit our work. * * * *

On further consideration I approve most fully of you new orders for commencing the Arabic. A year ago was not adequate to it ; my labours in the Persian an other studies have in the wisdom of God been the mean of qualifying me. So now, favente Deo, we will begi to preach to Arabia, Syria, Persia, India, Tartar China, half of Africa, all the south coast of the Med terranean, and Turkey, and one tongue shall suffice fc them all.

Your's, ever affectionately,

H. Martyn.

CXLVIII.

TO THE REV. D. BROWN.

Cawnpore, October 23, 1809.

DEAREST SIR,

Your letter of the 13th is just come to hand. Dear Mrs. Brown! by this time she has received the melancholy intelligence. But Oh! the God whom she serves will comfort her. He will enable her to submit, without repining, to the severest dispensations, and though she is now in heaviness, with the rest of the church of God, through manifold afflictions, her faith thus tried by fire, shall be found unto praise, and honour, and glory, at the appearing of Jesus Christ. *It is the Lord,* —let this silence every murmur. Charge her to cherish her precious life, not for her family only, but the church in India. You are essential to us, and she to you. She must live therefore, and must for the general good dismiss all earth-born woes, ere they prey on the little remnant of her strength. * * *

As to piecemeal translations, you have explained yourself fully, and I am aware of the necessity imposed upon us.

Though I sicken at the thought of coming forward with promises and palaver, after the manner of the apostles of the nineteenth century, instead of exhibiting the deep full silent tide of mighty works, like the apostles as the first, I must do something of the kind.

But save me as much as possible from every rencontre with the * * * If I set my foot in the arena, let it be the first and last time ; and this I say, not because I am afraid of them, or any man living, but because I hate war, and most of all war in the church. * * *

Your's, ever affectionately,

H. Martyn.

CXLIX.

TO THE REV. D. CORRIE.

October 30, 1809.

You are now doing my work, crossing rivers and traversing jungles, while I sit quietly in my bungalow, and the sweet song of Zion soothes my spirit. Yet I am with you in spirit, and lift my heart to God to keep you in all places whithersoever you go, and to make known by you the savour of Christ's name in every place. If you should not have time to get back to Chunar by next Lord's day, or even if you have, I should much wish you to preach at P—— on that day. You should make some memorandums of your conversation with ——. It is highly important. He is considered as such an oracle in all Sanscrit learning, that his testimony would be received without hesitation. Yesterday we had service at head-quarters. I preached from the parable of the pounds; on the accountableness of man. —— was pleased to say that it was a very good sermon, but the praises of men of that stamp have no charms for me. His commendation gave me real displeasure, so much so, that I hardly concealed my chagrin. Alas! thought I, the sermon has done you no good, it has not made you uneasy. At night I spoke to them on "Enoch walked with God." My soul breathed after the same holy happy state. O that the influence were more abiding; but I am the man that seeth his natural face in a glass.

H. Martyn.

CL.

TO THE REV. D. BROWN.

Cawnpore, Nov. 4, 1809.

MY DEAR SIR,

Your last bungy parcel, containing Mahommed Ras heed's translation and letter, is just come to hand. I must own that I feel a little for poor Sabat on this oc casion, and think that Rasheed's letter would engende choler in one of less bilious temperament. I dare no show him the papers, without preparing him for th shock, and mean to get the Epistle to the Roman fairly away to you before the commencement of th storm. Rasheed says that the translator has not facility in writing Persian, hence his style is destitut of ease and elegance. Yet it is intelligible, and the worl not absolutely good for nothing :—by no means, howeve worthy of admiration. He says, that the translator o the divine books should aim at perspicuity, in which I agree with him ; but perspicuity is not the only requi site ; a certain portion of grace is desirable, and dignit indispensable. I am now about to mention Rasheed' own production, but I must keep a tight reign on my self, lest you should suppose I have imbibed Sabat' spirit, as it is probable I have in some degree. Is it pos sible that Mr. H. can approve such low, miserable, bazaa language ? Where can Mahommed Rasheed show a book written in this style, except perhaps the Tootel Nameh ! Did he ever read a letter written so meanly

Why, Sir, it appears to me below the style in which the Mahometans speak their Hindoostanee. He mentions Sadi, I think, as a writer of the simple kind. Let him produce any chapter in Sabat's work, that has half as many high Arabic words, as Sadi's preface to the Gulistan. If the Scriptures are to be given in this form, we need not be giving away three hundred rupees to Sabat. A moonshee at fifteen rupees per month will answer our purpose ; nay, a Hindoo Cargater at five rupees. And this was your opinion, my dear Sir, you will remember, when I used to communicate my fears to you, that there was a redundance of Arabic. After all, I think it more than probable, that more Persian words would materially improve the work, and I shall endeavour to persuade Sabat to alter it accordingly. But we need never expect that he will come down to the point of depression which Rasheed would bring him to.

Now, dearest Sir, you, or rather we, all are in a dilemma. Who shall decide? To make Sabat's scale preponderate, I will remind you of two things. First, the side on which Sabat errs, is the safer side. A mean style puts it in the power of every blockhead to ridicule it, though the words may be pure, and the rendering exact. Who can help smiling, sometimes, at good Wickliffe's simple language. * * * * Secondly, The Mahometans are more affected with sound, than even the Greeks. They have no other argument for the truth of the Koran, but its eloquence. They are therefore accustomed to expect it in every divine book. By and bye, perhaps, when Persia shall become a Christian nation, and a synod of her bishops shall be held at Teheran, a translation more adapted to the capacity of the lower people will be deemed advisable ; but at first, their ridiculous prejudices require t be humoured, and we may do it innocently, we may be come all things to all men, that we may gain some. hope you will be able to find the Persians. Their opinio may have some weight with Sabat, but Rasheed's neve will, if Sabat sees his translation. I hope you wil cause my Hindoostanee to undergo a vigorous scrutiny and get written opinions upon it. Sabat does not worl half hard enough for me. I feel grieved and ashame that we produce so little, but the fault is not mine. would never willingly be employed about anything else but Sabat has no ardour. The smallest difficulty dis courages him, the slightest head-ache is an excuse fo shutting up his books, and doing nothing for days. I mak strong representations to him, which he does not tak in good part, thinks my temper soured, and so on. I is a comfort, however, to me, for which I desire to b thankful, that his temper is much better than it was.

* * * * *

Pray for Sabat and me.

Your ever affectionate,

H. Martyn.

CLI.

TO THE REV. D. BROWN.

Cawnpore, Nov. 14, 1809.

Dearest Sir,

Mr. Grant's letter is really refreshing to me. I had no notion that he possessed such a tender spirit, and now I grieve that he is so old. Why cannot he put on fresh feathers, like the moulting eagle? 'This is the third brought up under my wing who hath taken a splendid flight before me.' Fine remark! and from the sovereign of Hindoostan.

It appears that Dr. B.'s memoir has not been in vain, if four additional chaplains are to be sent. * * * Sabat is gone off again to Lucknow. * * * I dare not promise much from him, because there is no depending upon him. When he was safely in his palanquin commencing his journey, I put into his hands Rasheed's remarks, with an injunction not to open the parcel till he had crossed the river. * * *

* * * * *

I have just heard from Sabat. Among other remarks he says, 'Ah, and pity that a pearl should be set in the shop of an ironsmith!' 'They said that I am a beginner in Persian, which I spoke, sucking milk.'

Yours, ever affectionately,

H. Martyn.

CLII.

TO THE REV. W. CLARK, CAMBRIDGE.

Dinapore, November, 1809.

MY DEAR FRIEND,

* * * I could willingly convers with you a little on some part of your letter, but it ha probably all passed out of your mind long before this Respecting my heart, about which you ask, I mus acknowledge that H. Martyn's heart at Dinapore is th same as H. Martyn's heart at Cambridge. The teno of my prayer is nearly the same, except on one subject the conversion of the heathen. At a distance from th scene of action, and trusting too much to the highly coloured description of missionaries, my heart used t expand with rapture at the hope of seeing thousands o the natives melting under the word as soon as it shoul be preached to them. Here I am called to exercis faith—that so it shall one day be. My former feeling on this subject were more agreeable, and at the sam time more according with the truth ; for if we believ the prophets, the scenes that time shall unfold, 'thoug surpassing fable, are yet true.' While I write, hop and joy spring up in my mind. Yes, it shall be ; yon der stream of Ganges shall one day roll through tract adorned with Christian churches, and cultivated b Christian husbandmen, and the holy hymn be hear beneath the shade of the tamarind. All things ar working together to bring on the day, and my part i

he blessed plan, though not at first exactly consonant o my wishes, is, I believe, appointed me by God. To ranslate the word of God is a work of more lasting enefit than my preaching would be. But besides that, am sorry to say that my strength for public preaching is almost gone. My ministrations among the Europeans at this station have injured my lungs, and I am now obliged to lie by except on the Sabbath-days, and nce or twice in the week. * * However, am sufficiently aware of my important relations to the natives, and am determined not to strain myself any nore for the Europeans. This rainy season has tried ny constitution severely. The first attack was with pasms, under which I fainted. The second was a ever, from which a change of air, under God, recovered ne. There is something in the air at the close of the ains so unfavourable, that public speaking at that time s a violent strain upon the whole body. Corrie passed lown a few weeks ago to receive his sister. We enjoyed nuch refreshing communion in prayer and conversaion on our dear friends at and near Cambridge, and ound peculiar pleasure in the minutest circumstances ve could recollect about you all. I seldom receive a etter from Europe ; so that you cannot do me a greater avour than to write and mention all our common riends. I remember them with you always in my rayers, and beg the continuance of your's for me.

I am, dear Clark,

Affectionately yours,

H. MARTYN.

CLIII.

TO THE REV. D. BROWN.

Cawnpore, Dec. 4, 1809.

My Dear Sir,

You will see by Sabat's letter that he is ready to alte the words which are rather uncommon. But if all th Indian moonshees in Calcutta should unite in conside ing Aboolfarl's book as the standard of plain style, fear Sabat would not value their opinion a straw. 'H did not come from Persia to India to learn Persian ! Yet Mr. B. must not suppose that Sabat, with all his ex travagant vanity, thinks his performance immaculat or that his future translations will not be better for th castigation he has gone through for the failure of hi first effort. On the contrary, I am persuaded, that a he grows in age, in wisdom, in grace, and knowledge c God's word, he will see that it stands in no need of taw dry ornament. * * * *

The Psalms we must leave till the end of the Ne Testament, for this solid reason, that I do not unde stand one quarter of that book. Perhaps half of i may be rightly translated. It appears to me, that th two royal authors have suffered more from the plebeia touch of their interpreters, than even the prophets c any others but Job. Hebrew is my constant medita tion day and night. I have been sometimes three week at one verse, and thought myself richly rewarded if was made to understand the meaning of it. *

I hope to be able to send you the Hindoostanee New Testament, part the first, as soon as you are ready for printing.

Upon the whole, Sir, let us praise God. Though we have many difficulties and disappointments, he will help us through.

Your ever affectionate,

H. Martyn.

CLIV.

TO THE REV. D. CORRIE.

December 11, 1809.

Last Tuesday night I dined at the General's wit Shumsher Bahadoor. As there was no person preser able to criticise, I spoke to him boldly in Persian ; bu my dialect was infinitely too fine for him. I was sui prised to find a Nawaub so illiterate ; but I have sinc learnt that he is of Hindoo extraction ; moreover, a du young man, who has thrown away his time in fightin the English. Some of his moonshees were introduce after dinner, and with them I had something like conversation, chiefly of a moral kind ; reflections abou death, and the transition that would then take plac from the music and wine and glare in which we wer sitting, to the dark abodes of the grave, seemed to affec them in much the same way as it would us. I feel un happy, not because I do nothing, but because I am nc willing to do my duty. The flesh must be mortifiec and I am reluctant to take up the cross. Sabat said t me yesterday, 'Your beggars are come, why do nc you preach to them, it is your duty?' I made ex cuses ; but why do not I preach to them? My carna spirit says, that I have been preaching a long tim without success to my servants, who are used to m tongue ; what can I expect from them, the very dreg of the people? But the true cause is shame : I an afraid of exposing myself to the contempt of Saba my servants, and the mob, by attempting to speak in a language which I do not speak well. To-day in prayer, one consideration has been made of some power in overcoming this shameful backwardness :—these people, if I neglect to speak to them, will give me a look at the last day, which may fill me with horror. Alas! brother, where is my zeal?

H. Martyn.

CLV.

TO THE SAME.

January 1, 1810.

A change of date that calls for serious though Another year gone, dear brother. How soon the tal will be told!

Well, if our days must fly
  We'll keep their end in sight,
We'll spend them all in wisdom's way,
  And let them take their flight.

They'll waft us sooner o'er
  This life's tempestuous sea,
Soon we shall reach the blissful shore
  Of blest eternity.

May every succeeding year find us increasingly laboriou and holy, so that when time shall be no more, an rolling years shall cease to move, we may rest as faith ful servants of our Lord, who have done their work Well, but now for my congregation of the poor, th blind, the maimed, and the lame. I went without fea trusting to myself and not to the Lord, and accordingl I was put to shame; that is, I did not read half as wel as the preceding days. I shuffled and stammered, an indeed I am persuaded that there were many sentence the poor things did not understand at all. I spoke o the dry land, rivers, &c.; here I mentioned Gunga (Ganges) 'a good river' but there were others as good

God loves Hindoos, but does he not love others also? He gave them a good river, but to others as good. All are alike before God.' This was received with applause. On the work of the fourth day, 'Thus sun and moon are lamps. Shall I worship a candle in my hand? As a candle in the house so is the sun in the sky.' Applause from the Mahommedans. There were also hisses, but whether these betokened displeasure against me or the worship of the sun I do not know. I then charged them to worship Gunga and sun and moon no more, but the honour they used to give to them, henceforward to give to God their Maker. Who knows but even this was a blow struck, at least a branch lopped from the tree of heathenism. The number was about 550. You need not be deterred, dear brother, if this simple way of teaching do any good.

H. MARTYN.

CLVI.

TO THE SAME.

February 12, 1810.

Yesterday I had my usual services; first to the dragoons, then at head-quarters; in the afternoon to the beggars. The number was considerably increased, I suppose from the people's coming from the country to the Mohurrun. I spoke to them again on the promise of a Saviour, in expectation, and went on to the murder of Abel. There are no plaudits now. As for my once beloved Hebrew studies, discouragement has damped my ardour. I am now reading with great impetuosity and eagerness the Septuagint of the Psalms. There I see many more prophecies of Christ than in the English. In short I labour in vain to trace the connection between the verses of any of the mournful Psalms, except by applying them to Christ. Sabat goes on tolerably well. He has made a vow not to eat his dinner till one chapter in Arabic is done. Of course he finds no difficulty in keeping it. He prayed to-day for the conversion of the nations with great ardour, in such a way indeed, that my heart warmed.

H. MARTYN.

CLVII.

TO THE SAME.

February 26, 1810.

One day this week I dined with the ——'s; they, with a large party of the chiefs, had long been contemplating a trip to Culpee, and had fixed the day of their departure for Sunday next, the 25th. I was determined to make an effort to prevent this public profanation of the Lord's day; and accordingly, in the drawing-room, with the ladies after dinner, where I seldom appear, I opened my batteries, and experienced an obstinate resistance for some time. At last conscience turned the scale with them, it was put off till Monday, and most of the party came to church yesterday. Sunday week I spoke to my Hindoostanee congregation on the corruption of human nature, "The Lord saw that every imagination," &c. In the application I said, 'hence all outward works are useless while the heart remains in this state. You may wash in Gunga, but the heart is not washed.' Some old men shook their heads in much the same way as we do when seriously affected with any truth. The number was about seven hundred. The servants told me it was nonsense to give them all rice, as they were not all poor; hundreds of them are working people, among them was a whole row of Brahmins. I spoke to them about the flood; this was interesting, as they were very attentive, and at the end said, 'Shabash wa wa' (well said.) H. Martyn.

CLVIII.

TO THE REV. D. BROWN.

Cawnpore, March 3, 1810.

MY DEAR SIR,

Thomason tells me wonders of yourself and you doings ; your ardour, and ability, and more than I ca repeat. Blessed be the Lord our head, who in wisdor dispenses his gifts, making some evangelists, and som pastors and teachers, some directors, and some transla tors, for the edifying of the body of Christ. M thoughts are now constantly on Hebrew, as I perceiv that without some very great increase of knowledge, w shall be reduced to a dilemma in our translations. Th Arabic version of the Psalms, now in the hands of al the Christians of the East, follows the Septuagint, whic in every single Psalm, differs very materially from th English. Which sense of the Hebrew are we to take For my part, considering that the Septuagint has bee sanctified as it were, by the quotations of the Apostle and that the English is in many places unintelligibl where the Greek is plain,—I would rather translat from the latter than the former.

How do the missionaries get on ? D——, in a lette he sent us, tells us that he is translating the epistle into Orissa. You must be on your guard against al epistle-translations. It costs us days, to make one chap ter in the epistles intelligible in the Hindoostanee.

Let me hear something about the children ; I ough

to demand a half-yearly report of them, as you do from me. How I should rejoice to sit with them at S——'s feet ! but we sit at the feet of a better master.

Believe me to be, dearest Sir,

Yours ever,

H. Martyn.

CLIX.

TO THE REV. D. CORRIE.

March 5, 1810.

I lament your detention at Chunar, and the cause o it. So you are to go to Agra to be the founder of Christian church, I hope, in that great Nineveh. Youn —— and the —— must be near you. I wish you ma all come together, that I may experience a great rusl of joy ; such a conflux of saints in the Dooab has no been known, I suppose, since Jumna and Gunga unite their streams. Yesterday I had to preach to two ver small congregations at the General's artillery-barracks their aggregate not fifty. You, I suppose, were laid up and P—— perhaps on a sand-bank, so that little wa done in Hindoostan Proper yesterday. But such fruit less days shall not continue much longer. If it canno be said that the day has broke, let us hope that we se the morning star. I was not very well pleased witl my discourse to the beggars yesterday. I fear I hur their prejudices without removing them. On God' grant of flesh to Noah for meat, I said, 'Therefore we kil and eat. If God had considered one animal more hol than another, why did not he say so ? If, for instance the cow had been excepted, why was it not said so I say not, that in eating cow is any benefit, nor in nc eating it any loss ; but if you see others eat, do not thin it a sin.' There was a dead silence, and nothing sai after it. I have been labouring a good deal this wee to understand Romans vi. 7, 8. I am astonished at my ignorance of a subject of such vast importance. The whole of a believer's sanctification is interwoven with the work and person of Christ, and yet I do not know that I ever had two clear ideas upon the subject. Blessed be the goodness of the Lord, who carries on his work, though his poor saints hardly know by what name to call it.

H. Martyn.

CLX.

TO THE REV. D. BROWN.

Cawnpore, March 20, 1810.

DEAREST SIR,

The case of the Tanjore Christians is truly affecting It called for instant relief; you rose at the call, an God was with you. Lord, increase our faith! Wh are we not always more bold in our God? The readi ness of the Calcutta people associates them in my min with the loving Philippians, and goes a good way t reconcile me to a residence amongst them. As a symp tom, it is very important. It is a feature of apostoli times.

I hope the private communications from me, yo were pleased to insert in the report, will not cross th seas; lest my pert remarks, concerning the existin versions of the Psalms; should excite disgust. Yet it i but too true, that I do not understand one half, or hal of one half; and the same must be said of the prophet

I fear when —— begins to find what Sanscrit gram mar is, he will take a hasty farewell of it. I was si months at it, without getting out of the dark. Saba creeps on, and smokes his hookah with great compla cency, if he gets through a chapter a day. I grieve a this hireling spirit, but for peace-sake I have lon ceased to say anything. H. M.

CLXI.

TO MISS L. GRENFELL.

Cawnpore, March 30, 1810.

Since you kindly bid me, my beloved friend, consider you in the place of that dear sister, whom it has pleased God in his wisdom to take from me, I gratefully accept the offer of a correspondence, which it has ever been the anxious wish of my heart to establish. Your kindness is the more acceptable, because it is shown in the day of affliction. Though I had heard of my dearest sister's illness, some months before I received the account of her death, and though the nature of her disorder was such as left me not a ray of hope, so that I was mercifully prepared for the event; still the certainty of it fills me with anguish. It is not that she has left me, for I never expected to see her more on earth. I have no doubt of meeting her in heaven, but I cannot bear to think of the pangs of dissolution she underwent, which have been unfortunately detailed to me with too much particularity. Would that I had never heard them, or could efface them from my remembrance. But oh, may I learn what the Lord is teaching me by these repeated strokes. May I learn meekness and resignation. May the world always appear as vain as it does now, and my own continuance in it as short and uncertain. How frightful is the desolation which death makes, and how appalling his visits when he enters one's family. I would rather never have been born, than be born and die, were it not for Jesu: the prince of life, the resurrection and the life. Ho inexpressibly precious is this Saviour, when eternit seems near! I hope often to communicate with yo on these subjects, and in return for your kind and con solatory letters, to send you from time to time, account of myself and my proceedings. Through you, I ca hear of all my friends in the west. When I first hea of the loss I was likely to suffer, and began to refle on my own friendless situation, you were much in m thoughts,—whether you would be silent on this occasio or no? whether you would persist in your resolution Friends indeed I have, and brethren, blessed be God but two brothers cannot supply the place of one siste When month after month passed away, and no lett came from you, I almost abandoned the hope of eve hearing from you again. It only remained to wait th result of my last application through Emma. Yo have kindly anticipated my request, and, I need scarcel add, are more endeared to me than ever.

Of your illness, my dearest Lydia, I had heard no thing, and it was well for me that I did not.

Your's most affectionately,

H. MARTYN.

CLXII.

TO THE REV. D. BROWN.

Cawnpore, April 3, 1810.

DEAREST SIR,

I do not know whether my spirits were low or not, when I last wrote to you, but this I know, that I need not go so far as Calcutta for occasions of sorrow. Everybody would suppose Sabat improved : I fancy I see the worldly principle more predominant. Do not tell him any more that he is a learned man, the fact itself begins to be doubtful to me ; but however that may be, it can only tend to strengthen his abominable pride, to tell him that he is what he thinks he is.

As you will not part with Shalome for five or six months yet, we shall have time to consider of the expediency of his coming to me. I have no hope of getting anything from him, when all the versions and targum of the Polyglott are insufficient to afford me aid. The books however which you mention, I shall expect with impatience. Street's version ; Hammond, who is a learned man. Horne is all words. Now next to oriental translations, my wish and prayer is, that I may live to give a new English version of the Bible, from Job to Malachi, and after that, to lead men to search for the principles of all true philosophy in the Bible. Such are some of my modest desires. Schultens on the Proverbs, I long so much to see, that I would go two hundred miles to fetch it. Do send it up by bungy. Also G. Liomlas' version of the Psalms For these two I would give their weight in gold. Th gospels of Matthew and Mark, with errata, were sen off by dawk. The Epistle to the Romans in Arabic i translating for you.

I have had several letters from England this week o a mournful nature : my long-lost Lydia, however, con sents to write to me again. My health, through mercy is very well, notwithstanding all my vexations an fatigues. My church is almost ready for the organ an the bell.

Old Mirza gives me more satisfaction than any on in Cawnpore. He seems to take great pleasure in seein an intricate sentence of the Epistles unravelled.

Your's ever most affectionately,

H. Martyn.

CLXIII.

TO THE SAME.

Cawnpore, April 16, 1810.

Dearest Sir,

*   *   *   *   *   *

*   *   *   *   *   *

Is it possible that they can have been so ignorant of the languages, in which they have been sending forth versions. I am anxious to see their Epistle to the Romans in Hindoostanee, which I see from their circular letter they have done. It will then be more easy to judge of their real powers, because the four gospels are merely Fitrut's a little altered.

18. I do not know whether I may venture to tell you that I have a pain in my breast, occasioned, I fear, from over-exertion of my lungs on the Sundays: the Sunday before last it made its first appearance, and I was tolerably careful the whole week. Last Sunday it came on again at night, and I was obliged to leave my men in the midst. To-day (Wednesday) it is not gone. Such a symptom in my constitution is alarming; but let me assure you that in future I will be as careful as possible, if it be not too late. I do not know whether it is really a love to my work, or only the love of life, but I should be more contented to depart if I had finished the translation of the Epistles. The will of our God be done! Pray for me. Prayer lengthened Hezekiah's life, perhaps it may mine.

Your's ever affectionately,

H. Martyn.

CLXIV.

TO MISS L. GRENFELL.

Cawnpore, April 19, 1810.

I begin my correspondence with my beloved Lydia not without a fear of its being soon to end. Shall I venture to tell you, that our family complaint has again made its appearance in me, with more unpleasant symptoms than it has ever yet done? However, God, who two years ago redeemed my life from destruction, may again, for his Church's sake, interpose for my deliverance. Though, alas! what am I, that my place should not instantly be supplied with far more efficient instruments. The symptoms I mentioned are chiefly a pain in the chest, occasioned I suppose by over-exertion the two last Sundays, and incapacitating me at present from all public duty and even from conversation. You were mistaken in supposing that my former illness originated from study. Study never makes me ill—scarcely ever fatigues me—but my lungs! death is seated there; it is speaking that kills me. May it give others life. "Death worketh in us, but life in you." Nature intended me, as I should judge from the structure of my frame, for a chamber-counsel, not for a pleader at the bar. But the call of Jesus Christ bids me cry aloud, and spare not. As his minister, I am a debtor both to the Greek and the Barbarian. How can I be silent, when I have both ever before me, and my debt not paid? You would suggest that energies more restrained will eventually be more efficient. I am aware of this, and mean to act upon this principle in future, if the resolution is not formed too late. But you know how apt we are to outstep the bounds of prudence, when there is no kind monitor at hand to warn us of the consequences.

Had I been favoured with the one I wanted, I might not now have had occasion to mourn. You smile at my allusion, at least I hope so, for I am hardly in earnest. I have long since ceased to repine at the decree that keeps us as far asunder as the east is from the west, and yet am far from regretting that I ever knew you. The remembrance of you calls forth the exercise of delightful affections, and has kept me from many a snare. How wise and good is our God, in all his dealings with his children! Had I yielded to the suggestions of flesh and blood, and remained in England, as I should have done, without the effectual working of his power, I should without doubt have sunk with my sisters into an early grave; whereas here, to say the least, I may live a few years, so as to accomplish a very important work. His keeping you from me, appears also, at this season of bodily infirmity, to be occasion of thankfulness. Death, I think, would be a less welcome visitor to me, if he came to take me from a wife, and that wife were you. Now if I die, I die unnoticed, involving none in calamity. O that I could trust him for all that is to come, and love him with that perfect love, which casteth out fear; for to say the truth, my confidence is sometimes shaken. To appear before the Judge of quick and dead is a much more awful thought in sickness than in health. Yet I dare not doubt the all-sufficiency of Jesus Christ, nor can I, with the utmost ingenuity of unbelief, resist the reasonings of St. Paul, all whose reasons seem to be drawn up on purpose to work into the mind, the persuasion that God will glorify himself by the salvation of sinners through Jesus Christ. I wish I could more enter into the meaning of this 'chosen vessel.' He seems to move in a world by himself, and sometimes to utter the unspeakable words, such as my natural understanding discerneth not; and when I turn to commentators, I find that I have passed out of the spiritual, to the material world, and have got amongst men like myself. But soon, as he says, we shall no longer see as in a glass, by reflected rays, but see as we are seen, and know as we are known.

25th. After another interval, I resume my pen. Through the mercy of God I am again quite well, but my mind is a good deal distressed at Sabat's conduct. I forbear writing what I think, in the hope that my fears may prove groundless; but indeed the children of the East are adepts in deceit. Their duplicity appears to me so disgusting at this moment, that I can only find relief from my growing misanthropy by remembering Him, who is the faithful and true witness; in whom all the promises of God are yea and amen; and by turning to the faithful in Europe—children that will not lie. Where shall we find sincerity in a native of the East? Yesterday I dined in a private way with ——. After one year's inspection of me, they begin to lose their dread, and venture to invite me. Our conversation was occasionally religious, but topics of this nature are so new to fashionable people, and those upon which they have thought so much less, than on any other, that often from the shame of having nothing to say, they pass to other subjects where they can be more at home. I was asked after dinner if I liked music. On my professing to be an admirer of harmony, cantos were performed and songs sung. After a time I inquired if they had no sacred music. It was now recollected, that they had some of Handel's, but it could not be found. A promise however was made, that next time I came, it should be produced. Instead of it, the 145th Psalm-tune was played, but none of the ladies could recollect enough of the tune to sing it. I observed, that all our talents and powers should be consecrated to the service of Him who gave them. To this no reply was made, but the reproof was felt. I asked the lady of the house if she read poetry, and then proceeded to mention Cowper, whose poems it seems were in the library, but the lady had never heard of the book. This was produced, and I read some passages. Poor people! here a little, and there a little, is a rule to be observed in speaking to them.

26th. From speaking to my men last night, and again to-day conversing long with some natives, my chest is again in pain, so much so that I can hardly speak. Well! now I am taught, and will take more care in future. My sheet being full, I must bid you adieu. The Lord ever bless and keep you. Believe me to be, with the truest affection,

Yours ever,

H. Martyn.

CLXV.

TO THE REV. D. CORRIE.

May 1, 1810.

I bless God that you are better. For myself, I re main in a doubtful state. I had but two services o Sunday, yet was much exhausted. The occasional du ties here are very great at this time. I am willing t hope that the extraordinary weather is the cause of m pulmonary weakness. I have been out a good deal thi week. Last Monday I dined at a large party; made resolution never to dine in a large party again if possi ble. Next day at Col. ——'s in private. This wa more agreeable because more profitable. I read Cowpe to them, and made them play some Psalms. As peopl begin to be less afraid of me than they were, and begi to invite me, a new field of usefulness is opened; bu alas! I have not strength to do half my work.

H. Martyn.

CLXVI.

TO THE REV. D. BROWN.

Cawnpore, May 2, 1810.

Dearest Sir,

Your request for a list of books has almost blinded me. Anxious to demonstrate that I am on the alert, warm in the cause, and ready to run wherever you like to send me, I have been on the search night and day for books. I have written to Baillie's to know what is to be had at Lucknow. I have been interrogating Marcellino, a Padre just come from them, about the remains of the Jesuit library, but from him I learn nothing. If you mean to solicit any out of the pale of translators, and of those whose hearts are translating, I think you must not call it a translation library. Let it be proposed to form a library consisting of such books as do not form a part of private collections. Dictionaries and other books of reference, learned works particularly, in other languages, because such are more rarely met with in India ; in short, it should be such a library as may compensate for the privations, which the chaplains and others of literary habits suffer by leaving England Travels into the East will be of use, because they tell us where Christians may be found, and in what state they are. So much for the library at present. I object to the Latin names of the Bible Depositary ; if any be necessary, I should think Bibliotheca sufficient. If Bible is applied *κατ εξοχην* to the Holy Scriptures, Bibliotheca may be to the Theca of the Sacred Scriptures.

You have set me a most unpalatable task, in makin me a critic, though I did propose to commence wit Marshman about it. Since the receipt of your order, read a little with Mirza, who desires me to tell you tha it would be a great sin to publish their translation ; fo when it is gone forth there is no recalling it.

You shall have my remarks on the said chapters a soon as possible. I should have said, that I am gettin better, though not yet well. I do not expect to be s till we have the hot winds. But every day added to m life is undeserved grace.

3rd. Since writing the above, I have looked over th chapters. I had no conception they were so bad ; bu I may be mistaken, and most happy shall I be to fin that I am—for next to the Chinese there is none of thei works I have so much at heart. The blunder in chapter v. 32, is so important that I wish you would ge some one else to look at it ; for I can hardly believe m own eyes. I begin to despair of the ——'s works altogether. Nothing is yet done for India, absolutely nothing, if their Bengalee is like this. But let me see b all means their Epistle to the Romans in Hindoostanee

If you wish a critique on their Sanscrit from thi part of India, I can perhaps procure it. Send me a copy of the *Habe Hindee* Psalter. You are kind in proposing to help me in paying Fitrut, but there is no occasion—let me have the honour of presenting the Bibl Society with a Hindoostanee New Testament, free o expense. When Fitrut has finished the New Testament if you like, we two with Corrie and Parsons may clut together to make him a present of 200 rupees. I hav now left nothing unsaid. The Lord be with you.

Yours, ever affectionately,

H. Martyn.

CLXVII.

TO THE SAME.

Cawnpore, May 14, 1810.

Dearest Sir,

Remission of vocal labour, and the increasing heat of the air are restoring me to my strength, through the mercy of God; but every cold too often produces shooting pains in my chest. We are "in deaths oft" from other causes. Last night my horse, which had not been mounted some days, went off with such joy, that the saddle-girths broke. With the saddle I was precipitated to the earth, and a Persian, who was witness to the scene, thought I had fallen to rise no more; but I am again well, with no other effect than lameness. Sabat was much affected, and gave thanks to God in fervent prayer with me. My last critique on the ——'s Hindoostanee renders it unnecessary for me to return to that subject. A sheet large enough to contain all the emendations, would be larger than the work itself. Your plans, as they develope themselves, claim and possess my approbation and applause; as the eyes of servants look unto the hands of their master, so may our eyes wait upon the Lord our God. You have weathered the wintry storm, and now you live to see the blossoms of the spring. "The flowers appear on the earth, the time of singing is come, and the voice of the turtle is heard in our land."

Three translations will be a great deal to propose at

the first set out, as they will require perhaps not mucl less than half a lac of rupees, but we must not be dis trustful. If you set up but two, I fear the Hindoostane must be left out, which is a pity, as it is so much mor forward than the rest. Have you any informatio about the Malayim ? is it done well ? The Syrians ar brethren, and must not be neglected in the daily minis tration. " If any provide not for his own, and especiall for those of his own house, he hath denied the faith, an is worse than an infidel." A collection for them woul have no prejudices to encounter, the proposal woul rather meet the ideas of people in general. Perhaps som of the Bible Society's funds might be appropriated t the Hindoostanee. But I write without seeing half wa into things, though you take so much pains to instruc me. The Arabic New Testament may be all translate by the end of the year, and will, if our lives are spared but then it will not be all ready for the press ; we ca however, keep the press constantly employed, if tha will do, for the gospels will not require much attention and the epistles scarcely any, if, as we intend, Saba translates them with me ; alone he could do nothin with them. I cannot say that I have found Sabat no learned in Arabic ; I am clear that I have no right ye to judge him, my own acquaintance with the languag being so imperfect. What made me uneasy was tha I discovered eight or ten grammatical errors in th Epistle to the Romans, which after some anger an shame he was obliged to acknowledge. This would no disturb me if I were sure of making none myself, but I cannot be sure of any such thing. These are the thing that European scholars will detect, while errors in idiom lie beyond their ken. Arabic scholars in Indi are notorious for their false concords ; even Mr. Baillie' books are not exempt. What, however, is my opinion on the whole? Why that we shall never find in India so good a man as Sabat; and it will be wonderful indeed, if, with all the imperfections of his work, it is not decidedly superior to former versions. It will be a satisfaction to you to know, that Mr. Baillie has the highest opinion of Sabat's Arabic, and speaks in his praise to every body. I inclose the last letter I had from him.

I can hardly tell what the Colonel intends to do; he would rather give a donation than subscribe, but I want subscribers, that hereafter when they go home they may, once a year at least, be reminded of the existence of the Bible. Mirza is become restive again, and wants to throw me off. He will stay to finish the New Testament, and then he talks of going. He pleads half a promise I made him, that at the end of the New Testament I would use my interest with some judge or collector to get him a place; in which case he would come to me from time to time to correct what I have got ready; but to work every day will blind him. He frets as often as he thinks of Sabat's salary; wants me to write a petition to the College Council for him; every day he is turning up some new stone. I pity the old man, and really think the company or the College Council ought to do something for him. As they once employed him to translate the four gospels, might not they be disposed to allow him something for going on with the rest? Albert Schultens and Street—Street is good for nothing, and you may have him back as soon as you please; so much for him. But Schultens must remain with me, though after a cursory look at his learned notes, I despair of ever learning Hebrew from books. I sit as before, hours alone, contemplating this mysterious language. If light does not break upon m at last it will be a great loss of time, as I never rea Arabic or Persian. I have no heart to do it; I cannc condescend any longer to tread in the paths of ignc rance and lying grammarians. I sometimes say in m; vain heart, I will either make a deep cut in the min of philology, or I will do nothing; but you shall hea no more of Scriptural philology, till I make som notable discoveries. If Doederlein's Hebrew Bible i small, and you do not use it, I shall be glad to see it but there is no immediate necessity for it. Shall I sen back Street or no.

I hope you have not dropped your design of visit ing us.

Your's, ever affectionately,

H. Martyn.

CLXVIII.

TO THE SAME.

Cawnpore, June 11, 1810.

DEAREST SIR,

The excessive heat, by depriving me of my rest at night, keeps me between sleeping and waking all day. This is one reason why I have been remiss in answering your letters. It must not however be concealed that the man Daniel Corrie has kept me so long talking that I have had no time for writing since his arrival.

Your idea about presenting splendid copies of the Scriptures to native great men has often struck me, but my counsel is, not to do it with the first edition. I have too little faith in the instruments to believe that the first editions will be excellent; and if they should be found defective, we cannot after once presenting the great men with one book, repeat the thing.

Before the second edition of the Arabic, what say you to my carrying the first with me to Arabia, having under the other arm the Persian, to be examined at Shiraz or Tehran.

By the time they are both ready I shall have nearly finished my seven years, and may go on furlough.

I am glad to find you promising to give yourself wholly to your plans. I always tremble, lest Mrs. Brown should order you home; but I must not suspect her, she has the soul of a missionary. If you go soon, we shall all droop and die. Your Polyglot speculations are fine, but Polyglots are bible-luxuries, intended fo the gratification of men of two tongues or more. W must first feed those that have but one, especially a single tongues are growing upon us so fast.

12. To-day I have requested the Commander of th forces to detain D. Corrie here to assist me; he said h did not like to make innovations, but would keep hi here for two or three months. This will be a great re lief to my labouring chest, for I am still far from bein out of the fear of consumption. Tell me that you hav prayed for me.

Yours, &c.

H. Martyn.

CLXIX.

TO THE SAME.

Cawnpore, August 13, 1810.

Dearest Sir,

As you are determined to have a new type for the Arabic, it may as well be beautiful. I hope to procure from Baillie a specimen of small Arabic, from the best writer in Lucknow. You say, 'We cannot print except you come down.' I say in return, we cannot translate except we stay here. If you unsettle Sabat now, he will not recover his wits for three months. Oh that he had a little of your zeal, or even mine. I feel with you, like a bad rider upon a fiery horse; you carry me on with great rapidity, but I am in constant dread of breaking my neck. You and good Dr. Buchanan drag me, prematurely, I fear, into the light, and deaf to the cries of timidity, post me to the world as an Arabic scholar. Should some egregious blunder hereafter proclaim me an ignoramus, the fault will be yours, the disgrace mine. However, I am all obedience, and what is more, my heart is with you in all things—only give me a moment to consider and correct. There is no depending on Sabat for an accurate copy, even after the translation is selected. The seven chapters he brought to me, as a fair copy, had twice as many faults as lines. It is incredible the trouble I have to get anything correct. But all labour in the glorious cause is delightful; I only lament the delay.

Yours, ever affectionately,

H. Martyn.

CLXX.

TO MISS L. GRENFELL.

Cawnpore, August 14, 1810.

With what delight do I sit down to begin a letter to my beloved Lydia! Yours of the fifth of February, which I received a few days ago, was written, I perceive, in considerable embarrassment. You thought it possible it might find me married, or about to be so. Let me begin therefore, with assuring you, with more truth than Gehazi did his master, "Thy servant went no whither:" my heart has not strayed from Marazion, or Gurlyn, or wherever you are. Five long years have passed, and I am still faithful. Happy would it be if I could say that I had been equally true to my profession of love for Him who is fairer than ten thousand and altogether lovely. Yet, to the praise of his grace let me recollect that twice five years have passed away since I began to know him, and I am still not gone from him. On the contrary, time and experience have endeared the Lord to me more and more, so that I feel less inclination, and see less reason for leaving him. What is there, alas! in the world, even were it everlasting?

I rejoice at the accounts you give me of your continued good health and labours of love. Though you are not so usefully employed as you might be in India yet as that must not be, I contemplate with delight your exertions at the other end of the world. May 'ou be instrumental in bringing many sons and daughers to glory. What is become of St. Hilary, and its airy scenes ? When I think of Malachy, and the old nan, and your sister, and Josepha, &c., how some are ead, and the rest dispersed, and their place occupied y strangers, it seems all like a dream.

15th. It is only little intervals of time that I can nd for writing ; my visitors, about whom I shall write resently, taking up much of my leisure, from necesary duty. Here follow some extracts from my journal.

* * * * * * *

Here my journal must close. I do not know whether ou understand from it how we go on. I must endeaour to give you a clearer idea of it.

We all live here in Bungalows, or thatched houses, n a piece of ground enclosed. Next to mine is the hurch, not yet opened for public worship ; but which 'e make use of at night with the men of the 53rd. 'orrie lives with me, and Miss Corrie with the Sher'oods. We usually rise at day-break, and breakfast t six. Immediately after breakfast we pray together, fter which I translate into Arabic with Sabat, who ves in a small bungalow on my ground. We dine at welve, and sit recreating ourselves with talking a little bout dear friends in England. In the afternoon, I 'anslate with Mirza Fitrut into Hindoostanee, and orrie employs himself in teaching some native Chrisan boys whom he is educating with great care, in opes of their being fit for the office of catechist. I ave also a school on my premises, for natives ; but it not well attended. There are not above sixteen :indoo boys in it at present ; half of them read the book ' Genesis. At sunset we ride or drive, and then meet t the church, where we often raise the song of praise, with as much joy, through the grace and presence c our Lord, as you do in England. At ten we are al asleep. Thus we go on. To the hardships of mission aries, we are strangers, yet not averse, I trust, to en counter them, when we are called. My work at presen is evidently to translate; hereafter I may itinerate Dear Corrie, I fear, never will, he always suffers fron moving about in the day-time. But I should have sai something about my health, as I find my death wa reported at Cambridge. I thank God, I am perfectl well, though not very strong in my lungs; they d not seem affected yet, but I cannot speak long withou uneasiness. From the nature of my complaint, if i deserves the name, it is evident that England is the las place I should go to. I should go home only to find grave. How shall I therefore ever see you more on thi side of eternity? Well! be it so, since such is th will of God: we shall meet, through grace, in th realms of bliss.

I am truly sorry to see my paper fail. Write as ofte as possible, every three months at least. Tell me wher you go, and whom you see, and what you read.

17th. I am sorry to conclude with saying, that m yesterday's boasted health proved a mistake; I wa seized with violent sickness in the night, but to-day an better. Continue to pray for me, and believe me to b

Your ever affectionate,

H. Martyn.

CLXXI.

TO MR. G——.

Cawnpore, August 17, 1810.

MY DEAR G——,

I rejoice exceedingly in your kind remembrance of me, but above all that you stand fast in the Lord, and are still pressing towards the mark, for the prize of the high calling of God in Christ Jesus. Your letter of the 23rd of February, enclosing one from your sister, I received, and could have wished for a little more time to answer it rather more at length, but if I let this day's post go, I fear the Georgian will have sailed. In answer to your affectionate inquiries about my health, I may say that I am tolerably well. The sickness and faintness in which I was obliged to conclude the inclosed letter, are now nearly removed; but I am resolved to quit, for a while, my native assistants, mere exhausters of my strength, and recreate myself on the river—though alas! it will be no recreation to me—for I am never so miserable as when idle. This last short sickness, has, I trust, been blessed much to me. I sought not immediately for consolations, but for grace, patiently to endure and to glory in tribulation; in this way I found peace. Oh this surely is bliss, to have our will absorbed in the divine will. In this state are the spirits of just men made perfect in heaven. The spread of the gospel in these parts is now become an interesting subject to you—such is the universal change.

I have not much to say about it. All the English mis sionaries and chaplains, confine their attention almos exclusively to the translation of the Scriptures, thi appearing at present the first thing to be done. T preach so as to be understood, is no easy matter ; no even to translate. Do not omit writing a few lines i the covers of your sister's letters, as I shall be mucl interested abut you.

Believe me to be, yours affectionately,

H. Martyn.

CLXXII.

TO THE REV. D. BROWN.

Cawnpore, August 22, 1810.

DEAREST SIR,

Shall I come down, or shall I not? I have an aversion to Calcutta, with all the talking and preaching to which I shall be tempted there; yet you insist upon it, and sooner or later I must pass through you to the sea, or I shall be buried here. Again, if we stir this year from Cawnpore, my promise to the Bible Society will not be fulfilled. Sabat will revel in the confusion of moving, and our fields will lie fallow.

We hope to be on the river in a day or two; not to go far from Cawnpore. On Sunday I preached twice, and have hardly recovered my breath yet. I want silence and diversion, a little dog to play with; or what would be best of all, a dear little child, such as Fanny was when I left her. Perhaps you could learn when the ships usually sail for Mocha. I have set my heart upon going there; I could be there and back in six months.

H. MARTYN.

CLXXIII.

TO THE SAME.

Cawnpore, September 8, 1810.

DEAREST SIR,

I cannot undertake at this moment to reply at lengtl to your letter of the 25th of August. The twelve learne sections would require as many sheets to do justice t the subject. Your tide rolls on with terrifying rapidity at least I tremble while committing myself to it. Yo look to me, and I to Sabat; and Sabat I look upon a the staff of Egypt. May I prove mistaken! All, how ever, does not depend upon him. If my life is spared there is no reason why the Arabic should not be don in Arabia, and the Persian in Persia, as well as the Indian in India. But all this is inconsistent with you plans of return. I inquired truly what would be th result of your consulting me about ——. The rollin tide swept away my proposals bodily: well, let then go, since they deserved no notice. You are a perfec Lord Wellesley amongst his nominal counsellors.

I am well and strong, except that the lungs ache afte sermon; yet I go to sea (D.V.) to be stronger: the 1s of November we begin to float down: the middle of December shall be with you, and in a week be at sea; tha is I; for Sabat must not persecute me upon the high seas. If Mocha cannot be seen, may I not have you permission to visit the Syrian Christians. I might be back again in April or May, and leave you with the rains. Unless you think the company of three or four jaundiced pilot-men sufficiently refreshing to me, chalk out some plan for me by which I may see something, or learn, or do some good. I hope your Shalome has not left you. I promise myself great advantage in reading Hebrew and Syriac with him. All your orders shall be executed with all convenient dispatch.

Yours ever most affectionately,

H. MARTYN.

CLXXIV.

TO THE SAME.

Cawnpore, Sept. 9, 1810.

DEAREST SIR,

Yours of the 27th ult. is a heart-breaking business Though I share so deeply in Sabat's disgrace, I fee more for you than myself, but I can give you no com fort, except by saying, " It is well that it was in thin heart." Your letter will give a new turn to my life Henceforward I have done with India. Arabia shal hide me till I come forth with an approved New Testa ment in Arabic. I do not ask your advice, because I have made up my mind, but shall just wait your an swer to this, and come down to you instantly. I hav been calculating upon the means of support, and fin that I shall have wherewithal to live. Besides the Lor will provide. Before him I have spread this affair, an do not feel that I shall be acting contrary to his will.

It is now almost needless to return to the subject o Sabat. When we come to Calcutta let him be con fronted with his accusers, and let us hear his defence It is just possible that things may not be so bad ; but I have little hope. The truest character of Sabat is just that, 'He possesses astonishing powers of conversation but is not learned.' Let me know what are the obsta cles to my plans, and what the facilities ; that I may have some certain ground to go upon in ruminating upon my future life. Will government let me go away for three years before the time of my furlough arrives? If not, I must quit the service, and I cannot devote my life to a more important work than that of preparing the Arabic Bible.

Dear Corrie will write to-morrow. If anything occurs to me I will write it in his letter.

Yours ever affectionately,

H. Martyn.

CLXXV.

TO THE SAME.

Cawnpore, Sept. 17, 1810.

DEAREST SIR,

Herewith you will receive the first seven chapters i Persian and Hindoostanee, though I suppose you hav ceased to wish for them. The Persian will only prov that Sabat is not the man for it. I have protested agains many things in it; but instead of sending you my ob jections, I inclose a critique by Mirza, who must remai unknown. I am somewhat inclined to think the Ara bic not quite so hopeless. Sabat is confident, and eage to meet his opponents. His version of the Romans wa certainly not from the old one, because he translated i all before my face, from the English; but then, as hinted long ago, he is inaccurate, and must not be de pended upon. He entirely approves of my going t Bassorah with his translations, and the old one, confi dent that the decision there will be in his favour. I hopes of getting away in November from Calcutta, shall make every exertion to leave this the 1st of nex month, though no budgerows are to be had. So now dear Sir, take measures for transmitting me with th least possible delay; detain me not, for the King's busi ness requires haste. My health in general is good, bu the lungs not strong. One loud dispute brings on pain

Yours ever affectionately,

H. MARTYN.

CLXXVI.

TO THE REV. D. CORRIE.

Allahabad, Oct. 3, 1810.

Thus far are we come in safety ; but my spirits tell me that I have parted with friends. Your pale face as it appeared on Monday morning is still before my eyes, and will not let me be easy till you tell me you are strong and prudent. The first night there blew a wind so bleak and cold, through and through my boat and bed, that I rose, as I expected, with a pain in the breast, which has not quite left me, but will, I hope, to-night, when I shall take measures for expelling it. There is a gate, not paid for yet, belonging to the church-yard, may you always go through it in faith, and return through it with praise. You are now (twenty minutes past seven,) in prayer with our men. The Lord be with you, and be always with you, dearest brother.

H. MARTYN.

CLXXVII.

TO MISS LYDIA GRENFELL.

From the Ganges, Oct. 6, 1810.

MY DEAREST LYDIA,

Though I have had no letter from you very lately nor have anything particular to say, yet having bee days on the water without a person to speak to, tire also with reading and thinking, I mean to indulge my self with a little of what is always agreeable to me, an sometimes good for me: for as my affection for you ha something sacred in it, being founded on, or at leas cemented by, an union of spirit in the Lord Jesus; s my separation also from you, produces a deadness t the world, at least for a time, which leaves a solem impression as often as I think of it. Add to this, tha as I must not indulge the hope of ever seeing you agai in this world, I cannot think of you without thinkin also of that world where we shall meet. You mentio in one of your letters my coming to England, as tha which may eventually prove a duty. You ought t have added, that in case I do come, you will conside it a duty, not to let me come away again without you But I am not likely to put you to the trial. Useless a I am here, I often think I should be still more so a home. Though my voice fails me, I can translate an converse. At home I should be nothing without bein able to lift up my voice on high. I have just left m station, Cawnpore, in order to be silent six months.]

have no cough, nor any sign of consumption, except that reading prayers, or preaching, or a slight cold, brings on pain in the chest. I am advised therefore to recruit my strength by rest. So I am come forth, with my face towards Calcutta, with an ulterior view to the sea. Nothing happened at Cawnpore after I wrote to you in September, but I must look to my journal.

I think of having my portrait taken in Calcutta, as I promised Mr. Simeon five years ago. Sabat's picture would also be a curiosity. Yesterday I carried Col. Wood to dine with me, at the Nabob Bahir Ali's. Sabat was there. The Colonel, who had been reading by the way the account of his conversion, in the Asiatic and East Society Report which I had given him, eyed him with no great complacency, and observed in French, that Sabat might not understand him, 'Il a l'air d'un sauvage.' Sabat's countenance is indeed terrible ; noble when he is pleased, but with the look of an assassin when he is out of humour. I have had more opportunities of knowing Sabat than any man has had, and I cannot regard him with that interest which the "Star in the East" is calculated to excite in most people. Buchanan says, I wrote (to whom I do not know) in terms of admiration and affection about him. Affection I do feel for him, but admiration, if I did once feel it, I am not conscious of at present. I tremble for everything our dear friends publish about our doings in India, lest shame come to us and them.

November 5. *Calcutta.* A sheet full, like the preceding, I had written, but the moment that it is necessary to send off my letter, I cannot find it. That it does not go on to you is of little consequence, but into whose hands may it have fallen ? It is this that grieves me. It was the continuance of my journal to Calcutta, where I arrived the last day in October. Constant cor versation with dear friends here has brought on th pain in the chest again, so that I do not attempt t preach. In two or three weeks I shall embark for th Gulf of Persia, where, if I live, I shall solace myself i my hours of solitude, with writing to you.

Farewell, beloved friend ; pray for me, as you do am sure, and doubt not of an unceasing interest in th heart and prayers of your ever affectionate,

H. Martyn.

CLXXVIII.

TO THE REV. D. CORRIE.

Aldeen, Nov. 1, 1810.

I continue my narrative from Ghazipore. The men came down at night, about nine of them, and I spoke a good deal to them, and exhorted them to return and with full purpose of heart to cleave unto the Lord; but where there is no shepherd I am not sanguine in my hopes that they will keep together—the sheepfold will fall to pieces. Next day at Boglipore with Antonio. He has translated the Four Gospels, Acts, and Missal, into Hindoo exceedingly well. He had written it out in the worst kind of Nagree, but read it off fluently, exactly like a Brahmin. I was much delighted with his doings, but especially with his modesty. 25th. Entered the Hooghly with something of those sensations with which I should come in sight of the white cliffs of England. 26th. Spent the evening with P——. Next called on the Roman Catholics at Hooghly; at last came to Aldeen at sun-set. Children jumping, shouting, and convoying me in troops to the house. They are a lovely family indeed, and I do not know when I have felt so delighted as at family worship last night. To-day Mr. Brown and myself have been consulting at the Pagoda.

H. MARTYN.

CLXXIX.

TO THE REV. D. BROWN.

Calcutta, January 1, 1811.

At the going down of yesterday's sun, I ascended the roof, not doubting but that I should hear some more wisdom from a certain Patriarch ; but he was gone. I felt considerable pain ; but something within me said Should I grieve at being left alone with God ?

Believe that I was not yesterday at roots. On Sundays I try to let them sleep deep in earth, and regale myself with the fruits and flowers.

I am well enough, but look so pale that Mr. T—— advises me to stay at home this evening. I see no necessity for it, but I was very willing to be persuaded.

My best love to all the invalids, and best wishes for their speedy recovery.

Yours ever affectionately,

H. Martyn.

CLXXX.

TO THE REV. D. CORRIE.

January 1, 1811.

At last I have a moment's leisure, and nothing shall prevent my employing it in communicating with Cawnpore. You will guess what has occupied me. Mr. Brown, foreseeing I should have to stay one new year's day, ordered me to preach for the British and Foreign Bible Society. In consequence, I prepared an unwieldy sermon, which has just been delivered. None of the great were present; none of the clergy, though public notice was given; but it does not much matter, as the sermon is to be printed, and sent to beg from Meerut to Cape Comorin. It is to be called the claims of Christian India, or an appeal in behalf of eight hundred thousand native Christians in India. Since writing the above we have received two thousand six hundred rupees in donations. We proceed without delay to form an Auxiliary Bible Society. Why do I say *we*, for, take notice, you are not likely to see me for two years. After consulting the Patriarch, I waited this morning on Lord M. and made a statement to Colonel C——, for the Commander-in-chief, respecting my views about going to Persia, and obtained their sanction, so that it strikes me a way is opened, and an intimation given of the will of God. May my journey be for the prosperity of Zion! My ship has dropped down.

5. I have received yours of the 21st; five thousand

rupees have been already subscribed to the Britisl and Foreign Bible Society, by the few who were a church.

6. We go to-night. As the time approaches fo leaving you, I feel my heart drawn nearer to yoı than ever.

Adieu ! from your ever-affectionate,

H. Martyn.

CLXXXI.

TO MISS L. GRENFELL.

At sea, Coast of Malabar, Feb. 4, 1811.

The last letter I wrote to you, my dearest Lydia, was dated November 1810. I continued in Calcutta to the end of the year, preaching once a week, and reading the word in some happy little companies, with whom I enjoyed that sweet communion, which all in this vale of tears have reason to be thankful for, but especially those whose lot is cast in a heathen land. On New-year's day, at Mr. Brown's urgent request, I preached a sermon for the Bible Society, recommending an immediate attention to the state of the native Christians. At the time I left Calcutta they talked of forming an Auxiliary society. Leaving Calcutta was so much like leaving England, that I went on board my boat without giving them notice, and so escaped the pain of bidding them farewell. In two days I met my ship at the mouth of the river, and we put to sea immediately. Our ship is commanded by a pupil of Schwartz, and manned by Arabians, Abyssinians and others. One of my fellow-passengers is Mr. Elphinstone, who was lately Ambassador at the court of the King of Cabul, and is now going to be resident at Poonah, the capital of the Mahratta empire. So the group is rather interesting, and I am happy to say not averse to religious instruction ; I mean the Europeans. As for the Asiatics, they are in language, customs, and religion, as far removed from us as if they were inhabitants of another planet I speak a little Arabic sometimes to the sailors, bu their contempt of the Gospel, and attachment to thei own superstition, make their conversion appear impossible. How stupendous that power, which can mak these people the followers of the Lamb, when they so nearly resemble Satan in pride and wickedness. Th first part of the voyage I was without employment, an almost without thought, suffering as usual so much from sea-sickness, that I had not spirits to do anythin but sit upon the poop, surveying the wide waste o waters blue. This continued all down the bay of Bengal. At length in the neighbourhood of Ceylon w found smooth water, and came to an anchor off Columbo, the principal station in the island. The captain having proposed to his passengers that they should g ashore and refresh themselves with a walk in the Cinnamon gardens, Mr. E. and myself availed ourselves o the offer, and went off to inhale the cinnamon breeze The walk was delightful. The huts of the natives, wh are, (in that neighbourhood, at least) most of them Protestants, are built in thick groves of cocoa-nut-tree with openings here and there, discovering the sea Every thing bore the appearance of contentment. contemplated them with delight, and was almost gla that I could not speak with them, lest further acquaintance should have dissipated the pleasing ideas thei appearance gave birth to. In the gardens I cut off piece of the bark for you. It will not be so fragrant a that which is properly prepared ; but it will not hav lost its fine smell, I hope, when it reaches you.

At Captain R.'s, the Chief Secretary to Government we met a good part of the European society of Columbo The party was like most mixed parties in England where much is said that need not be remembered. The next day we stretched across the gulf of Manaan, and soon came in sight of Cape Comorin, the great promontory of India. At a distance the green waves seemed to wash the foot of the mountain, but on a nearer approach little churches were seen, apparently on the beach, with a row of little huts on each side. Was it these maritime situations that recalled to my mind Perran church and town in the way to Gurlyn; or that my thoughts wander too often on the beach to the east of Lamorran? You do not tell me whether you ever walk there, and imagine the billows that break at your feet, to have made their way from India. But why should I wish to know! Had I observed silence on that day and thenceforward, I should have spared you much trouble and myself much pain. Yet I am far from regretting that I spoke; since I am persuaded that all things will work together for good. I sometimes try to put such a number of things together as shall produce the greatest happiness possible, and I find that even in imagination I cannot satisfy myself. I set myself to see what is that "Good for the sons of men, which they should do under heaven all the days of their life," and I find that paradise is not here. Many things are delightful, some things are almost all one could wish; but yet in all beauty there is deformity; in the most perfect, something wanting; and there is no hope of its ever being otherwise. "That which is crooked cannot be made straight, and that which is wanting cannot be numbered." So that the expectation of happiness on earth seems chimerical to the last degree. In my schemes of happiness I place myself of course with you, blessed with great success in the ministry, and seeing all India turning to the Lord. Yet it is evident that with these joys there would be mingled many sorrows. The care of all the churches was a burden to the mighty mind of St. Paul. As for what we should be together, I judge of it from our friends. Are they quite beyond the vexations of common life? I think not—still I do not say that it is a question, whether they gained or lost by marrying. Their affections will live when ours, (I should rather say mine) are dead. Perhaps it may not be the effect of celibacy; but I certainly begin to feel a wonderful indifference to all but myself. From so seldom seeing a creature that cares for me, and never one that depends at all upon me, I begin to look round upon men with reciprocal apathy. It sometimes calls itself deadness to the world, but I much fear that it is deadness of heart. I am exempt from worldly cares myself, and therefore, do not feel for others. Having got out of the stream into still water, I go round and round in my own little circle. This supposed deterioration you will ascribe to my humility; therefore I add, that Mr. Brown could not help remarking the difference between what I am and what I was; and observed on seeing my picture, which was taken at Calcutta for Mr Simeon, and is thought a striking likeness, that it was not Martyn that arrived in India, but Martyn the recluse.

10. To-day my affections seem to have revived a little. I have been often deceived in times past, and erroneously called animal spirits, joy in the Holy Ghost. Yet I trust that I can say with truth, "To them who believe, He is precious!" "Yes, thou art precious to my soul, my transport and my trust." No thought now is so sweet as that which those words suggest—"*In Christ.*" Our destinies thus inseparably united with those of the Son of God! What is too great to be expected: "All things are yours, for ye are Christ's!" We

nay ask what we will, and it shall be given to us. Now, why do I ever lose sight of him! or fancy myself withut him, or try to do anything without him? Break ff a branch from a tree, and how long will it be before t withers? To-day, my beloved sister, I rejoice in you efore the Lord, I rejoice in you as a member of the nystic body, I pray that your prayers for one who is nworthy of your remembrance may be heard, and ring down tenfold blessings on yourself. How good is he Lord in giving me grace to rejoice with his chosen, ll over the earth; even with those who are at this noment going up with the voice of joy and praise, to read his courts and sing his praise. There is not an obect about me but is depressing. Yet my heart expands vith delight at the presence of a gracious God, and the ssurance that my separation from his people is only emporary. On the 7th we landed at Goa, the capital of he Portuguese possessions in the east. I reckoned much n my visit to Goa; expecting, from its being the resience of the Archbishop and many ecclesiastics, that I hould obtain such information about the Christians in ndia as would render it superfluous to make inquiries lsewhere, but I was much disappointed. Perhaps it vas owing to our being accompanied by several officers, English and Portuguese, that the Archbishop and his rincipal agents would not be seen, but so it was, that I scarcely met with a man who could make himself inelligible. We were shown what strangers are usually hown, the churches and monasteries, but I wanted to ontemplate man, the only thing on earth almost that ossesses any interest for me. I beheld the stupendous nagnificence of their noble churches without emotion, xcept to regret that the Gospel was not preached in hem. In one of the monasteries we saw the tomb of

Francis Xavier, the Apostle of India, most richly ornamented, as well as the room in which it stands, with paintings and figures in bronze, done in Italy. The Friar who showed us the tomb, happening to speak of the grace of God in the heart, without which, said he as he held the sacramental wafer, the body of Christ profits nothing, I began a conversation with him which, however, came to nothing.

We visited among many other places the convent of Nuns. After a long altercation with the lady-portress we were admitted to the ante-chamber, in which was the grate, a window with iron-bars, behind which the poor prisoners made their appearance. While my companions were purchasing their trinkets, I was employed in examining their countenances, which I did with great attention. In what possible way, thought I, can you support existence, if you do not find your happiness in God. They all looked ill and discontented, those at least whose countenances expressed anything. One sat by reading, as if nothing were going on. I asked to see the book, and it was handed through the grate. Finding that it was a Latin Prayer Book, I wrote in Latin something about the love of the world, which seclusion from it would not remove. The Inquisition is still existing at Goa. We were not admitted as far as Dr. Buchanan was, to the Hall of Examination ; and that because he printed something about the inquisitors, which came to their knowledge. The priest in waiting acknowledged that they had some prisoners within the walls, and defended the practice of imprisoning and chastising offenders, on the ground of its being conformable to the custom of the Primitive Church. We were told that when the officers of the Inquisition touch an individual, and beckon him away, he dares not resist ; if he does not come out again, no one must ask about him ; if he does, he must not tell what was done to him.

18. (Bombay.) Thus far I am brought in safety. On this day I complete my 30th year. "Here I raise my Ebenezer ; Hither by thy help I'm come." It is sweet to reflect that we shall at last reach our home. I am here amongst men who are indeed aliens to the commonwealth of Israel, and without God in the world. I hear many of those amongst whom I live, bring idle objections against religion, such as I have answered a hundred times. How insensible are men of the world to all that God is doing! How unconscious of his purposes concerning his church! How incapable, seemingly, of comprehending the existence of it! I feel the meaning of St. Paul's words—"Hath abounded toward us in all wisdom and prudence, having made known to us the mystery of his will, that he would gather in one all things in Christ.." Well! let us bless the Lord—"All thy children shall be taught of the Lord, and great shall be the peace of thy children." In a few days I expect to sail for the gulf of Persia in one of the Company's sloops of war.

Farewell, my beloved Lydia, and believe me to be ever,

Your's, most affectionately,

H. Martyn.

CLXXXII.

TO THE REV. D. BROWN.

Goa, February 8, 1811.

Dearest Sir,

All down the bay of Bengal I suffered so much from sea-sickness, that I had not spirits to prepare a letter for you. This is the reason you did not hear from Ceylon We did not touch at Point de Galle, but passed on to Columbo, where we arrived on the 22nd. Mr. Elphinstone and myself went ashore to refresh ourselves with a walk in the cinnamon-gardens. In our way thither I did not forget, you may be sure, to enquire, whether the vine flourished and the pomegranate budded; but I was disappointed in not meeting with any who could give me the information I wanted. Mr. Twisleton was not at home, and General Maitland was ill at Mount Lavinia. From our Cingalese guide, who spoke English very well, Mr. E. was endeavouring to learn something about Boodh and his temples. Sir, said the man, I am a Christian, a Protestant, and do not worship stocks and stones. My heart bounded at hearing this I got nearer and began to question the sable brother touching the common faith. He did not, however, seem to know much, or to have felt as I hoped he had. One thing I learnt from him, that they had all the Scriptures in Cingalese and Malabar. A Portuguese who attended us, said the same, and told me that the Malabar spoken at Cochin was the high Malabar, not understood by the Cingalese of the Tamul; further my informants knew nothing.

A little out of the road a funeral party was seen retiring from a church-yard. I went off instantly and accosted the Catechist; he spoke a little English, but so little that I could gain nothing from him. He shewed me the neighbouring church; it was spacious, but low, with a double row of pillars, and at the south end a porch. On our return from the garden to the fort we met some of the society of Columbo at Captain Rodney's, Chief Secretary to the Government. In hopes of seeing Mr. Twisleton there,—for they told me he was expected,—I staid as long as possible; but as he did not come I wrote to him, requesting information about the state of the Christians, the version of the Sacred Scriptures, &c. and added a request that he would communicate with you upon these points. I regretted much that I could not stay a little longer in order to ascertain what this Malabar version is. Whatever it be, my note on Cordiner about its being the Tamul had better be cancelled. It is sufficient for us that it is not the Malayalim. We arrived at Alapan, or Alapee, the 26th. It is a miserable place; all I could learn there, was, that there were 300 Christians who spoke Portuguese, and besides them the caste of Christian fishermen. The distinction is worth observing, as it proves that all Christians are not included under the name of Portuguese. The Padre does not live there.

This place has most miserably disappointed me. I did not care about churches or convents, but I did expect to find men, Bishops and Archbishops, learned friars and scowling inquisitors; but Goa, as I had imagined it, does not exist. Perhaps the train of officers, &c. that attended us deterred many from appearing, but certain it is, that though we have been shewn all the finery of the churches, not a person have we seen that was able to give us the smallest particle of information. Wherever we went, a black padre was deputed to shew us the church, and if a white one appeared it was only to shew his ignorance. At the Inquisition we were just admitted within the gates and that was all. I intreated the padre to let us see the hall; but no—no Englishman now was allowed to go there.

H. Martyn.

CLXXXIII.

TO THE REV. D. CORRIE.

February 26, 1811.

I write just now because I am in your neighbourhood, and must say a last farewell before I lose sight of your country and mine, ill-fated India as —— calls it. I long to be with you again at Cawnpore for many reasons. Peacefully preaching the word of life to a people daily edified is the nearest approach to heaven below. But to move from place to place, hurried away without having time to do good, is vexatious to the spirit as well as harassing to the body. The sea, too, I loath. I was scarcely well any part of the voyage, which was six weeks, and consequently did little but sit the live-long day upon the poop, looking at the flying fish, and surveying the wide waste of waters blue. Under the pressure of sea-sickness I resolved, that if ever I got back safe to India, it should not be a trifle that should move me from it again. We had prayer in the cabin every night, with all the passengers. About the end of the week we sail, if God will, for the Gulf. Had I been a little sooner, Sir J. O. might have taken me in the Lion man-of-war; but what is clearly the appointment of Providence I do not repine at. I went aboard my ship to-day, the Mercury. There is no accommodation for passengers, but I am to have part of the captain's cabin. Though most of the crew are Europeans, twelve artillerymen are to be sent to help work the guns, and another cruizer with like comple ment is to accompany her, and a third is to follow, s strong and desperate are these pestilent Ishmaelites Hearing last Saturday that some sons of Belial, mem bers of the Bapre Hunt, intended to have a great rac the following day, I informed Mr. ——, at whose hous I was staying, and recommended the interference of th secular arm. He accordingly sent to forbid it. Th messengers of the Bapre Hunt were exceedingly exas perated; some came to church, expecting to hear a ser mon against hunting, but I merely preached to them o " the one thing needful." Finding nothing to lay hol of, they had the race on Monday, and ran *Hypocrit* against *Martha* and *Mary*. And now, dearest brothe may God abundantly bless you in your work, and i your own soul. Keep you in health and strength, tha if it be his will, we may have the comfort of meetin once more here below.

H. Martyn.

CLXXXIV.

TO THE SAME.

Bombay, March 26, 1811.

I have just time to send you a bit of a letter. It is ıow nearly six months since I left you, and I am not yet .elivered from Bombay, when I expected to be on my eturn from Arabia. I am reconciled to this delay by he consideration that I could do nothing were I at ;awnpore. My chest is not at all stronger, but I ıave no doubt it would be if I could flee the haunts of nen. At this place I am visited from morning to ıight by the learned natives, who are drawn hither by ın Arabic tract, which I was drawing up merely for ;abat, to help him in his book, but which the scribe I mployed has been showing all about. At church on ;unday some of the 47th appeared; they put me in nind of my dear men at Cawnpore; my kind love to hem all. It is said that we are to go immediately, but here is no believing what is said. General Malcolm ıas given me letters to great men at Bushire, Shiraz, ınd Ispahan; moreover queries respecting things on vhich he wants further information. Perhaps I shall ›e taken up and hanged as a spy. As it is probable, ıay almost certain, that I shall be detained at Bushire ı month before I can receive the ambassador's permis-ion to enter Persia, you may direct to me there, via Bombay.

H. MARTYN.

CLXXXV.

TO MISS L. GRENFELL.

Muscat, April 22, 1811.

My dearest Lydia,

I am now in Arabia Felix ; to judge from the aspect of the country, it has few pretensions to the name, unless burning barren rocks convey an idea of felicity ; but perhaps, as there is a promise in reserve for the sons of Joktan, their land may one day be blest indeed.

We sailed from Bombay on Lady-day ; and on the morning of Easter saw the land of Mekran in Persia. After another week's sail across the mouth of the Gulf, we arrived here, and expect to proceed up the Gulf to Bushire, as soon as we have taken in our water. You will be happy to learn that the murderous pirates against whom we were sent, having received notice of our approach, have all got out of the way ; so that I am no longer liable to be shot in a battle, or decapitated after it, if it be lawful to judge from appearances. These pestilent Ishmaelites indeed, whose hand is against every man's, will escape, and the community suffer ; but that selfish friendship of which you once confessed yourself guilty, will think only of the preservation of a friend. This last marine excursion has been the pleasantest I ever made, as I have been able to pursue my studies with less interruption than when ashore. My little congregation of forty or fifty Europeans does not try my strength on Sundays ; and my wo companions are men who read their bible every ay. In addition to all these comforts, I have to bless od for having kept me more than usually free from he sorrowful mind. We must not always say with Vatts, 'the sorrows of the mind be banished from this lace'; but if freedom from trouble be offered us, we ay choose it rather. I do not know anything more deghtful than to meet with a Christian brother, where nly strangers and foreigners were expected. This leasure I enjoyed just before leaving Bombay; a ropeaker who had just come from England, understood om my sermon that I was one he might speak to; so e came and opened his heart, and we rejoiced together. n this ship I find another of the household of faith. n another ship which accompanies us there are two rmenians who do nothing but read the Testament. ne of them will, I hope, accompany me to Shiraz in ersia, which is his native country.

We are likely to be detained here some days, but the hip that will carry our letters to India sails immeditely, so that I can send but one letter to England, and ne to Calcutta. When will our correspondence be esablished? I have been trying to effect it these six ears, and it is only yet in train. Why there was no etter from you among those dated June and July 1810, cannot conjecture, except that you had not received ny of mine, and would write no more. But I am not et without hopes that a letter in the beloved hand ill yet overtake me somewhere. My kindest and most ffectionate remembrances to all the western circle. Is because he is your brother that I love —— so much? r because he is the last come into the number? The ngels love and wait upon the righteous who need no epentance; but there is joy whenever another heir of salvation is born into the family. Read Eph. i. I cannot wish you all these spiritual blessings, since they are already all yours; but I pray that we may have the spirit of wisdom and knowledge to know that they are ours. It is a chapter I keep in mind every day in prayer. We cannot believe too much or hope too much. Happy our eyes that they see, and our ears that they hear.

As it may be a year or more before I shall be back, you may direct one letter after receiving this, if it be not of a very old date, to Bombay, all after to Bengal as usual. Believe me to be ever, my dearest Lydia,

Your most affectionate

H. Martyn.

CLXXXVI.

TO THE REV. D. BROWN.

Muscat, April 23, 1811.

Dearest Sir,

I left India on Lady-day, looked at Persia on Easter Sunday, and seven days after found myself in Arabia Felix. In a small cove, surrounded by bare rocks, heated through, out of the reach of air as well as wind, lies the good ship Benares, in the great cabin of which, stretched on a couch, lie I. But though weak, I am well—relaxed but not disordered. Praise to His grace, who fulfils to me a promise which I have scarcely a right to claim—"I am with thee, and will keep thee in all places whether thou goest." My voyage from Bombay hither has been most agreeable. My companions in the cabin, namely, the Captain, and his cousin a Captain of Artillery, let me expound to them every night, and read the Bible themselves. On Sundays we have forty or fifty Europeans at church on the quarter-deck. There are just enough to animate me without exhausting my strength. All the way I have been as usual, Hebraizing; indeed, I must make the same complaint of my mind, that Anacreon does of his harp. He struck one string, and the harp replied from another. I resolve to read Arabic and Persian, but, or ever I am aware, I am thinking about Hebrew. I have translated Psalm xvi. and but for one part, which wants more support than I can yet find for it, I should have sent it to that obstinate lover of antiquity, the Rev. T. Thc mason, whose potent touch has dissolved so many of m; fabrics heretofore, that I do not like to submit an; thing to him which is not proof. With my kindes love to him, tell him that I cannot write now. H directed me to remember first our beloved Daniel in th north, and if I have time I will; but the ship whic carries this to Bombay sails immediately.

Last night I went ashore for the first time with Cap tain Lockett; we walked through the bazaar, and u the hill, but saw nothing but what was Indian o worse. The Imaun or Sultan is about thirty miles of fighting, it is said, for his kingdom, with the Wahabees

You will be happy to learn that the pirates whon we were to scourge, are got out of our way, so that may now hope to get safe through the Gulf withou being made to witness the bloody scenes of war.

From Bushire, where my land-journey commences you may expect to hear again; till then, believe me t be ever,

Yours most affectionately,
H. MARTYN.

CLXXXVII.

TO THE REV. D. CORRIE.

Muscat, April 24. 1811.

I rejoice that an unexpected detention of the ship going to Bombay enables me to assure you of my unceasing regard, and to make inquiries about the men whom you are taking care of for me. May I hear of their affairs, that they stand fast, and have their conversation as becometh the Gospel of Christ! I have now to write to my friends in India. I quitted that country on Lady-day. We stood out directly to the westward, and lost sight of land that night. For the first two or three days I was more than usually ill, but the rest of the passage compensated for the unpleasantness of the beginning. Smooth waters and light airs left me at liberty to pursue my studies as uninterruptedly as if I were on shore; and more so, as my companions in the great cabin being sufficient company for each other, and studious and taciturn withal, seldom break my repose. Every day, all day long, I Hebraize. On Sundays we have had a good congregation, about fifty Europeans; many of whom, however, are foreigners. The carpenter is a methodist, lately from Gosport. My attention was called to him, from observing his disrespectful behaviour and extraordinary loquacity. Thinking, I suppose, that there was no one on board who knew what practice became his principles, he gave way to his tempers more freely. Lately he has become

more consistent. My captain and his cousin, a captai
of artillery, are such sort of men as I have not ofte
met with. They do not seem to feel at all in religion
never speak about it, nor discover any interest in wha
I say to them. Yet except when they are at thei
lunars, they read their Bible with a paraphrase, an
pray at nights, and avoid every thing immoral in con
versation. On Easter day we came in sight of Tiz: th
whole coast was rock et præterea nihil: no appearanc
of animated or vegetable nature. The Sunday after, w
entered this cove. So I am now with Sabat's amiabl
countrymen. Monday night I went ashore with Lockett
who is going to Bagdad. We went through the bazaa
and mounted a hill to look at it, but saw nothing bu
what was hideous. The town and houses are mor
mean and filthy than any in India, and in all the envi
rons of the place, I counted three trees, date-trees
suppose. The Iman or Sultan is about two or thre
days off, fighting with the Wahabees for his kingdom
About five thousand of them came a few days ago, an
sacked one of his towns, which is now in our sight. H
is aided by another Arab king, but victory alway
declares for the Wahabees. The Iman of Muscat mur
dered his uncle, and sits on the throne in the place o
his elder brother, who is here a cypher. Last night th
captain went ashore to a council of state, to conside
the relations subsisting between the government o
Bombay and these mighty chieftains. I attended a
interpreter. The Company's agent is an old Hindo
who could not get off his bed. An old man in whon
pride and stupidity seemed to contend for empire, sa
opposite to him. This was the Wazeer. Between then
sat I, opposite to me the captain. The Wazeer utterec
something in Arabic, not one word of which could

understand. The old Hindoo explained in Persian, for he has almost forgot his Hindoo, and I to the captain in English. We are all impatient to get away from this place. Through God's mercy I am tolerably well, but have lost the greatest part of every night's sleep since I have been here ; at this time the smoke from the galley is trying to suffocate and blind me, but all shall not prevent me from exerting myself amongst you in the form of a letter.

SHIRAZ.

Page 377.

CLXXVIII.

TO THE SAME.

S[illegible], *June* 2[illegible], 1811.

[illegible] precedent [illegible] from which I write will lead you [illegible] I am in [illegible], and think and dream [illegible] of [illegible] Bulbul, roses and [illegible] that [illegible] that Sir Gore Ouseley, who [illegible] and [illegible] greater enthusiast in Persian than I [illegible] wish [illegible], as well as myself, completely [illegible] of Pars and with the men [illegible] The unfa[illegible] which has been made upon my [illegible], prompts me to say nothing of [illegible] but what is [illegible] on further consideration I [illegible] inclined to [illegible]. As for their wickedness and [illegible], it is [illegible] nature unveiled, its [illegible] and per[illegible] the [illegible] under which they groan. A [illegible] after my letter to you from Muscat we [illegible] the Gulf and continued [illegible] in sight of [illegible] Arabia [illegible] 22nd of May we [illegible] at Bushire, and took [illegible] lodging with Mr. [illegible] We are now in a [illegible] situation. Mrs. — and her sister, both Arme[illegible] [illegible] speaking but Persian at table; [illegible] down the [illegible] One day a party of [illegible] [illegible] my hand,—the usual [illegible] I was [illegible] explain [illegible] duty. The Armenian [illegible] was

CLXXXVIII.

TO THE SAME.

Shiraz, June 24, 1811.

The poetical region from which I write will lead you to imagine that I am in extasies, and think and dream only of Gool and Bulbul, (roses and nightingales,) but so it is, that Sir Gore Ouseley, who is now here, and is a far greater enthusiast in Persian than I ever wish to be, is, as well as myself, completely disgusted with the land of Fars, and with the men thereof. The unfavourable impression which has been made upon my mind, prompts me to say nothing of Persia but what is evil, but on farther consideration I am inclined to pity them. As for their wickedness and misery, it is only human nature unveiled, its depravity heightened perhaps by the superstition under which they groan. A few days after my letter to you from Muscat, we sailed for the Gulf, and continued cruizing a month, generally in sight of Persia or Arabia, sometimes of both. On the 22nd of May we landed at Bushire, and took up our lodging with Mr. ——. We are now in a new situation. Mrs. —— and her sister, both Armenians, spoke nothing but Persian at table; the servants and children the same. One day a party of Armenian ladies came to kiss my hand,—the usual mark of respect shewn to their own priests: I was engaged at the time, but they begged to have it explained that they had not been deficient in their duty. The Armenian priest was as dull as they usually are. He sent for me one Sunday evening to come to church; though he was ministering when I entered, he came out, and brought me within the rails of the altar; and at the time of incense, censed me four times, while the others were honoured with only one fling of the censer: this the old man begged me afterwards to notice. But though his civility was well meant, I could hardly prevail upon myself to thank him for it. It was due, he said, to a *Padre:* thus we provide for the honour of our own order, not contented with that degree of respect which really belongs to us. Walking afterwards with him by the sea-shore, I tried to engage him in a conversation respecting the awful importance of our office; but nothing could be more vapid and inane than his remarks.

One day we called on the Governor, a Persian Khan: he was very particular in his attentions, seated me in his own seat, and then sat by my side. After the usual salutations and inquiries, the calean (or hookah) was introduced; then coffee, in china cups placed within silver ones, then calean, then some rose-water syrup, then calean. As there were long intervals, often, in which nought was heard but the gurgling of the calean, I looked round with some anxiety for something to discourse upon, and observing the windows to be of stained glass, I began to question him about the art of colouring glass, observing that the modern Europeans were inferior to the ancient in the manufactory of that article. He expressed his surprise that Europeans, who were so skilful in making watches, should fail in any handicraft work. I could not help recollecting the Emperor of China's sarcastic remark on the Europeans and their arts, and therefore dropped the subject. On his calean,—I called it hookah at first, but he did no understand me,—I noticed several little paintings o the Virgin and Child, and asked him, whether such things were not unlawful among the Mahometans? He answered very coolly, 'Yes;' as much as to say 'What then?' I lamented that the Eastern Christian should use such things in their churches. He repeated the words of a good man, who was found fault with fo having an image before him while at prayer: 'God i nearer to me than that image, so that I do not see it. We then talked of the ancient Caliphs of Bagdad; thei magnificence, regard for learning, &c. This man, I afterwards found, is, like most of the other grandees o the east, a murderer. He was appointed to the govern ment of Bushire, in the place of an Arab Shekh, i whose family it had been for many years. The Persian dreading the resentment of the other Arab families invited the heads of them to a feast. After they had regaled themselves a little, he proposed to them to take off their swords, as they were all friends together: they did so, a signal was given, and a band of ruffians mur dered them all immediately. The Governor rode of with a body of troops to their villages, and murdered or secured their wives and children. This was abou two years and a half ago.

Abdalla Aga, a Turk, who expects to be Pacha o Bagdad, called to examine us in Arabic; he is a grea Arabic scholar himself, and came to see how much w knew; or rather, if the truth were known, to shew hov much he himself knew. There was lately a conspiracy at Bagdad, to murder the Pacha. He was desired t add his name, which he did by compulsion, but secured himself from putting his seal to it, pretending he had lost it: this saved him. All the conspirators were dis covered and put to death; he escaped with his life, but was obliged to fly to Bushire.

On the 30th of May, our Persian dresses were ready, and we set out for Shiraz. The Persian dress consists of, first, stockings and shoes in one, next, a pair of large blue trowsers, or else a pair of huge red boots; then the shirt, then the tunic, and above it the coat, both of chintz, and a great coat. I have here described my own dress, most of which I have on at this moment. On the head is worn an enormous cone, made of the skin of the black Tartar sheep, with the wool on. If to this description of my dress I add, that my beard and mustachios have been suffered to vegetate undisturbed ever since I left India,—that I am sitting on a Persian carpet, in a room without tables or chairs,—and that I bury my hand in the pillau, without waiting for spoon or plate, you will give me credit for being already an accomplished Oriental.

At ten o'clock on the 30th, our cafila began to move. It consisted chiefly of mules, with a few horses. I wished to have a mule, but the muleteer favoured me with his own pony; this animal had a bell fastened to its neck. To add solemnity to the scene, a Bombay trumpeter, who was going up to join the embassy, was directed to blow a blast as we moved off the ground; but whether it was that the trumpeter was not an adept in the science, or that his instrument was out of order, the crazy sounds that saluted our ears had a ludicrous effect. At last, after some jostling, mutual recriminations, and recalcitrating of the steeds, we all found our places, and moved out of the gate of the city in good order. The Resident accompanied us a little way, and then left us to pursue our journey over the plain. It was a fine moonlight night, the scene new, and perfectly oriental, and nothing prevented me from indulging my own reflections. I felt a little melancholy, but commended myself anew to God, and felt assured of his blessing, presence, and protection. As the night advanced, the cafila grew quiet; on a sudden one of the muleteers began to sing, and sang in a voice so plaintive, that it was impossible not to have one's attention arrested. Every voice was hushed. As you are a Persian scholar, I write down the whole, with a translation;

'Think not that e'er my heart could dwell
Contented far from thee:
How can the fresh-caught nightingale
Enjoy tranquillity?

O then forsake thy friend for nought
That slanderous tongues can say;
The heart that fixeth where it ought,
No power can rend away.'

Thus far my journey was agreeable: now for miseries. At sunrise we came to our ground at Ahmeda six parasangs, and pitched our little tent under a tree it was the only shelter we could get. At first the heat was not greater than we had felt in India, but it soon became so intense as to be quite alarming. When the thermometer was above 112°, fever heat, I began to lose my strength fast; at last it became quite intolerable. I wrapped myself up in a blanket and all the warm covering I could get, to defend myself from the external air; by which means the moisture was kept a little longer upon the body, and not so speedily evaporated as when the skin was exposed; one of my companions followed my example, and found the benefit of it. But the thermometer still rising, and the moisture of the body being quite exhausted, I grew restless, and thought

I should have lost my senses. The thermometer at last stood at 126°: in this state I composed myself, and concluded that though I might hold out a day or two, death was inevitable. Captain ——, who sat it out, continued to tell the hour and height of the thermometer; and with what pleasure did we hear of its sinking to 120°, 118°, &c. At last the fierce sun retired, and I crept out, more dead than alive. It was then a difficulty how I could proceed on my journey; for besides the immediate effects of the heat, I had no opportunity of making up for the last night's want of sleep, and had eaten nothing. However, while they were loading the mules I got an hour's sleep, and set out, the muleteer leading my horse, and Zechariah, my servant, an Armenian, of Isfahan, doing all in his power to encourage me. The cool air of the night restored me wonderfully, so that I arrived at our next munzil with no other derangement than that occasioned by want of sleep. Expecting another such day as the former, we began to make preparation the instant we arrived on the ground. I got a tattie made of the branches of the date-tree, and a Persian peasant to water it; by this means the thermometer did not rise higher than 114°. But what completely secured me from the heat was a large wet towel, which I wrapped round my head and body, muffling up the lower part in clothes. How could I but be grateful to a gracious Providence, for giving me so simple a defence against what, I am persuaded, would have destroyed my life that day. We took care not to go without nourishment, as we had done; the neighbouring village supplied us with curds and milk. At sun-set, rising up to go out, a scorpion fell upon my clothes; not seeing where it fell, I did not know what it was; but Captain —— pointing it out, gave the alarm, and I struck it off, and he killed it. The night before we found a black scorpion in our tent; this made us rather uneasy; so that though the cafila did not start till midnight, we got no sleep, fearing we might be visited by another scorpion.

The next morning we arrived at the foot of the mountains, at a place where we seemed to have discovered one of nature's ulcers. A strong suffocating smell of naptha announced something more than ordinarily foul in the neighbourhood. We saw a river;—what flowed in it, it seemed difficult to say, whether it were water or green oil; it scarcely moved, and the stones which it laved, it left of a greyish colour, as if its foul touch had given them the leprosy. Our place of encampment this day was a grove of date-trees, where the atmosphere, at sun-rise, was ten times hotter than the ambient air. I threw myself down on the burning ground, and slept: when the tent came up I awoke, as usual, in a burning fever. All this day I had recourse to the wet towel, which kept me alive, but would allow of no sleep. It was a sorrowful sabbath; but Captain —— read a few hymns, in which I found great consolation. At nine in the evening we decamped. The ground and air were so insufferably hot, that I could not travel without a wet towel round my face and neck. This night, for the first time, we began to ascend the mountains. The road often passed so close to the edge of the tremendous precipices, that one false step of the horse would have plunged his rider into inevitable destruction. In such circumstances, I found it useless to attempt guiding the animal, and therefore gave him the rein. These poor animals are so used to journeys of this sort, that they generally step sure. There was nothing to mark the road, but the rocks being a little more worn in one place than in another. Sometimes my horse, which led the way, as being the muleteer's, stopped, as if to consider about the way: for myself, I could not guess, at such times, where the road lay, but he always found it. The sublime scenery would have impressed me much, in other circumstances; but my sleepiness and fatigue rendered me insensible to every thing around me. At last we emerged *superas ad auras*, not on the top of a mountain, to go down again,—but to a plain or upper world. At the pass, where a cleft in the mountain admitted us into the plain, was a station of Rahdars. While they were examining the muleteer's passports, &c. time was given for the rest of the cafila to come up, and I got a little sleep for a few minutes. We rode briskly over the plain, breathing a purer air, and soon came in sight of a fair edifice, built by the king of the country for the refreshment of pilgrims. In this caravansera we took our abode for the day. It was more calculated for eastern than European travellers, having no means of keeping out the air and light. We found the thermometer at 110°. At the passes we met a man travelling down to Bushire with a load of ice, which he willingly disposed of to us. The next night we ascended another range of mountains, and passed over a plain, where the cold was so piercing, that with all the clothes we could muster, we were shivering. At the end of this plain, we entered a dark valley, contained by two ranges of hills converging to one another. The muleteer gave notice that he saw robbers. It proved to be a false alarm; but the place was fitted to be a retreat for robbers; there being on each side caves and fastnesses from which they might have killed every man of us. After ascending another mountain, we descended by a very long and circuitous route into an extensive valley, where we were exposed to the sun till eight o'clock. Whether from the sun, or from continued want of sleep, I could not, on my arrival at Carzeroon, compose myself to sleep; there seemed to be a fire within my head, my skin like a cinder, and the pulse violent. Through the day it was again too hot to sleep; though the place we occupied was a sort of summer-house, in a garden of cypress-trees, exceedingly well fitted up with mats and coloured glass. Had the cafila gone on that night, I could not have accompanied it; but it halted here a day; by which means I got a sort of night's rest, though I awoke twenty times to dip my burning hand in water. Though Carzeroon is the second greatest town in Fars, we could get nothing but bread, milk, and eggs, and those with difficulty. The governor, who is, under great obligations to the English, heard of our arrival, but sent no message.

June 5.—At ten we left Carzeroon, and ascended a mountain: we then descended from it, on the other side, into a beautiful valley, where the opening dawn discovered to us ripe fields of wheat and barley, with the green oak here and there in the midst of it. We were reminded of an autumnal morning in England. Thermometer, 62°.

June 6.—Half way up the Peergan mountain we found a caravansera. There being no village in the neighbourhood, we had brought supplies from Carzeroon. My servant Zachary got a fall from his mule this morning, which much bruised him; he looked very sorrowful, and had lost much of his garrulity. Zachary had become remarkable throughout the cafila for making speeches; he had something to say to all people and on all occasions.

June 7.—Left the caravansera at one this morning

and continued to ascend. The hours we were permitted to rest, the musquitoes had effectually prevented me from using; so that I never felt more miserable and disordered; the cold was very severe; for fear of falling off, from sleep and numbness, I walked a good part of the way.—We pitched our tent in the vale of Dustarjan, near a crystal stream, on the banks of which we observed the clover and golden cup: the whole valley was one green field, in which large herds of cattle were browsing. The temperature was about that of spring in England. Here a few hours sleep recovered me, in some degree, from the stupidity in which I had been for some days. I awoke with a light heart, and said, "He knoweth our frame, and remembereth that we are but dust. He redeemeth our life from destruction, and crowneth us with loving-kindness and tender mercies. He maketh us to lie down on the green pastures, and leadeth us beside the still waters." And when we have left this vale of tears, there is "no more sorrow, nor sighing, nor any more pain." "The sun shall not light upon thee, nor any heat: but the Lamb shall lead thee to living fountains of waters."

June 8.—Went on to a caravansera, three parasangs, where we passed the day. At night set out upon our last march for Shiraz. Sleepiness, my old companion and enemy, again overtook me. I was in perpetual danger of falling off my horse, till at last I pushed on to a considerable distance beyond the cafila, planted my back against a wall, and slept I know not how long, till the good muleteer came up and gently waked me.

'In the morning of the 9th we found ourselves in the plain of Shiraz. We put up at first in a garden, but are now at Jaffier Ali Khan's.'

CLXXXIX.

TO MISS L. GRENFELL.

Shiraz, June 23, 1811.

My dearest Lydia,

How continually I think of you, and indeed convers with you, it is impossible to say. But on the Lord' day in particular, I find you much in my thoughts because it is on that day that I look abroad, and take view of the universal church, of which I observe tha the saints in England form the most conspicuous part On that day too, I indulge myself with a view of th past, and look over again those happy days, when i company with those I loved, I went up to the house o God with a voice of praise. How then shall I fail t remember her who, of all that are dear to me, is th dearest. It is true that I cannot look back upon man days, nor even many hours passed with you ;—woul they had been more ;—but we have insensibly becom more acquainted with each other, so that, on my par at least, it may be said that separation has brought u nearer to one another. It was a momentary interview but the love is lasting, everlasting. Whether we eve meet again or not, I am sure that you will continue t feel an interest in all that befals me.

After the death of my dear sister, you bid me consider that I had one sister left while you remained ; an you cannot imagine how consolatory to my mind thi assurance is. To know that there is one who is willin to think of me, and has leisure to do so, is soothing to a degree, that none can know but those who have, like me, lost all their relations.

I sent you a letter from Muscat in Arabia, which I hope you received; for if not, report will again erase my name from the catalogue of the living, as I sent no other to Europe. Let me here say with praise to our ever-gracious heavenly Father, that I am in perfect health; of my spirits I cannot say much; I fancy they would be better were 'the beloved Persis' by my side. This name, which I once gave you, occurs to me at this moment, I suppose because I am in Persia, entrenched in one of its vallies, separated from Indian friends by chains of mountains and a roaring sea, among a people depraved beyond all belief, in the power of a tyrant guilty of every species of atrocity. Imagine a pale person seated on a Persian carpet, in a room without table or chair, with a pair of formidable mustachios, and habited as a Persian, and you see me.

26. Here I expect to remain six months. The reason is this, I found on my arrival here, that our attempts at Persian translation in India were good for nothing; at the same time they proposed, with my assistance, to make a new translation. It was an offer I could not refuse, as they speak the purest dialect of the Persian. My host is a man of rank, his name Jaffier Ali Khan, who tries to make the period of my captivity as agreeable as possible. His wife, for he has but one, never appears; parties of young ladies come to see her, but though they stay days in the house, he dare not go into the room where they are. Without intending a compliment to your sex, I must say that the society here, from the exclusion of females, is as dull as it can well be. Perhaps, however, to a stranger like myself, the

most social circles would be insipid. I am visited by all the great and the learned; the former come out of respect to my country, the latter to my profession. The conversation with the latter is always upon religion, and it would be strange indeed, if with the armour of truth on the right hand and on the left, I were not able to combat with success, the upholders of such a system of absurdity and sin. As the Persians are a far more unprejudiced and inquisitive people than the Indians and do not stand quite so much in awe of an Englishman, as the timid natives of Hindoostan, I hope they will learn something from me; the hope of this reconciles me to the necessity imposed on me of staying here about the translation I dare not be sanguine. The prevailing opinion concerning me is, that I have repaired to Shiraz in order to become a Mussulman. Others more sagacious, say that I shall bring from India some more, under pretence of making them Mussulmans, but in reality, to seize the place. They do not seem to have thought of my wish, to have them converted to my religion; they have been so long accustomed to remain without proselytes to their own. I shall probably have very little to write about, for some months to come, and therefore I reserve the extracts of my journal since I last wrote to you, for some other opportunity, besides that the ambassador, with whose dispatches this will go, is just leaving Shiraz.

July 2. The Mahomedans now come in such numbers to visit me, that I am obliged, for the sake of my translation-work, to decline seeing them. To-day one of the apostate sons of Israel was brought by a party of them, to prove the divine mission of Mahommed from the Hebrew Scriptures; but with all his sophistry he proved nothing. I can almost say with St. Paul, I feel continual pity in my heart for them, and love them for their fathers' sake, and find a pleasure in praying for them. While speaking of the return of the Jews to Jerusalem, I observed that the "gospel of the kingdom must first be preached in all the world, and then shall the end come." He replied with a sneer, 'And this event, I suppose you mean to say, is beginning to take place by your bringing the gospel to Persia.'

5. I am so incessantly occupied with visitors and my work, that I have hardly a moment for myself. I have more and more reason to rejoice at my being sent here, there is such an extraordinary stir about religion throughout the city, that some good must come of it. I sometimes sigh for a little Christian communion, yet even from these Mahomedans I hear remarks that do me good; to-day, for instance, my assistant observed, 'How he loved those twelve persons!' Yes, said I, and not those twelve only, but all those who shall believe in him; as he said, "I pray not for these alone, but for all them who shall believe on me through their word." Even the enemy is constrained to wonder at the love of Christ. Shall not the object of it say, What manner of love is this?

I have learned that I may get letters from England much sooner than by way of India. Be so good as to direct to me, to the care of Sir Gore Ouseley, Bart. Ambassador at Tehran, care of J. Morier, Esq. Constantinople, care of G. Moon, Esq. Malta. I have seen Europe newspapers of only four months date, so that I am delightfully near you. May we live near one another in the unity of the Spirit, having one Lord, one hope, one God and Father. In your prayers for me, pray that utterance may be given me, that I may open my mouth boldly, to make known the mysteries of the gospel. I often envy my Persian hearers th freedom and eloquence with which they speak to me Were I but possessed of their powers, I sometimes thinl that I should win them all ; but the work is God's and the faith of his people does not stand in the wisdon of men, but in the power of God. Remember me a usual with the most unfeigned affection to all my dea friends. This is now the seventh letter I send you without having received an answer.

Farewell, your's

Ever most affectionately,

H. Martyn.

CXC.

TO THE REV. D. BROWN.

Shiraz, June 24, 1811.

DEAREST SIR,

I believe I told you that the advanced state of the eason rendered it necessary to go to Arabia circuitously y way of Persia. Behold me therefore in the Athens f Fars, the haunt of the Persian man. Beneath are he ashes of Hafiz and Sadi ; above, green gardens and unning waters, roses and nightingales.

Does Mr. Bird envy my lot? Let him solace himself vith Aldeen. How gladly would I give him Shiraz or Aldeen ; how often, while toiling through this miseable country, have I sighed for Aldeen. If I am ever ermitted to see India once more, nothing but dire necesity or the imperious call of duty, will ever induce ne to travel again.

One thing is good here, the fruit ; we have apples nd apricots, plumbs, nectarines, greengages and cheries, all of which are served up with ice and snow. When I have said this for Shiraz, I have said all.

But to have done with what grows out of the soil, et us come to the men. The Persians are, like ourselves, mmortal ; their language has passed a long way beond the limits of Iran. The men of Shiraz propose o translate the New Testament with me. Can I refuse o stay?

After much deliberation, I have determined to remain

here six months. It is sorely against my will, but I feel it to be a duty. From all that I can collect, there appears no probability of our ever having a good translation made out of Persia. At Bombay I showed Moollah Feeroz, the most learned man there, the three Persian translations, viz. the Polyglott, and Sabat's two. He disapproved of them all. At Bushire, which is in Persia, the man of the greatest name was Seid Hosyn. Of the three he liked Sabat's Persian best, but said it seemed written by an Indian. On my arrival at this place I produced my specimens once more. Sabat's Persian was much ridiculed; sarcastic remarks were made on the fondness for fine words so remarkable in the Indians, who seemed to think that hard words made fine writing. His Persic also was presently thrown aside, and to my no small surprise the old despised Polyglott was not only spoken of as superior to the rest, but it was asked, What fault is found in this? —this is the language we speak. The king has also signified, that it is his wish that as little Arabic as possible may be employed in the papers presented to him. So that simple Persian is likely to become more and more fashionable. This is a change favourable certainly to our glorious cause. To the poor the Gospel will be preached. We began our work with the gospel of St. John, and five chapters are put out of hand. It is likely to be the simplest thing imaginable; and I dare say the pedantic Arab will turn up his nose at it; but what the men of Shiraz approve who can gainsay? Let Sabat confine himself to the Arabic, and he will accomplish a great work. The fore-mentioned Seid Hosyn of Bushire is an Arab. I showed him Erpenius's Arabic Testament, the Christian Knowledge Society's, Sabat's, and the Polyglot. After rejecting ll but Sabat's, he said, This is good, very good, and hen read off the 5th of Matthew in a fine style, giving t unqualified commendation as he went along. On my proposing to him to give a specimen of what he thought he best Persian style, he consented ; but, said he, give ne this to translate from, laying his hand on Sabat's Arabic. At Muscat an Arab officer who had attended is as guard and guide, one day when we walked into he country, came on board with his slave to take leave of us. The slave who had argued with me very strenuously in favour of his religion, reminded me of a pronise I had made him of giving him the Gospel. On ny producing an Arabic New Testament, he seized it and began to read away upon deck, but presently topped, and said it was not fine Arabic. However, he carried off the book.

The Governor of Shiraz is one of the princes. The ambassador, Sir Gore Ouseley, who is here on his way o Tehran, offered to take me to court a few days ago, but as it was Sunday I declined going. It will be proper however that I should be acknowledged by him, and I shall therefore accompany his suite the next time hey pay a visit. Sir Gore said of himself that he should take care to commend me to the prince and his ninisters before he went away ; offered to assist me in ny inquiries by taking a list of queries with him, and promised me a guard if I would let him know my intended route.

Now, good Sir, seeing that I am to remain six months n captivity, comfort me with a letter now and then, a Christian Observer, or an Evangelical Magazine, and direct to the care of —— Bruce, Esq. Resident, Bushire. I have nothing to assist me in the translation : no commentator or annotator,—a just judgment upon me,

Thomason will say, for my want of respect for that learned body,—perhaps you may be able to send me the little French Testament.

My kindest remembrances to Mrs. Brown and her children, Mrs. Thomason and her's; Udneys, Hamptons, Myers, Edmund, Forsythe, Marshman, &c. For the particulars of my journey here I must refer you to a letter I have written to Corrie, if you think it worth while to send for it. My MSS. on 'Grace Reigns,' would be acceptable, for if not I must write on that text again, which takes time.

H. Martyn.

CXCI.

TO MISS L. GRENFELL.

Shiraz, Sept. 8, 1811.

A courier on his way to the capital, affords me the unexpected pleasure of addressing my most beloved friend. It is now six months since I left India, and in all that time I have not heard from thence. The dear friends there, happy in each other's society, do not enough call to mind my forlorn condition. Here I am still, beset by cavilling infidels, and making very little progress in my translation, and half disposed to give it up, and come away. My kind host, to relieve the tedium of being always within a walled town, pitched a tent for me in a garden a little distance, and there I lived amidst clusters of grapes, by the side of a clear stream, but nothing compensates for the loss of the excellent of the earth. It is my business, however, as you will say, and ought to be my effort, to make saints, where I cannot find them. I do use the means in a certain way, but frigid reasoning with men of perverse minds, seldom brings men to Christ. However, as they require it, I reason, and accordingly challenged them to prove the divine mission of their prophet. In consequence of this, a learned Arabic Treatise was written, by one who was considered as the most able man, and put it into my hands; copies of it were also given to the college and the learned. The writer of it said that if I could give a satisfactory answer to it, he would become a Christian, and at all events, would make my reply as public as I pleased. I did answer it, and after some faint efforts on his part to defend himself, he acknowledged the force of my arguments, but was afraid to let them be generally known. He then began to inquire about the Gospel, but was not satisfied with my statement. He required me to prove from the very beginning, the divine mission of Moses, as well as of Christ; the truth of the Scriptures, &c. With very little hope that any good will come of it, I am now employed in drawing out the evidences of the truth; but oh, that I could converse and reason, and plead, with power from on high. How powerless are the best-directed arguments, till the Holy Ghost renders them effectual.

A few days ago I was on the eve of my departure for Ispahan, as I thought, and my translator had consented to accompany me as far as Bagdad, but just as we were setting out, news came that the Persians and Turks were fighting thereabouts, and that the road was in consequence impassable. I do not know what the Lord's purpose may be in keeping me here, but I trust it will be for the furtherance of the Gospel of Christ, and in that belief I abide contentedly.

My last letter to you was dated July. I desired you to direct to me at Tehran. As it is uncertain whether I shall pass anywhere near there; you had better direct to the care of S. Morier, Esq., Constantinople, and I can easily get your letters from thence.

I am happy to say that I am quite well, indeed never better; no returns of pain in the chest since I left India. May I soon receive the welcome news, that you also are well, and prospering even as your soul prospers. I read your letters incessantly, and try to find out something new, as I generally do, but I begin to look with pain at the distant date of the last. I cannot tell what to think, but I cast all my care upon him who hath already done wonders for me, and am sure that come what will, it shall be good, it shall be best. How sweet the privilege, that we may lie as little children before him. I find that my wisdom is folly, and my care useless, so that I try to live on from day to day, happy in his love and care. May that God who hath loved us, and given us everlasting consolation, and good hope through grace, bless, love, and keep my ever-dearest friend; and dwelling in the secret place of the Most High, and abiding under the shadow of the Almighty, may she enjoy that sweet tranquillity which the world cannot disturb. Dearest Lydia! pray for me, and believe me to be ever most faithfully and affectionately your's,

H. Martyn.

CXCII.

TO THE REV. D. CORRIE.

Shiraz, Sept. 12, 1811.

DEAREST BROTHER,

I can hardly conceive, or at least am not willing t believe, that you would forget me six successive months I conclude therefore that you must have written, thoug] I have not seen your handwriting since I left Calcutta

The Persian translation goes on but slowly. I an my translator have been engaged in a controversy witl his uncle, which has left us little leisure for anythin else. As there is nothing at all in this dull place t take the attention of the people, no trade, manufactures or news, every event at all novel is interesting to them You may conceive, therefore, what a strong sensatio was produced by the stab I aimed at the vitals of Ma hommed. Before five people had seen what I wrote defences of Islam swarmed into ephemeral being fron all the Moulwee maggots of the place, but the mor judicious men were ashamed to let me see them. On Moollah, called Aga Acber, was determined to distin guish himself. He wrote with great acrimony on th margin of my pamphlet, but passion had blinded hi reason, so that he smote the wind. One day I was or a visit of ceremony to the prime minister, and sitting ir great state by his side, fifty visitors in the same hall and five hundred clients without, when who should make his appeaance, but my tetric adversary, the said

Aga Acber, who came for the express purpose of presenting the minister with a piece he had composed in defence of the prophet, and then sitting down, told me he should present me with a copy that day. There are four answers, said he, to your objection against his using the sword. Very well, said I, I shall be glad to see them, though I made no such objection. Eager to display his attainments in all branches of science, he proceeded to call in question the truth of our European philosophy, and commanded me to show that the earth moved, and not the sun. I told him that in matters of religion, where the salvation of men was concerned, I would give up nothing to them, but as for points in philosophy, they might have it all their own way. This was not what he wanted; so after looking at the minister, to know if it was not a breach of good manners to dispute at such a time, and finding that there was nothing contrary to custom, but that on the contrary, he rather expected an answer, I began, but soon found that he could comprehend nothing without diagrams. A moonshee in waiting was ordered to produce his implements, so there was I, drawing figures, while hundreds of men were looking on in silence.

But all my trouble was in vain—the Moollah knew nothing whatever of mathematics, and therefore could not understand my proofs. The Persians are far more curious and clever than the Indians. Wherever I go, they ask me questions in philosophy, and are astonished that I do not know everything. One asked me the reason of the properties of the magnet, I told him I knew nothing about it; 'But what do your learned men say?' *They* know nothing about it. This he did not at all credit.

I do not find myself improving in Persian, indeed,

I take no pains to speak it well, not perceiving it to be of much consequence. India is the land where we can act at present with most effect. It is true that the Persians are more susceptible, but the terrors of an inquisition are always hanging over them. I can now conceive no greater happiness than to be settled for life in India, superintending native schools, as we did at Patna and Chunar. To preach so as to be readily understood by the poor, is a difficulty that appears to me almost insuperable, besides which, grown-up people are seldom converted. However, why should we despair. If I live to see India again, I shall set to and learn Hindee in order to preach. The day may come, when even our word may be with the Holy Ghost and with power. It is now almost a year since I left Cawnpore, and my journey is but beginning: when shall I ever get back again? I am often tempted to get away from this prison, but again I recollect, that some years hence, I shall say, When I was at Shiraz, why did not I get the New Testament done?—what difference would a few months have made? In August I passed some days at a vineyard, about a parasang from the city, where my host pitched a tent for me, but it was so cold at night, that I was glad to get back to the city again. Though I occupy a room in his house, I provide for myself. Victuals are cheap enough, especially fruit; the grapes, pears, and water-melons are delicious; indeed, such a country for fruit I had no conception of. I have a fine horse, which I bought for less than a hundred rupees, on which I ride every morning round the walls. My vain servant, Zechariah, anxious that his master should appear like an ameer, furnished him, *i. e.* the horse, with a saddle, or rather a pillion, which fairly covers his whole back; it has all the colours of the rainbow, but

ellow is predominant, and from it hang down four
rge tassels, also yellow. But all my finery does not
efend me from the boys. Some cry out, Ho, Russ!
hers cry out, Feringee! One day a brickbat was
ung at me, and hit me in the hip with such force, that
felt it quite a providential escape. Most of the day I
n about the translation, sometimes in a leisure hour
ying at Isaiah, in order to get help from the Persian
ews. My Hebrew reveries have quite disappeared,
erely for want of leisure. I forgot to say that I have
een to visit the ruins of Persepolis, but this, with many
her things, must be reserved for a hot afternoon at
awnpore.

What would I give for a few lines from you, to say
ow the men come on, and whether their numbers are
creasing, whether you meet the S——'s at the evening
past as when I was there. My kindest love to them,
our sister, and all that love us in the truth. May the
race of the Lord Jesus Christ be with your spirit, and
ith your faithful and affectionate brother,

H. MARTYN.

CXCIII.

TO MISS L. GRENFELL.

Shiraz, October 21, 1811.

* * * It is, I think, about a month sinc I wrote to you, and so little has occurred since, that find scarcely anything in my journal, and nothing wort transcribing. This state of inactivity is becoming ver irksome to me. I cannot get these Persians to work and while they are idle, I am sitting here to no purpos Sabat's laziness used to provoke me excessively, bu Persians I find are as torpid as Arabs, when their salar does not depend on their exertions, and both very infe rior to the feeble Indian, whom they affect to despis My translator comes about sunrise, corrects a little, an is off, and I see no more of him for the day. Meanwhil I sit fretting, or should do so, as I did at first, were i not for a blessed employment which so beguiles th tediousness of the day, that I hardly perceive how i passes. It is the study of the Psalms in the He brew. I have long had it in contemplation, in the as surance, from the number of flat and obscure passage that occur in the translations, that the original has no been hitherto perfectly understood. I am delighted t find that many of the most unmeaning verses in ou version turn out, on close examination, to contain direct reference to the Lord our Saviour. The testimon of Jesus is indeed the spirit of prophecy. He is neve lost sight of. Let them touch what subject they wil

they must always let fall something about him. Such should we be, looking always to him. I have often attempted the 84th Psalm, endeared to me on many accounts, as you know, but have not yet succeeded. The glorious 16th Psalm I hope I have mastered. I write with the ardour of a student, communicating his discoveries, and describing his difficulties to a fellow-student.

I think of you incessantly, too much, I fear, sometimes, yet the recollection of you is generally attended with an exercise of resignation to His will. In prayer I often feel what you described five years ago as having felt,—a particular pleasure in viewing you as with me before the Lord, and intreating our common Father to bless both his children. When I sit and muse, my spirit flies away to you, and attends you at Gurlyn, Penzance, Plymouth Dock, and sometimes with your brother in London. If you acknowledge a kindred feeling still, we are not separated, our spirits have met and blended. I still continue without intelligence from India; since last January I have heard nothing of any one person whom I love. My consolation is, that the Lord has you all under his care, and is carrying on his work in the world by your means; and that when I emerge, I shall find that some progress is made in India especially, the country I now regard as my own. Persia is in many respects, a field ripe for the harvest. Vast numbers secretly hate and despise the superstition imposed on them, and as many of them as have heard the Gospel, approve it; but they dare not hazard their lives for the name of the Lord Jesus. I am sometimes asked whether the external appearance of Mahomedanism might not be retained with Christianity; and whether I could not baptize them without their believing in the divinity of Christ? I tell them, No.

Though I have complained above of the inactivity o my translation, I have reason to bless the Lord that h thus supplies Gibeonites for the help of his true Israel They are employed in a work, of the importance o which they are unconscious, and are making provisio for future Persian saints, whose time is, I suppose, nov near. "Roll back, ye crowded years, your thick array!' Let the long, long period of darkness and sin at las give way to the brighter hours of light and liberty which wait on the wings of the Sun of Righteousness Perhaps we witness the dawn of the day of glory, an if not, the desire that we feel, that Jesus may be glori fied, and the nations acknowledge his sway, is the ear nest of the Spirit, that when He shall appear, we shal also appear with him in glory. Kind love to all th saints who are waiting his coming.

Your's with true affection,

My ever dearest Lydia,

H. Martyn.

It is now determined that we leave Shiraz in a week and as the road through Persia is impassable througl the commotions which are always disturbing some par or other of this unhappy country, I must go back t Bushire.

CXCIV.

TO THE REV. D. CORRIE.

Shiraz, December 12, 1811.

DEAREST BROTHER,

Your letters of January 28 and April 22, have just eached me. After being a whole year without any idings of you, you may conceive how much they have ended to revive my spirits. Indeed I know not how o be sufficiently thankful to our God and Father for iving me a brother, who is indeed a brother to my oul, and thus follows me with affectionate prayers vherever I go, and more than supplies my place to the recious flock, over whom the Holy Ghost hath made ıs overseers. There is only one thing in your letters hat makes me uneasy, and that is, the oppression you omplain of in the hot weather. As you will have to ass another hot season at Cawnpore, and I do not know ıow many more, I must again urge you to spare yourelf. I am endeavouring to learn the true use of time n a new way, by placing myself in idea twenty or hirty years in advance, and then considering how I ught to have managed twenty or thirty years ago. In acing violently for a year or two and then breaking lown? In this way I have reasoned myself into conentment about staying so long at Shiraz. I thought t first, what will the Government in India think of ny being away so long, or what will my friends think?

Shall I not appear to all a wandering shepherd, leaving the flock and running about for my own pleasure? But placing myself twenty years on in time, I say, Why could not I stay at Shiraz long enough to get a New Testament done there, even if I had been detained there on that account three or six years. What work of equal importance can ever come from me? So that now I am resolved to wait here till the New Testament is finished, though I incur the displeasure of Government, or even be dismissed the service. I have been many times on the eve of my departure, as my translator promised to accompany me to Bagdad; but that city being in great confusion he is afraid to trust himself there; so I resolved to go westward through the north of Persia, but found it impossible, on account of the snow which blocks up the roads in winter, to proceed till spring. Here I am therefore, for three months more; our Testament will be finished, please God, in six weeks. I go on as usual, riding round the walls in the morning, and singing hymns at night over my milk and water, for tea I have none, though I much want it. I am with you in spirit almost every evening, and feel a bliss I cannot describe in being one with the dear saints of God all over the earth, through one Lord and one Spirit.

They continued throwing stones at me every day, till happening one day to tell Jaffier Ali Khan, my host, how one as big as my fist had struck me in the back, he wrote to the Governor, who sent an order to all the gates, that if any one insulted me, he should be bastinadoed, and the next day came himself in state to pay me a visit. These measures have had the desired effect; they now call me the Feringee Nabob, and very civilly offer me the Calean; but indeed the Persian common-

.lity are very brutes ; the Soofies declare themselves .nable to account for the fierceness of their country-nen, except it be from the influence of Islam. After peaking in my praise, one of them added, 'and there .re the Hindoos too (who have brought the guns) when saw their gentleness I was quite charmed with them ; ut as for our Iranees, they delight in nothing but tor-nenting their fellow-creatures.' These Soofies are quite he methodists of the East. They delight in every hing Christian, except in being exclusive. They con-ider that all will finally return to God, from whom hey emanated, or rather of whom they are only dif-erent forms. The doctrine of the Trinity they admired, ut not the atonement ; because the Mahommedans, they ay, consider Iman Hosyn as also crucified for the sins f men ; and to every thing Mahommedan they have particular aversion. Yet withal they conform exter-ally. From these things, however, you will perceive how he first Persian church will be formed, judging after the nanner of men. The employment of my leisure hours s translating the Psalms into Persian. What will poor 'itrut do when he gets to the poetical books ? Job, I ope, you have let him pass over. The Books of Solo-non are also in a very sorry condition in the English. 'he Prophets are all much easier, and consequently better one. I hear there is a man at Yezid that has fallen nto the same way of thinking as myself about the etters, and professes to have found out all the arts and ciences from them. I should be glad to compare notes vith him. It is now time for me to bid you good night. We have had ice on the pools some time, but no snow et. They build their houses without chimneys, so if ve want a fire we must take the smoke along with it. prefer wrapping myself in my sheepskin.

Your accounts of the progress of the kingdom of God among you are truly refreshing. Tell dear H——, and the men of both regiments, that I salute them much in the Lord, and make mention of them in my prayers. May I continue to hear thus of their state, and if I am spared to see them again, may we make it evident that we have grown in grace. Affectionate remembrances to your sister and S——, I hope they continue to prosecute their labours of love. Remember me to the people of Cawnpore who inquire, &c. Why have not I mentioned Colonel P——? It is not because he is not in my heart, for there is hardly a man in the world whom I love and honour more. My most Christian salutations to him.

May the grace of the Lord Jesus Christ be with your spirit, dearest brother.

Yours affectionately,

H. Martyn.

CXCV.

TO THE REV. C. SIMEON.

Tebriz, July 12, 1812.

MY DEAREST FRIEND AND BROTHER,

The Tartar courier for Constantinople, who has been delayed some days on our account, being to be dispatched instantly, my little strength also being nearly exhausted by writing to Mr. Grant a letter to be laid before the court,—I have only to notice some of the particulars of your letter of February of this year. It is not now before me, neither have I strength to search for it among my papers; but from the frequent attentive perusals I gave it during my intervals of ease, I do not imagine that any of it has escaped my memory. At present I am in a high fever, and cannot properly recollect myself. I shall ever love and be grateful to Mr. Thornton for his kind attention to my family.

The increase of godly young men is precious news. If I sink into the grave in India, my place will be supplied an hundred-fold. You will learn from Mr. Grant that I have applied for leave to come to England on furlough; a measure you will disapprove; but you would not, were you to see the pitiable condition to which I am reduced, and knew what it is to traverse the continent of Asia in the destitute state in which I am. If you wish not to see me, I can say that I think it most probable that you will not; the way before me being not better than that passed over, which has nearl killed me.

I would not pain your heart, my dear brother, bu we who are in Jesus have the privilege of viewing lif and death as nearly the same, since both are one ; an I thank a gracious Lord that sickness never came at time when I was more free from apparent reasons fo living. Nothing seemingly remains for me to do bu to follow the rest of my family to the tomb. Let no the book written against Mahomedanism be publishe till approved in India. A European who has not live amongst them cannot imagine how differently they see think, reason, object, from what we do. This I ha full opportunity of observing during my eleven month residence at Shiraz. During that time I was engage in a written controversy with one of the most learne and temperate doctors there. He began. I replie what was unanswerable ; then I subjoined a secon more direct attack on the glaring absurdities of Mahom medanism, with a statement of the nature and evidence of Christianity. The Soofies then, as well as himsel desired a demonstration from the very beginning, of th truth of any revelation. As this third treatise con tained an examination of the doctrine of the Soofie and pointed out that their object was attainable by th Gospel, and by that only, it was read with interest an convinced many. There is not a single Europeanis in the whole that I know of, as my friend and interpre ter would not write any thing that he could not pe fectly comprehend. But I am exhausted ; pray for m beloved brother, and I believe that I am, as long as li and recollection lasts,

Yours affectionately,

H. Martyn.

CXCVI.

TO MISS LYDIA GRENFELL.

Tebriz, July 12, 1812.

My dearest Lydia,

I have only time to say that I have received your letter of February 14. Shall I pain your heart by adding, that I am in such a state of sickness and pain, that I can hardly write to you? Let me rather observe, to obviate the gloomy apprehension my letters to Mr. Grant and Mr. Simeon may excite, that I am likely soon to be delivered from my fever. Whether I shall gain strength enough to go on, rests on our heavenly Father, in whose hands are all my times. Oh, his precious grace! His eternal unchanging love in Christ to my soul, never appeared more clear, more sweet, more strong. I ought to inform you that in consequence of the state to which I am reduced by travelling so far over-land, without having accomplished my journey, and the consequent impossibility of returning to India the same way, I have applied for leave to come on furlough to England. Perhaps you will be gratified by this intelligence; but oh, my dear Lydia, I must faithfully tell you, that the probability of my reaching England alive, is but small; and this I say, that your expectations of seeing me again may be moderate, as mine are of seeing you. Why have you not written more about yourself? However, I am thankful for knowing that you are alive and well. I scarcely know how to desire you to direct. Perhaps Alexandria ir Egypt will be the best place ; another may be sent t‹ Constantinople, for though I shall not go there, I hop‹ Mr. Morier will be kept informed of my movements Kindest love to all the saints you usually mention.

Your's ever most faithfully and affectionately,

H. Martyn.

CXCVII.

TO THE REV. C. SIMEON.

Tebriz, August 8, 1812.

MY DEAREST BROTHER AND FRIEND,

Ever since I wrote, about a month I believe, I have been lying upon the bed of sickness for twenty days or more; the fever raged with great violence, and for a long time every species of medicine was tried in vain. After I had given up every hope of recovery, it pleased God to abate the fever; but incessant head-aches succeeded, which allowed me no rest day or night. I was reduced still lower, and am now a mere skeleton; but as they are now less frequent, I suppose it to be the will of God that I should be raised up to life again. I am now sitting in my chair, and wrote the will with a strong hand; but as you see I cannot write so now. Kindest love to Mr. John Thornton, for whose temporal and spiritual prosperity I daily pray.

Your ever affectionate friend and brother,

H. MARTYN.

CXCVIII.

TO MISS L. GRENFELL.

Tebriz, Aug. 28, 1812.

I wrote to you last, my dear Lydia, in great disorde
My fever had approached nearly to delirium, and m
debility was so great, that it seemed impossible I coul
withstand the power of disease many days. Yet it ha
pleased God to restore me to life and health again ; no
that I have recovered my former strength yet, but con
sider myself sufficiently restored to prosecute my jour
ney. My daily prayer is, that my late chastisemen
may have its intended effect, and make me all the res
of my days more humble, and less self-confident. Sel
confidence has often let me down fearful lengths, an
would, without God's gracious interference, prove m
endless perdition. I seem to be made to feel this evi
of my heart, more than any other at this time. I
prayer, or when I write, or converse on the subject
Christ appears to me my life and strength, but at othe
times, I am as thoughtless and bold, as if I had all lif
and strength in myself. Such neglect on our par
works a diminution of our joys ; but the covenant, th
covenant ! stands fast with Him, for his people eve
more. I mentioned my conversing sometimes on divin
subjects, for though it is long enough since I have see
a child of God, I am sometimes led on by the Persian
to tell them all I know, of the very recesses of the san
tuary, and these are the things that interest them. Bu

to give an account of all my discussions with these mystic philosophers, must be reserved to the time of our meeting. Do I dream! that I venture to think and write of such an event as that! Is it possible that we shall ever meet again below? Though it is possible, I dare not indulge such a pleasing hope yet. I am still at a tremendous distance; and the countries I have to pass through, are many of them dangerous to the traveller, from the hordes of banditti, whom a feeble government cannot chastise. In consequence of the bad state of the road between this and Aleppo, Sir Gore advises me to go first to Constantinople, and from thence to pass into Syria. In favour of this route, he urges, that by writing to two or three Turkish governors on the frontiers, he can secure me a safe passage at least half way, and the latter half is probably not much infested. In three days, therefore, I intend setting my horse's head towards Constantinople, distant about thirteen hundred miles. Nothing I think, will occasion any further detention here, if I can procure servants who know both Persian and Turkish; but should I be taken ill on the road, my case would be pitiable indeed. The ambassador and his suite are still here; his, and Lady Ouseley's attentions to me, during my illness, have been unremitting. The Prince Abbas Mirza, the wisest of the king's sons, and heir to the throne, was here some time after my arrival; I much wished to present a copy of the Persian New Testament to him, but I could not rise from my bed. The book will, however, be given to him by the Ambassador. Public curiosity about the gospel, now for the first time, in the memory of the modern Persians, introduced into the country, is a good deal excited here, at Shiraz, and other places; so that upon the whole, I am thankful for having been led hither, and detained ; though my resi dence in this country has been attended with man unpleasant circumstances. The way of the kings o the east is preparing. Thus much may be said witl safety, but little more. The Persians also will pro bably take the lead in the march to Zion, as they are ripe for a revolution in religion as well a politics.

Sabat, about whom you inquire so regularly, I hav heard nothing of this long time. My friends in Indi have long since given me up as lost or gone ou of reach, and if they wrote, they would probably no mention him, as he is far from being a favourite witl any of them. ——, who is himself of an impatien temper, cannot tolerate him ; indeed I am pronounced to be the only man in Bengal who could have lived witl him so long. He is, to be sure, the most tormentin creature I ever yet chanced to deal with—peevish proud, suspicious, greedy ; he used to give daily mor and more distressing proofs of his never having receive the saving grace of God. But of this you will sa nothing ; while his interesting story is yet fresh in th memory of people, his failings had better not be men tioned. The poor Arab wrote me a querulous epistl from Calcutta, complaining that no one took notice o him, now that I was gone ; and then he proceeds t abuse his best friends. I have not yet written to re prove him for his unchristian sentiments, and when do, I know it will be to no purpose, after all the privat lectures I have given him. My course from Constan tinople is so uncertain that I hardly know where to de sire you to direct to me ; I believe Malta is the onl place, for there I must stop in my way home. Soon w shall have occasion for pen and ink no more ; but I trus

I shall shortly see thee face to face. Love to all the saints.

Believe me to be yours ever
most faithfully and affectionately,
H. MARTYN.

At Tocat, on the 16th of October, Mr. Martyn entered into his rest.

TOCA.

TOCAT.

JOHN HUSS;

Or, The Workings of Popery in the Fourteenth and Fifteenth Centuries,
Translated from the German.
By MARGARET ANNE WYATT.
With an Introductory note on Popery. By a Beneficed Clergyman of the Anglican Church.
In Foolscap 8vo. Price 3s. 6d. in cloth.

THE SUPPRESSION OF THE REFORMATION IN FRANCE,

As exhibited in De Rulhiére's "Historical Elucidations," and various other Documents.
Complied, translated, and edited by DAVID DUNDAS SCOTT, Esq.
In 12mo. Price 6s. in cloth.

NOTICES OF THE REFORMATION IN THE SOUTH-WEST PROVINCES OF FRANCE.

BY ROBERT FRANCIS JAMESON. In 12mo. Price 5s. 6d. in cloth.

THE PROTESTANT'S ARMOURY;

Being a Collection of Extracts from various Writers on the Church of Rome; Chiefly designed to shew its Apostate, Idolatrous, and Anti-Christian Character.
Compiled by A LAY MEMBER OF THE CHURCH OF ENGLAND.
In 12mo. Price 7s. in cloth.

LUTHER, AND THE LUTHERAN REFORMATION

With Portraits. In Two Vols. Foolscap 8vo. Price 12s. in cloth.
By the Rev. JOHN SCOTT, M.A. Vicar of North Ferriby, and Minister of St. Mary's, Hull.

BY THE SAME AUTHOR,

CALVIN AND THE SWISS REFORMATION.

With Portrait. In Foolscap. 8vo. Price 6s. in cloth.

ESSAYS ON ROMANISM.

In foolscap 8vo. Price 5s. in cloth.

HOLY SCRIPTURE,

THE ULTIMATE RULE OF FAITH TO A CHRISTIAN MAN.

By the Rev. W. FITZGERALD, M.A., Trinity College, Dublin.

In foolscap 8vo. Price 4s. 6d. in cloth.

EPISCOPACY AND PRESBYTERY.

BY ARCHIBALD BOYD, M.A.

Curate of the Cathedral of Derry.

In one Volume, octavo. Price 10s. 6d. cloth.

THE CHURCHMAN'S GUIDE IN PERILOUS TIM

Or, the Thirty-nine Articles of the Church of England explained a commented on.

By the Rev. JAMES PIGOT, A.M., Incumbent of St. Helen's, Lanca:
In foolscap 8vo. Price 3s. in cloth.

USHER ON THE SACRAMENTS.

Extracted from his " Body of Divinity."
Foolscap. Price 2s.

SECRETA MONITA SOCIETATIS JESU.

THE SECRET INSTRUCTIONS OF THE JESUITS.

Edited by BISHOP COMPTON.

A new Edition. Price 3s. boards.

CPSIA information can be obtained
at www.ICGtesting.com
Printed in the USA
BVHW081616120819
555665BV00014B/1162/P

9 781318 701865